IN MY GARDEN

IN MY GARDEN

CHRISTOPHER LLOYD

Edited by Frank Ronan

BLOOMSBURY

This edition first published 1993

Copyright © Christopher Lloyd and Frank Ronan 1993

The moral right of the authors has been asserted
Bloomsbury Publishing Ltd, 2 Soho Square, London W1V 5DE
A CIP catalogue record for this book is available from the British Library
ISBN 0 7475 16596

Typeset in Great Britain by Hewer Text Composition Services, Edinburgh
Printed in Great Britain by Clays Ltd, St Ives plc, Bungay, Suffolk

The pieces by Christopher Lloyd first appeared in *Country Life* between
1963 and 1993.
Illustrations by Simon Unglass

Contents

CONTENTS

PREFACE

It was lucky for me when Frank Ronan suggested that he would be prepared to make a collection of my pieces. I had made two such attempts before, in *The Well-Tempered Garden* and *The Adventurous Gardener*, but in these I felt it necessary both to update and to elaborate, so that much of their content was new. And that is a lot of work. On the whole it is easier and fresher to write entirely from scratch.

Frank's method has been to reproduce exactly what I wrote, even before it passed through the subeditors' hands. He has gone back to the original typescripts. This now seems a good idea, though allowance needs to be made for the passing of time, the changing of facts and of opinions. I may be opinionated and have often been called so, but I am always ready to change my opinions.

As an author himself (of novels, which often make me exclaim or laugh with pleasure), Frank has tended to select the well-made piece. He likes an article to be rounded off, the conclusion often bringing the reader back to the opening. There are two main reasons for my writing often failing to do this. The chief is that I am anxious to impart information, if possible based on my own experience. Gardening information, that is, and in many cases I liked it to be relevant to the actual season as it was being experienced. When I first started *In My Garden*, I was writing only eleven days ahead of publication. It is now fifteen days (such is progress), but even so, close enough to give the feel of immediacy. Often I'm not specially interested in whether the piece is rounded off or not. Such articles have therefore tended to be passed over, in a retrospective collection.

The other reason, valid at one time but now no longer, was that editing often necessitates excising and that in the old days,

1

before we could juggle around with a computer at will, cuts were most easily and cheaply made from the end of an article. The felicitous rounding off phrase was therefore a waste of time. One might just as well write as though cut off in mid flow, since that would probably be the case in any event.

The net result, so far as this book is concerned, is a selective bias, but a bias which probably makes me more readable to a wider public than would be the case if a technically orientated horticulturist had done the job. I would rather have Frank on it, any day.

I enjoy my gardening (and have been enormously lucky in my opportunities) and I enjoy writing in our wonderfully expressive, albeit ambiguous, English language. I am passionate about my subject matter, but not (heaven forfend) solemn. I find it impossible to take either myself or anyone else too seriously. Gardening, like living, should be fun. It can't be, much of the time, but we can do our best to make it so.

I am most grateful to *Country Life* for allowing these pieces to be reproduced. They have sometimes had to restrain me from being libellous, but have always shown great sympathy for my intentions and I have never felt more at home than when writing for their readership.

Christopher Lloyd
September 1993

INTRODUCTION BY FRANK RONAN

This is about pleasure and nothing else. There are those of us who get some of our keenest pleasure from reading, and there are those of us for whom gardening has become a dependence of embarrassing proportions (and, I suppose, there may be some who are beyond these pales, but that is their loss). It is rare that the craving of these two classes of hedonist can be satisfied in one work: that the reader who doesn't know *Eucryphia* from *Euphorbia* (poor sap) can be riveted by the prose, while the red-blooded gardener who thinks that an oxymoron is a nineteenth-century synonym for *Leucanthemum vulgare* (how sad can you get?) thinks he has laid his hands on the nearest equivalent in the horticultural world to pornography. It is rare that a garden writer can make you laugh; rarer still that this writer will be someone who really knows what he is talking about and is capable of imparting his knowledge to you, and, as far as I know, it is unique that the joke will be delivered in a beautifully made sentence. So, for those of us who are both bookish and plant-minded, Christopher Lloyd is a psychiatric balm, making the double life of our pleasures whole.

I should declare an interest. Christopher Lloyd is a friend of mine, but that should not detract from my opinion of his work, since our friendship began after I had formed that opinion, and, to some extent, because I had formed that opinion. It was while I was staying with him last year that he showed me a piece he had just written for *Country Life*. The distractions of Dixter being what they are, I did not read it straight away but stowed it in my baggage, from where it emerged several weeks later (with me, packing takes minutes and unpacking takes months). I read it and was horrified. The article was the one called 'Long-flowering Plants', and it was better than anything

I had read for some time. It was the waste that horrified me; the idea that only subscribers to *Country Life* would get to see some of Christopher Lloyd's best work. I immediately wrote to him, and somehow, between one thing and another, finished up reading through nearly one and a half million words, and whittling them down to eighty-five thousand or so.

It was not as difficult a job as you might imagine. In the first place there was pleasure in all of it, and in the second place there was so much material that I was free to choose only what I considered perfect. I admit that my chief criterion was literary rather than horticultural, since it seemed that the extraordinary thing about Christopher Lloyd's writing was its literary merit. And I also admit, as a non-academic, that I judged this merit, not by deconstruction and measuring of the sub-clauses, but by the pleasure given to me by the sentences and the ideas. There were easy choices, like 'The Anatomy of Pears', a piece of writing which is so infused with sensuality that you can almost feel the juice of it run down your chin as you read. There is 'Peel Me a Walnut', which I would pit against any love story I have ever read; better than that, because you are not told it is a love story and hit over the head with men and women swooning and gasping, it is a story about the quality of love with no indication that it is a story at all. In 'Blue Beauty Queens the Waters', we are told of acquisitive passion (but not of the ending: the project was a failure, though these days there is more grinning than grieving at the memory of it), and elsewhere we are constantly reminded that the Lloyd philosophy is not the philosophy of the collector, but of the enthusiast, of one who is at his best when the plant in question enthuses in return.

Here is a garden of the five senses. Vision, yes, first and foremost. Vision is the easiest passion, and the most freely shared and discussed, and gardening is primarily about learning to see what you are looking at. So, here, we have yellow daisies, which are a Lloyd trademark. There should have been pieces about crocuses and tulips and the other Lloyd fixations, but I thought the pieces about lupins and phloxes were better. Of the other senses, scent and taste are best covered. Christopher is particularly good at pinpointing a scent, and making you smell it more exactly. His sense of smell being an enthusiasm with him, he writes about it particularly well. As for taste, his enthusiasm for food is almost shameful, and I sometimes think that he would be as happy writing a cookery column as a gardening one. I tried to keep the gluttony pieces to a minimum, but there were too many of them that were too well written to leave out. And touch, and sound: you will find yourself repeating the word *Zingiber* in quiet moments, and listening out for the noise of gunnera leaves on windy days. Touch appears controversially, with a recommendation that cactuses be used in gardens for the blind. Read it, before you become incensed. If I ever lose my sight it is exactly the sort of attitude I would most like to encounter.

Much as I hate to, something should be said about nomenclature. This is not a work of botanical reference, and there is absolutely no reason that any plant name in it should be correct from a botanist's point of view (I've yet to meet two botanists who agree on a name anyway). Despite that, I have checked the plant names against the current thinking and, where it seemed appropriate and in consultation with Christopher Lloyd, changed them or left them alone. We are happy with it, and if you are the sort of nitpicker who thinks they have spotted a mistake (there's always one) we have no objection to you feeling smug about it, but would much rather you didn't bother us with your discovery.

The first of these pieces, 'Survivors from the Ice Age', appeared on 2 May 1963, and there has been one a week since, without fail. You'd never think, from reading them, that Kennedy was shot or that Vietnam was anything other than a place of mild botanical interest, or that the end of the world had been announced at least half a dozen times. Nor do you get the impression that this author is a fantasist in an ivory tower. Death and passion are here, but they are given their proper place within the universal laws of mutability. This is the writing of a man who has learned from his subject, and whose subject is a better one for his involvement.

JANUARY

DYING GRACEFULLY

HOWEVER prolonged the final scene, the heroes and heroines of opera can always be guaranteed to die gracefully and mellifluously. They have been carefully elevated to an ideal which we should like to be true while knowing very well that it is nothing of the sort. We have not always disguised the fate of our man-made flowers so successfully. At their peak, when we admire them on the show bench, they may elicit gasps of admiration. But their exit is often slow, painful and distressing. Of that we learn only when we come to grow them.

A correspondent deplores the fact that this failure to die cleanly is 'ignored in catalogue descriptions'. Here's one as an instance. It is of the once-flowering rambler rose 'Albertine': 'Seen in so many gardens in June–July. The deep coppery-red buds contrast with the sweetly fragrant soft salmon-pink full flowers which smother the vigorous growth of last year, withering and dying to a tasteful tobacco-stain brown without shedding, while next year's canes blotch grey with powdery mildew. Should be in every garden.'

Only I had to tack on that last bit. So many salesmen remain totally oblivious of their duty to their customers.

Actually my correspondent was especially worried about white flowers: 'The horror of a white buddleia past its best destroys all the delightful memories of its initial flowering.' True, because white turned to brown somehow makes a more insulting contrast than the change from any other colour. And anyway, cultivars of *Buddleia davidii* with names like 'White Bouquet', 'White Cloud' and 'White Profusion' have such enormous and coarse green leaves. The advantage of *B. fallowiana alba* is, first, that its flower spikes being slender and small, they don't become aggressively brown and anyway they are borne in a long succession so that opening buds can easily distract you in their

9

direction. Then, the grey-felted leaves are a beautiful and long-continuing feature in themselves. *B. f. alba* is not too far removed from the species that gave rise to it. The splendours and miseries of flower power have not here taken over.

The knock-out display usually has a twist in its tail. That's why we hear so much about the dead-heading of rhododendrons. In the greatest gardens this chore has become a way of life, a menial task that takes up weeks of some human's working time each year. Big flowers still tend (thank goodness) to be carried by big bushes (the breeders have not yet attained the triumphs here that they have with marigolds) and that entails a lot of step-ladder work. It is all amazingly costly and unproductive. The reason given for this exercise is that it promotes free flowering in the following year, but that is nonsense. You would need selectively to disbud your rhododendrons *now*, if you wanted to save their strength to flower next year instead. But nobody does that. Wanting to eat their cake and still have it, they wait till the rhododendrons have finished flowering and then remove the flower heads. By then the weakening damage has been done. New breaks below the flower trusses will not appear in time to bud up themselves the same year (I'm not writing of the despicable hybrids which flower all over every year whatever you do to them).

No, the real reason that rhododendrons are dead-headed is that the dead heads look such a fright.

The defect is more often tolerated in *Camellia japonica* and *C. reticulata* cultivars and hybrids, though I can't think why. It's always the weather that receives the blame: frost and wind. Year after year, the plants are excused; it's nature that has done the dirty on them. In fact it's the vicious nature of the beast that should be blamed. It simply does not know how to carry on.

I suppose I should get rid of my 'Madame Lemoine' lilac, and perhaps one day I shall*. She's stiff and ungainly, let alone the spitefully hideous browning off of her double white flowers. But I still have a soft spot for the old girl. Perhaps I'll cut her

---

* I now have.

down instead. That will at least disguise the ungainliness for a few years while allowing the neighbours a bit of a breather. She does have sharp elbows.

It isn't just of shrubs we need to think. Chrysanthemums die off in the centre of a multiple truss in the spray types and ruin the display if nothing is done about it. Dead-heading needs to be an ongoing operation. And you cannot do it just anyhow (not with dahlias either). If you just pull the heads off, as in the outdoor chrysanthemum trial at Wisley when I visited it two or three years ago, the task is quickly completed but the decapitated stalks look terrible. Nothing for it but to do the job intelligently with knife or secateurs.

Bearded irises need going over every day if their withered blossoms are not to detract from those that are fresh. Many of the large-flowered day lilies, also, not to mention gladioli. But with them you have the additional drawback, common to many flowers that bloom on spikes, that by the time the top half is blooming, the whole inflorescence looks unbalanced. Better, really, to remove the spike before its last flowers have opened, let alone died.

Ideally perhaps we should remove every display before it has even begun. Then there'd never be room for disappointment and we could always be making ready for the next non-event. Imagination could take the place of fact and failure.

Happy New Year!

2.1.86

GARDENING WITH FERNS INCLUSIVELY

ONCE you develop an interest in hardy ferns they almost become an obsession. I try to resist that; after all, it can't be healthy to be obsessed. You're no longer master of your passions, and anyway other plants tend to become unfairly excluded. But ferns, it seems to me, can find places in so many parts of the garden without excluding anything. They are of those ingredients, like bulbs, that add an extra dimension, an added richness, a deeper texture, setting off or alternating with other plants in or out of their seasons.

We have lately cut down the last remnants of a lot of hostas and veratrums growing in a north-west border in front of a wall. And there, revealed at the wall's foot, is a continuous chain of hart's-tongue ferns, *Asplenium scolopendrium*. No one planted them; they have sown themselves and clearly they love it there, for their rich green leather straps are long and upstanding. They must, of course, have been present all through the summer and autumn, but passed unnoticed while the large-leaved herbs in front of them held the stage. Now they have come into their inheritance.

Ferns that have sown themselves always do well. They wouldn't be there, otherwise. Their spores are so numerous and light that they are carried everywhere. Only when they settle in a congenial spot do they germinate and start new plants. Tight in the angle of a wall and a border is not the sort of place where one plants anything deliberately, unless it is a wall shrub or climber, and even then you more often plant a foot or more in front of the wall, thus enabling the shrub to make roots in all directions and to find its moisture and nutrients where they are most likely to be available. The ferns are making use of a piece of no-man's-land.

The common male fern does the same thing and I often use it as an indicator of where I might find a home for some new fern that I have not yet placed. After all, male ferns are two a penny. I don't despise them but I don't feel I owe them a living. So if I find, for instance, that one has established itself in and around the stems or trunk of a shrub rose, it is a sign. Here is a spot where, if I dig out the male fern, a fern replacement of somewhere near the same habit is likely to prosper. At the same time it will perform the useful function of occupying a gap that I hadn't spotted for myself *and* of hiding the ugliest part of any rose, its legs.

Having adjusted yourself to looking at your garden, and not

12

necessarily to its shady places, with fern eyes, you no longer feel inhibited about acquiring pretty well every new species and variety that you clap eyes on. A place for it is sure to turn up. And after all if I who says so am living in the comparatively dry south-east, how much truer of those who 'enjoy' (a mixed enjoyment, I know) a higher rainfall.

There's another point I should like to make about the common male fern, *Dryopteris filix-mas*. It often sows itself in the angle of a length of dry walling that abuts on a paved path where there is a terraced change of levels. This looks nice until the fern grows so hefty that its fronds hang out more than halfway across the path; then it becomes a nuisance.

In one place where this has happened, the visiting public were being forced, unless they walked in single file, to tread on the border on the path's other side. That was at the end of June, when the fronds were fully expanded. So we cut the whole lot hard back, right to the crown of the rhizomes. Almost immediately, new fronds were unfolded, but they were of only half the length of the original crop and therefore did not renew the problem. Furthermore, they appeared remarkably fresh at the late summer season when those that had unfurled in spring were dark and heavy. A photographer friend (not at my instigation) chose to photograph that piece of path when she was at Dixter on 9 August, and it was on seeing her picture, of which she sent me a copy, that I realised what an asset the rejuvenated ferns had become. Naturally this treatment weakens the plants, but they can afford to be weakened.

Our main planting of common male ferns is in a narrow border along the front of our fifteenth-century house where they receive virtually no sunshine at all. And very little water either, because they are overhung by a deep eave. This perfectly plain and simple planting was my mother's idea and it has been too successful to be changed in seventy years. As I write the fronds are still upstanding and unfrosted and they are slowly changing from green to pale-fawn. Where a building is of considerable merit, you had better refrain from fussing it with exciting foreground plantings. To eschew vegetation altogether is unnecessarily stark, but the ferns are a plain yet elegant solution.

And so I feel a bit of a traitor when I contemplate even a minor change. My mind runs on another native species which I consider superior. This is the golden-scaled male fern, *D. affinis* syn. *D. borreri*. You see it a great deal mixed up with common male ferns in Scotland and the north country and it stands out for many weeks in the earlier part of the growing season by dint of its lively gold-green colouring. But even after this has faded, the plant has a prouder carriage than *D. filix-mas* and the winter frosts have to be quite severe before it crumples.

That's one idea, and I have others; perhaps to use the taller shield fern, *Polystichum setiferum* and its sports, which are evergreen. But no; I must rein myself in. The last thing I want is for that border to look like a fern collection. To have a collection of ferns is one thing, and a great joy, but for it to look, from the way it is planted, like a fern collection is entirely second rate.

3.1.85

THE RECURRENT THEME OF WINTER

AT no time in the cycle of the seasons do you get that feeling of 'here we are again' so strongly as in winter. For one thing it is very quiet; there are few interruptions or distractions. Friends and visitors keep away – probably they don't want to be shaken from their illusion that in your garden it is always summer. Relations stay indoors.

It is in my rose garden that winter predominantly holds court. Enclosed by hedges, this area is isolated and, whereas it becomes stiflingly hot in summer, in winter it collects more frost and snow than anywhere. But one can usually prune and peg the roses. In doing so, I always try (being a moderate sybarite) to chase the sunlight. Until about 10.30 a.m., this scarcely counts but by eleven it is quite palpably warming, if you get yourself into just the right place. It seems a pity to have to go in to lunch at the best moment in a winter's day, because by two the sun is already failing and might just as well not be there at three.

Half the rose garden never catches the sun at all, in winter, and this I tend to deal with on dull, mild days. You can't have too much frost around for pegging, either, nor for picking up fallen rose leaves if you intend to do this. I have always been conscientious about it up to this year but have now rebelled. If they encourage slugs, let them. Slugs don't worry rose bushes. And as to harbouring disease – black spot in particular – I shall, as usual, counter this threat by applying a thick, smothering mulch, when pruning operations are at an end. There is short straw from some bales that were allowed to rot, which will be ideal for the purpose.

We hear and read a lot about the garden in winter but, speaking for myself, it gives me little actual pleasure. Nearly all pleasurable thoughts are in looking forward, in noting bulbs pushing through, the number of dormant flower buds on shrubs and trees and so on.

Anything that flowers in winter is tremendously welcome, of course, but mainly with the idea of bringing it into the house to be enjoyed under relaxed circumstances. A handful of evergreens looks well in the garden: the bay tree, the fatsias and the golden holly, for instance. But there is almost too much evergreen in this garden with its extensive architecture in yew hedging and topiary. Yew, we are always being told (and I have frequently said it myself) makes a sober and dignified background setting for borders of gay flowers. But where are the gay flowers? I haven't conditioned myself to using plastic yet. No, the yews in winter would look glum indeed but for one saving grace, and that is their irrepressibly cheerful contours. They have tried to imitate the man-made masonry of bricks and stone-work, but have failed triumphantly. Always they will bulge or lean or spread into comfortable obesity and the result is hilarious, giving the lie to all serious pretensions.

Still, I should really prefer a landscape garden at this time of year; to be able to look from my drawing-room window, as at Scotney Castle, down on to the wonderfully soft yet varied colouring of deciduous tree tops; trees of typical Kentish woodland and beyond to a grassy hillside set with a scattering of ancient-looking Scots pines. Is there a tree with more character, at maturity, than this?

Or to have water – a lake that really was a lake. Even at my own modest pondside I derive more satisfaction, in winter, from seeing the carmine dogwood stems and their reflections, than from any other garden feature. When the water is frozen over, the effect is ruined and the dogwoods become less than half themselves, but for most of a typical English winter, the water remains ice-free. The sun comes out between the depressions, and the whole scene vibrates with light and colour.

The dedicated flower gardener should never yearn for an open setting and a view, let's face it. Not for himself. All his efforts must be aimed at cutting down the devastating effects of living on a windy island. This is what has happened and is still happening in my garden, perched on its south-west-facing hillside. I have just planted another eight Leyland cypresses, to windward of us. We add and add and the trees grow and grow, so that little of the countryside remains to be seen even in winter, let alone in summer. What does remain are views of the half-timbered house, the oast house, the barn with the glow of its vast tiled roof and of other old farm buildings that were worked into the garden framework – views of these from the garden in the flattering light of low winter sunshine. For these we might well be envied. The buildings are full of warmth. In slate and millstone grit country, a comparable view might be chilly, but its inhabitants will have the compensation of mountain scenery and rushing streams; perhaps even of a natural rock garden and of running water that does not have to be pumped or measured or paid for.
11.1.68

GARDENING UNREST CURES

IF you paused to ask yourself, as well you might at this slack time of the year, how you could pull up your standards in gardening, my suggestion would be to take stock more often and more critically of your garden's appearance. I don't mean that everything should be in apple-pie order right now; I should be a terrible humbug if I did, because being dishevelled in winter comes as naturally to me as moulting to a bird in late summer.

Dormant plants whose top growth has been cut down disguise now the faults that will become apparent again when they really matter, which is when the garden is in fullest use, between spring and autumn. Try and visualise how your plants were and will again be looking at their peak. Two of the most likely defects in need of remedies are first that certain juxtapositions look pretty horrible and second (even more frequent) that you've not enough of any one kind of plant to look really effective. Your borders are suffering from the measles syndrome.

Good gardening and a quiet life seldom go hand in hand. To feel that you have at last achieved (even if by accident) some telling effect is a great fillip, but to go on feeling that you can just coast along with that same achievement year after year is a sure sign of mental sclerosis. Candid friends may rescue you off your pedestal but such friends are rare. Mostly they'll be thinking of the delicious wines with which you regale them and perhaps there'll be a chocolate roulade with the Beaumes de Venise. Candour is no match for competition of that sort. Spouses are candid, once the honeymoon is well out of the way, but discouragement is no help either and indifference is all too often the conjugal alternative. Nothing for it but to be your own severest critic.

When you acquire herbaceous perennials it is usually no more than one, two or three of a kind. You plant them where you hope they'll do well and there they'll remain for years to follow. Yet the chances that you've hit on their ideal role first shot are remote in the extreme, even with a lifetime's experience behind you and a vivid mind's eye which can picture the flowering scene when there's scarcely one helpful hint at the moment of planting.

Plants need to be moved around. You may have to move them half a dozen times before you get the position right (or before they give up the ghost) but that's nothing to be ashamed of. Trial and error may be a bit wasteful of time and energy but is far likelier to turn up the right answers than doing nothing at all. Plants can rarely be left to their own devices for long, anyway. They'll start going back or else aggressively muscle out their neighbours.

And how many big patches of any one plant can you boast of in your borders? I don't mean the invasive kinds, of which it is only too easy to have a lot and so has everyone else. I mean of things that are rather exciting in quantities like some of the better kniphofias or agapanthus or cardinal-flower-type lobelias or a dazzling cranesbill like the magenta-and-black *Geranium psilostemon*, or a vast quilt (covered with bees and butterflies) of *Sedum spectabile* instead of just two or three, and perhaps the spires of not one but ten or twelve blue perovskias behind them and somewhere not far distant a cohort of white cimicifuga spikes; ebullient buns of pink hydrangeas in a fermenting tumulus near by. One thought, one dream leads to another and this is the stuff of which gardening plans are made in January.

I know that they have to be brought to earth by the old cry 'We haven't the space,' but surely even with gardens of the dwindling size that we see around us today, more can be achieved than by pecking around with ones and twos. Plants love to be divided and reset in freshly improved soil. And this sort of propagation is of the simplest, yet the itch to be making more seems to be absent from the vast majority of garden owners. By all means start with just one plant. But then, when you see how beautiful it is, go on to the next step: 'I'm going to have a lot of that.' A feast, after all, is a great deal more fun than that puritanical enough which we are conned into believing as good.

Change is usually for the better unless it is of the reducing kind that is dishonestly presented to the world as streamlining. There's little call for that in our gardens for as long as we remain in reasonable health or can turn for assistance to younger, willing hands. That's not usually too difficult. Enthusiasm is infectious and gardening an inspiration as soon as you scratch beneath the surface.

Couldn't you make a once-and-for-all effort to have that deadly boring, drought-breeding, oppressively umbrageous tree removed this winter? The air will breathe so much freer without it. I appreciate the obstacles: undiscriminating tree worshippers around you, an awkward site for manipulation and extraction, how to get rid of the stump, the expense. But there must be some way, unless you prefer the alternative of removing yourself.

And I admit the possibility that the tree could be more valuable than you are, in which case we're back to the need for a second opinion and who's to give it?

12.1.84

GOING NATIVE

IN a way, I am glad that the British Isles have a very small number of truly native plant species. Otherwise there would be an outbreak of going British, as I find in other countries. All-Californian gardens are two a penny in California and lately I have had a heavy dose of the all-Australian garden.

What attracts people to this self-imposed strait-jacket? I can see that in California, over much of which summer drought is endemic, the choice of such plants will obviate the need for irrigation, but most of these drought resisters are mighty boring to live with. In Australia, where native plants have in many cases evolved to tolerate – indeed, to need – soils which are naturally extremely low in phosphates, it may be simpler to concentrate on these rather than upset them with a 'balanced' diet, suitable to exotic plants but not to them. That argument can easily be carried too far. I have seen Australian natives growing happily side by side with equally happy exotics.

For the ignorant gardener, confused by the wealth of plant material at his disposal, going native offers a simple restriction. But there is also a strong element of jingoism in this let's-stick-to-our-own-plants school.

After addressing a National Press Club luncheon in Canberra (the first time a horticulturist had ever spoken there), I was asked what I thought of native gardens. Having just been driven around the city by my kind host, to see what the form was, I was able to say that, judging by appearances, they were a disaster. This may not have pleased some of my audience but it aroused a cheer from quite a part of it. Next morning I appeared on the front page of *The Canberra Times* under the heading 'Canberra a Blot on the Landscape'.

The all-native front gardens I had seen – and there were plenty of them – consisted of tall, scrawny tree-shrubs, totally uncared for. 'So mournful,' as my host rightly remarked. The chief trouble obviously was that the owners had not the slightest interest in gardening. They planted their natives and there their duties ended. But how we should see and enjoy plants in our gardens is often entirely different from the way they grow in nature. Many Australian shrubs (and it often seems not to occur to Australians that there are many herbs and ground plants they could make their choices from) naturally grow tall, woody, upswept and of unpleasing habit. They lack character on account of their very rapid development.

In their first couple of years, after planting, these native shrubs are often of charming appearance, but they must be controlled, so as to keep them shapely. Then, compared with their prototypes in the bush, they may be incredibly beautiful.

To what extent they can be cut back into old wood I don't know, and this obviously depends on the species. Those of the myrtle family, like callistemons, will gladly respond to any amount of butchering. But hacking back need never become necessary if, every year, you tip the young growth and thus promote bushiness. As usual, after flowering is the time to get busy. In many cases you could probably shorten the shrub's youngest growth by a foot each year.

Successful native gardens are certainly possible. I saw an excellent example, belonging to George and Alvina Smith at Tyalge, Tynong North, east of Melbourne, Victoria. I was totally bemused by the range of unknown species yet delighted by their charm and by their excellent cultivation. Under 'Remarks' in their visitors' book, I wrote, 'Lost – but happy.'

But the gardens on which I made most detailed notes were mixed. There was Pat Learmonth's in West Victoria, with a stunning view, which she had carefully included within her garden scene, of a mountain in their Grampians. As well as Australian natives, there was abundance of roses, lavender and many other familiar plants. 'An excellent English garden,' I complacently remarked afterwards to Michael McCoy, my Australian friend and companion throughout the trip. 'Why English?' he queried. He was right. Like most of our gardens here, it was drawing on plant material appealing to its owner, from anywhere in the world and the result was great. Familiar, too, but that doesn't make it English.
14.1.93

TAKING OVER

IT is always fascinating to snoop around a lately vacated garden. Obviously the previous owners of the place which my great niece and nephew have now moved into were keen on 'the good life': a decrepit chicken house, a cow byre, a stable and paddock. They also liked their own vegetables. Having made a rather quick decision to quit, they had left parsnips about, calabrese and that awful tough curly kale, of which the best-known variety was so aptly known as 'Hungry Gap'. Indifferently grown vegetables (probably sown too late), although there was a compost heap at hand, on which marrows had roamed, and close to the house, where it could be admired from the sitting-room, a row of brilliant-blue plastic sacks in each of which a tomato had struggled. With sacks like that, what need of flowers?

Indeed, the principal flower was golden rod, but there was a random collection of conifers and other shrubs around the perimeter of an oblong lawn, and I was required (nothing would have stopped me) to pronounce on these.

The conifers pronounced on themselves. Most of them were eminently expendable: a pretty blue 'Boulevard' was about to grow out of the pretty stage; a nice dwarf golden cypress near by; an Irish juniper that had divided into two at an early age giving it a faintly raffish look; a Lawson and the statutory Leyland cypress (lucky there was only one – they usually go in coveys), and the bright-green, upswept cypress called 'Erecta Viridis' that develops hideous bare legs from early youth.

The only deciduous tree was – could it be otherwise? – the double pink 'Kanzan' cherry. It proclaims its identity by its stiffly ascending habit. As Cherry Ingram in his monograph pointed out, a more spreading habit can be encouraged by pruning repeatedly in youth to an outside bud. My relations' tree is now too large for any such modification, but it is a healthy specimen and, given another twenty years, will lose its stiffness and become spreading of its own accord. If and when they get tired of it, that will be the time to take action. For now it is a well-made piece of furniture in a bare room.

There's a bush laburnum, which will become a several-stemmed tree one day. I like that. Laburnums that have formed themselves can develop character.

A viburnum with all but one of its leaves shed is probably *Viburnum* × *burkwoodii*, and it has not suckered back to wayfaring tree stock, *V. lantana*, as so often happens. The latter looks well enough in its native chalk scrubland, but is a coarse, unlovely companion at close quarters. A friend at Ringmer, near Lewes, of whose garden I have written before, has one plonked bang in front of his sitting-out area where, despite the fact that he annually gives it the hedgehog haircut treatment, it effectively blocks the view. How appropriate that that view has now blossomed into a rash of new housing. I had long felt the want of exactly that, and, with retirement looming, it ties in neatly with his need for new neighbours to talk to over the fence.

These spring-flowering viburnums give notice six months ahead of how they intend to perform, with tight clusters of flower buds at the branch tips, so the shrub in Giny and Andrew's garden is a plus value. Not so a lilac, which is nothing but a thicket of suckers, the principal having long since departed. I would cut that lot down and apply Tumble-weed to the young shoots that would later develop.

A vigorous philadelphus, the mock orange, was still young enough not to have been spoilt by lack of pruning – and no pruning is anyway to be preferred to the ghastly botch that is generally made of this and a number of other strong-growing shrubs, by those who take fright at any plant growing larger than themselves.

I showed Andrew how to treat it, cutting out all the dead, flowered wood and leaving the strongest warm-brown, unbranched shoots intact. Then (the teacher in me ever anxious that his pupil should shine) made him show me how he would deal with another part of the bush. Should some of the young shoots be tipped? he asked. I refrained from screaming, as a spectral vision of the awful consequences processed before my inward eye. No, I said gently, the young shoots must be left full length and they will flower right to the tip. I did not go on to say that if tipped, they would, behind each cut, sprout a ridiculous and unbalanced umbrella frame of young shoots where no young shoots were wanted.

I wasn't sure of the next bush until I had squeezed one of its dormant buds and put it to my nose. Yes, it was a currant, the flowering *Ribes sanguineum*. Then we came to a shrub which, to my shame, I couldn't identify in its winter nakedness. Opposite buds; some sort of bush honeysuckle, I suspected. It'll have to wait till the growing season. Then another currant. 'Funny there should be currants and no forsythia,' I said. 'They usually hunt in couples.' But two paces on, there it was.

Predictably, the former owner had regularly cut it back to a dumpy 4 foot ball, so that it was covered with a mass of unbudded, watery young shoots of astounding vigour.

It is understandable treating a forsythia like this when there is not the space to allow it to show at least some grace of form (not a strong point in forsythias, aside from the underrated *Forsythia suspensa*). But in the present and many other cases, it could have grown as large as it liked without doing any harm to anyone. It wasn't even 'blocking the view' – the usual cry.

All that a forsythia needs is to have its oldest branches removed, allowing space for the production of new ones, these not to be tipped or interfered with until they themselves are ageing. If this sorting out is done in February, the removed branches can be brought into the house and gently forced into early flower.

21.1.88

A Diet of Roots

PLANNING ahead for vegetables is almost as exciting as planning ahead for flowers. Not quite, because you seldom plan your vegetable associations in the garden pictorially, though I toy even with this idea. I thought I might follow the dianthus-cum-Dutch iris planting in my main bedding-out border with ornamental vegetables. Nothing new about this, of course, but it would be new to me.

On the whole our vegetables are for steady guzzling. Fortunately Mrs C., who cooks my lunch, appreciates my appreciation of vegetables. To such an extent, indeed, that she seldom serves fewer than five kinds at a time. When it reaches seven I have to say, 'Only seven vegetables today, Mrs C.?' and then they drop back to four or five for a bit.

What to grow? The longer I live the easier I find it to dispense with potatoes, but one must have some, especially when there are visitors. Potatoes are a problem because the tastiest are the most difficult to grow. Furthermore they are likely to be prohibited for reasons which I forget, under EEC rules, so they tend to drop out of the lists. Also, the seed firms hate handling potatoes. Till now I've gone for 'Duke of York'. Taste and preference in potatoes is an extremely sensitive and individual matter – for those, that is, who notice what is in their mouth. I prefer a yellow waxy potato to a floury white one on every occasion except for baking in their skins. 'Duke of York' is yellow. So is 'Aura', my preference for a maincrop variety (I carry on with virus-riddled stock, not knowing where to procure any fresh and clean). But I must admit that 'Duke of York', although an early, does not inspire that feeling of elation, that something special in flavour which is the peculiar quality of most new potatoes. So I thought I would give the ancient 'Sharpe's Express' a run this year. Only to discover that it has just been dropped.

Nearest to the potato in appearance when cooked is the parsnip, which is perhaps why so many people regard it with undying hostility, having once in early childhood popped a parsnip in their little mouths thinking it would taste of potato and been shocked at the deception. But if you like parsnips you love them, glory in their goo, squelch their woolly fleeces between teeth, tongue and palate. I like parsnips. Unless you are growing them for show, which is a silly though faintly amusing waste of time (not as bad as growing prize pumpkins, however), there is no point, no metaphysical point in a long parsnip. Physically, of course, it is all point, its whole long taper being devised for that one end but this is not nearly as practical for growing and for preparing for the table as a short, rotund parsnip. My soil is clayish but even so is not unusual, I think, in being of better quality near the surface than lower down (on new building sites it is admittedly the other way about as builders seem to take a fiendish delight in burying top soil under yards of sub). This being the case I believe in growing root vegetables that naturally develop near the surface and the parsnip called 'Avonresister' does just that.

The same principle applies to beetroots and carrots. Nantes-type carrots are quick-maturing and stump-rooted. They are used for early cropping but are just as successful later in the season. Far more so with me, indeed, for by then the dreaded carrot fly has (up till now, anyway) gone to bye-byes and the carrots can be grown without that menace. So we sow all our carrot seed in June and July.

Youth is the essence of good white turnips. I am told that they deep-freeze very well, in which case it might be an idea to grow one large crop and freeze enough to last you through. Not that I always want the same vegetable the whole year round but convenience foods are an undoubted temptation, especially when you do not have the trouble of freezing them yourself. We still make a practice of sowing one lot of turnips 'early' (May is early in this set-up) and another in July.

As a result of the horrors of mush-slush swedes, endemic to institutional cooking, this is one of the few vegetables that I face up to reluctantly. A friend who is a gourmet assures me I am wrong and I can, by stretching my imagination to near snapping point, believe that swedes might, under ideal circumstances, be enjoyable but I do not intend to experiment. And why does he never serve swedes to me at his table?

I know onions are expensive but I still think they are a waste of space and effort inasmuch as the flavour of an onion is much the same wherever it has been grown whereas the majority of home-grown vegetables are vastly superior in this respect (and because, also, they are fresh) to anything you can buy. But celeriac is one of my most favourite root vegetables and this you must grow or go without in most areas. It has all the flavour of celery without any of the string and without any of the bore of growing celery properly. Again and again the slugs would defeat us. But if yours is a light, slug-repelling soil then perhaps there is a case for celery.

29.1.76

FEBRUARY

Catch Phrases and Covert Comments

THOSE readers who are aching to do the right thing at the right moment can look lower down the page. I can't help you with tips or suggestions for your seed order, not having yet got to grips with my own. I can, topically, report, that my first *Iris histrioïdes* 'Major' came out on 17 January, which was eight days earlier than in 1971. We have still had no winter to speak of: *Melianthus major* and the gazanias are plump and fresh as in summer.

So now let us dwell upon ourselves, for a little, and examine some of our jargon and clichés and the meaning that lies behind certain common gardening phrases and euphemisms.

First by visitors to your (or my) garden. An invariable question is 'How many gardeners have you?' or 'How many of you do all this?' or 'Do you do all this yourself?' (which is a bit fatuous at times, when the garden is 6 or 8 acres in extent and crammed with detail). This is a natural and innocent expression of curiosity, though the questioner will often be unable to apply the information when he has it, since he is no gardener himself and hasn't a clue about what work is involved. A less innocent remark on the same tack is 'You must find it very hard to get the labour, these days,' meaning that you have obviously let the place get out of control. Long grass, however intentional, always provokes this comment. Or there is the more pussy-ish 'You don't know what a comfort it is for a gardener like me to see weeds in a garden like yours.' Or 'Do tell me, what *is* the best time to come and see your garden?' (obviously not now or any other time I've tried). I think I shall take a leaf out of a friend's book: not having caught up with tidying her garden, she is now calling it an adventure playground.

Only yesterday I was asked by one of our rare winter visitors

'What do you do about the moss in your lawns?' when it must have been perfectly obvious that I do nothing about the moss in my lawns (except enjoy its bright emerald colouring in winter and lament its browning in spring). Come the spring, a visitor will look meaningfully at my (or your) hydrangeas and ask, 'When *is* the right time to dead-head hydrangeas?' which is supposed to sound better than 'It's time you dead-headed those hydrangeas, old cock.' Actually I don't find it sounds any better.

There is a kind of in-talk when two gardening friends are inspecting the garden belonging to one of them. The visitor will point with his foot and ask, 'What are you calling that?' which implies that he knows what to call it but that 'they', the systematic botanical name-twisters, may have been meddling. '*Reinoldii*' comes the brief reply (*Senecio reinoldii*, actually, but *Senecio* is understood between the two of them). 'Oh! but surely it's either *elaeagnifolius* or *rotundifolius*.' '*Rotundifolius* is the old name for the same thing.' 'I threw it out six or eight years ago.' 'It has a good leaf.'*

The last remark is one I find myself constantly making as an apology for a plant that has miserable flowers.

Writers on gardening matters have their own code. Their presumption is that the majority of gardeners have no outside assistance, are themselves congenitally idle and would rather not be gardening at all were it not for the neighbours. Hence all the emphasis on labour-saving ground-cover. But if you read that something makes 'excellent ground-cover in difficult places' (i.e., in dry shade) you may be fairly certain that an excessively boring plant is being recommended. 'Deserves wider recognition' is another desperate attempt to gain the reluctant reader's wandering attention. Any suggestion that a plant may need staking is taboo nowadays (except with bearded irises, when we are told that 'a small cane to each stem will provide all the necessary support'). If it is shapeless and messy or flops around we dwell upon its 'pleasant informality'.

* The name now being touted for this plant is *Brachyglottis rotundifolia*.

'Colourful' is an adjective widely brandished by purveyors of garden sundries: buckets, watering cans, wheelbarrows, string and every sort of implement. If these articles are in brilliant shades of red, green and yellow, they will help to keep your garden bright even when it has failed to produce flowers. The unusual 'container' (and 'containerisation' has reached the garden centre via the docks) is now as much a feature of the garden as of the flower arranger's world. Colourful fibre-glass wheelbarrows with drainage holes are constructed with the express and original intention of using them like pots or tubs.

I don't really mind speaking of the ubiquitous 'container' for flower arranging, where 'vase' would once have been the natural word. Vase is, after all, rather ugly-sounding. But three words in the floral art vocabulary that do fill me with foreboding and disgust are 'drapes', 'accessories' and 'figurines': a dread that will not be understood, let alone shared, by the floral artists themselves.
3.2.72

SERVANT OR MASTER

FLOWER photography arouses very mixed feelings in me. So do the photographers. I know, by now, where I stand with it myself. I take about six hundred or seven hundred transparencies of flowers and gardens a year, and they are useful, both for lectures or, if the quality is high enough, for reproduction in books and articles. Some book publishers insist on all the photographic work being done by the one professional engaged for that job. Even if I can produce an excellent – well, reasonably good – picture of an interesting subject particularly relevant to the text and not available to the official photographer, they'll have none of it.

But other publishers are glad to use as many decent pictures as I can muster. As they get them for nothing, this reduces the cost of the book. The advantage of using one's own photographs is that one knows exactly what is being represented. Most of the mistakes in a book or article occur in the captions, because the caption writer doesn't know what he is looking at and all too often the photographer doesn't either.

The fact that a professional photographer happens to specialise in plants and gardens seems to be more or less of an accident. He (or she, be it understood) is more interested in photographic effects than in the interest of a particular planting. He will know few plant names himself (while latching on repetitively to particular favourites, as it might be the snakeshead fritillary or the teazle, both having satisfying structures) and will depend for identifications on the garden owner, who is also fallible and may be a lot keener on what plants look like than on what they are called. There's plenty of room for howlers.

Most pros love low lighting, either to show dramatically long and spooky shadows or to take shots against the sun, so that his plant subject appears to be wearing a halo. I think we are all united in hating the glare of the midday sun, in summer, which makes flowers limp and appears to drain them of colour. As most gardens open to the public are visited at just these unflattering hours, an unfortunate mental or photographic impression is all too frequent.

Photography on location requires great patience. If conditions are ever just right, the moment is fleeting. Among the demands, cloud formations, the amount of sunshine and absence of wind are among the most important. Photographs are useful to me but I hate to 'waste' time in their taking, which is why I shall never be a good photographer. I am far too impatient (though not with my plants, be it added). On the other hand I'm not too bad at composing a picture in the view-finder as also, I flatter myself, I can arrange plants to make a satisfying planting.

What about you? What category of photographer are you? Do you habitually ruin a good garden feature by sticking a human figure in front of it? Oh well; I suppose the feature should feel flattered at being considered worthy of forming a background.

But that is not serious photography. The serious amateur photographer is a far greater problem, largely because he so seriously inflates the importance of his 'art' and is apt to forget other considerations. He is a slave to his hobby. When I give an illustrated talk, I naturally select those photographs which will make a decent impression and someone at the end is pretty sure to come up and ask for photographic details, starting with the camera. 'I've no idea,' I truthfully tell him. 'I know it's Japanese because I had to buy it in Japan, where I lost its predecessor.' Obviously I'm a hopeless case and am let off that hook forthwith.

The amateur photographer, with great devotion, lugs an enormous amount of equipment around. He has a generally dissatisfied air, squinting about him as though things could and should be better (we all know that). 'When *is* your garden at its best?' one heavily loaded young New Zealander enquired. 'Today; now,' was my firm reply.

I don't wonder that tripods are not allowed into some of the most visited gardens. Two human feet are bad enough without having three extras stuck into your borders. Professionals are nearly always considerate, in this and other respects. They know their continued acceptance depends on good behaviour. Not so the amateur, who blithely (except that there's nothing blithe about him) wades into and tramples down my meadow grass at its longest, in order to get a better viewpoint. I'm afraid I shout my protest when I see that happening.

When I see him taking close-up shots of flowers, I know it isn't the plant that interests him. A very small area in focus will be blown up to ten times its natural size for the admiration of fellow photographers and family members who have to admire out of duty. Orchids are favourite subjects, because of their flowers' complexity. Well, it is fascinating, but I query whether it is the more so for this grotesquely out-of-scale representation.

So engrossed are these people in their hobby that they

entirely fail to appreciate the garden they are in. So it is, also, with visitors from abroad who start clicking their cameras the moment they enter the garden precincts – or even before – but have precious little notion of what they have been taking or where until they get home and see their films developed. Even then, there must be a good deal of head scratching and 'Where was that?'s.

Which is not to deny that photographs are an invaluable record and aid to memory. What is the ideal way to see a garden, anyway? Not just with a camera but a notebook, also. And a companion with whom to discuss what you're seeing (and to have a few jokes with). If the garden owner is with you, that complicates matters in some ways. Perhaps your companion can take the pictures and notes while you concentrate on talking and looking. The owner's presence provides insights which often entirely alter your own perceptions. I suppose the most important thing is not to be in a hurry. As a photographer, I am.

4.2.93

THE POND IS STILL ALIVE

THE pond might not be thought a good subject for winter contemplation, except in a day-dreaming, fireside sense, looking ahead to summer warmth and lushness. But this is a mistake. Our pondside is one of the pleasantest places to linger, even now; particularly now, in some respects. It helps to catch your weather right, of course, but the only really dead periods are when the whole surface is muffled in ice and snow, which hasn't happened yet. Indeed, the surface has never been frozen over for more than a few hours at a time and thin ice is still beautiful, because you can admire the crystalline structure wherewith it formed. Reflections are still fairly bright and at the same time you can see through the ice to what's going on below.

Mostly the weather has been open, which is best of all, and the water has been able to live its double life to the full. You can alternately change your perspective between a world of reflections and a world of subaqueous activity. How clear the water is in winter! After all those brown and turbid months, a whole new dimension is revealed. You look through layers of submerged vegetation to the bottom of the pond itself. Now and again a fish moves listlessly across your line of vision. When the sun shines, there are shadows; one leaf against another, gradually thickening and darkening, down, down.

Very important, those submerged oxygenating aquatics, as they are inelegantly termed. Important to install the right one; the one whose leafy shoots appeal to you the strongest. Why can't I have several? you may ask, hoping for jam and butter on your bread, and perhaps honey and clotted cream as well. It doesn't really work with weeds, which is what we're talking about. Pond weeds are not companionable. Each likes to be top dog and sooner rather than later, one of them is.

My pond has the water violet, *Hottonia palustris*, and it suits me, which is lucky because it was there before I was born and every effort to get rid of it (my brother's, not mine) has been a triumphant failure. The weed positively enjoys persecution. After each fresh onslaught, there are always some bits that escape, and they do so much better for being relieved of the competition of what was removed (pigeon shooting is, topically, supposed to work in much the same way, benefiting rather than reducing the species). The water violet could hardly look less like a violet, unless it were a cactus. It has filigree leaves arranged in loose rosettes, and the rosettes are arranged in billowing feather-clouds of the richest green colouring – as luminous a green as any in the February garden. Imagine sunshine on this and then superimpose a stabbing red exclamation mark, made by a goldfish (and how did this supremely red fish ever come to be named gold?).

Goldfish appear not to become wholly torpid in winter. They are about; you can even see them moving under a skin of ice, and although the heron fishes here, there are so many fish for him to catch and so much cover, that it never seems to make much difference. That is in the horse pond, which is a fair size and has a mud bottom. Not so in our formal octagonal pool, alas, where I have my more precious hi-goi and golden orfe. The heron has been there, too, and I fear all may be lost. Most anti-heron devices are visually unacceptable, to my way of looking. The only possibility, if it works as it is said to (but you know what people will say), is the notion of a dummy heron standing in the pool. Real herons are alleged to stay away if they see another of their kind in occupation. But what sort of dummy? It could so easily descend to gnome level. On the other hand it might be such a beautiful work in bronze that someone would pinch it forthwith. Life is full of flies, as my father used to say.

But to return to the horse pond's vegetable contents: what amazes me is that dormancy is so very incomplete. You can see the waterlilies right from the floor to the surface because the hottonias won't tolerate the shade they cast but make a respectful circle round each colony. At this time of year the lilies are casting scarcely any shade, but they are growing. There are rich, reddish-purple young leaves at every stage of development from bottom to top; flower buds too, but when leaves and buds actually reach the surface they find the world less agreeable than they had been led to suppose, and wither.

Practically nothing is wholly without signs of living. The giant buttercup, *Ranunculus lingua*, which loves to roam about the pond bottom has submerged bunches of green leaves almost as broad as a dock's. From among the dead stems and leaves of *Cyperus longus*, there are green hints when you look into the centre of them and this bulks mainly as brown remnants 2 or 3 feet above the water's surface. It is a good foliage plant in its summer season, with leaves that radiate from their stem tops like the spokes of an umbrella.

On the bank, the gunnera's dark leaf remnants, folded over their crowns for protection, resemble the last remains of some decayed monster. Looking at them, a friend who wasn't wearing her spectacles remarked that we had evidently been doing some dredging.
10.2.72

SLOW: DOGS ABOUT

WHATEVER worries a dog may cause you in the garden, never forget that it is marvellous company, well worth a spot of trouble and anxiety. When I go forth to garden, I look something like the White Knight, except that I don't bother to wear a coal scuttle on my head. In one hand a large trug with trowel, secateurs, string, saw, mallet, kneeler, a board to stand on if the ground is wet and a garden fork balanced on top of that. Under my other arm, Tulipa's iron-framed bed complete with a couple of blankets.

Having explored as much as she feels inclined, she uses her bed as base and if she's tired or chilly, she gets right inside the blankets (a natural instinct in dachshunds) and becomes entirely invisible. Which is her best protection against the visiting public, who will pass by without knowing she is there; only sometimes she foolishly gives her presence away by growling. A growl rising from beneath layers of blanket sounds odd, and she is laughed at, which she hates. Dogs have no sense of humour.

If she's visible from the first, she lays herself open to every kind of attention, from being pursued or otherwise teased by sadistic children (what horrible little beasts they can be; I'm ashamed to think I was one myself) to being invited to 'come here, little doggie'. Funny how people seem to imagine that every dog should be their friend, even if neither has met the other before or ever will again. But dogs are as selective as we are.

There are visitors who think that if they talk to my dog for long enough they're bound to get a reaction from me. But they are wrong, unless to tell them to leave her alone. If they have something sensible to say or ask, that's quite another matter.

In summer, the bed is unnecessary. Tulipa can lie on my jacket (dogs become very possessive and rather unapproachable when on master's jacket) or, if it's too hot even for that, she'll stretch out on the lawn. Soon that'll be too hot and she'll creep into a border and flop under the shade of some plants. That'll soon be too cold and out she'll come again. Sun, shade, sun, shade; dogs have very poor thermostats.

'Do you mind dogs in your borders?' I am asked. 'Do you mind children in your borders?' you might equally ask. It depends on their size and behaviour. A standard dachshund is still quite a small animal and, with a somewhat reptilian glide, it can move among dense plantings doing no damage at all, unless you get worked up and frighten it. Then it may try to escape your wrath by the shortest route, which is certain to be the most destructive.

So my dogs are usually free to walk in the mixed borders. If it's a bedding-out area or some new planting that's being trespassed on, then they soon learn the meaning of a curt 'Off it!' Dogs are as sensible as children. They know when you mean it or whether you don't really, and react accordingly.

When I have two dogs, which I normally do, they keep each other company more, and me less, but are a lot of fun – when they're there. Dachshunds are inveterate hunters but they like to hunt in couples, at the least (more than two quickly becomes an unmanageable pack). When your eye is off them, they'll sneak away, returning hours later, horribly pleased with themselves and covered in mud and badgers' fleas – they always go to ground. Worth it? I suppose so, though I've lost a dog that way (the other returned with nasty badger bites) and had to dig another out.

If you can't fence your garden in, there'll always be some worry; the worst, that they'll stray on to the road, where there are such interesting scents from other dogs. My dachshunds have always been complete fools about traffic. Luckily we're in a cul-de-sac, but even so, farm traffic and tradesmen whizz up and down, always assuming, because they've done it so often before, that there can't be any obstacle to their progress.

I have bitches (I enjoy breeding from them) and they are far

40

less inclined to wander than dogs. Another difference is that a dog will lift its leg against the same unfortunate bush until that bush is killed, whereas a bitch makes brown patches, surrounded by a very vigorous green ring, in your lawn, which is preferable unless you're lawn proud.

And anyway, it doesn't have to be the lawn. Dogs are creatures of habit. Given early training, they'll do their jobs wherever you tell them, but you have to be firm and prepared to accompany them in bad weather to the selected area until they know and go there automatically. In a shrubbery is an obviously good spot, eventually providing nourishment for the shrubs.

When Crocus (Tulipa's grandmother) was a pup, it was January and she got so used to squatting on the snow that when it was melting she sought out the last remaining patches rather than use strange turf.

A smooth, short-haired dog, like a standard dachshund, is much the best to have around the garden. They pick up very little dirt, and what they do is easily rubbed off as soon as dry. Baths are not needed. I've only had one dachs that would plunge into the pond or any other piece of water at the slightest opportunity. Labradors are terrible like that, with the added embarrassment of preferring close human company when they come out to shake.

And smooth, short-haired dachshunds don't pick up burrs. When I was a child we had cocker spaniels and they collected horrible wads and mats of burdock burrs and agrimony seeds in their ears and feathers. We didn't grow acaenas (the much despised bidibid in New Zealand) in those days. I now have the carmine-red burrs of *Acaena novae-zelandiae* covering a large part of the sunk garden floor and cannot doubt that its barbs would be even more tiresome in a long-haired dog's coat than in my socks.

In the snow, your dog with feathered legs collects balls of ice. Their tinkling sounds pleasant but the dog hates them. No such trouble with dachshunds although, with their short legs, they can't be expected to like deep soft snow. For Tulipa, we clear a track to the bay tree, under which the snow is always thin. She can perform, there, if somewhat resentfully.

Dogs all have nasty habits, no matter how refined their owners. If seen rolling on the grass, you needn't imagine it's sheer joie de vivre. There'll be the added attraction of a glutinous bird's dropping, which you'll then have to sponge off.

As with children, you'll be worrying about what your animal is eating in the garden, especially when it is an inexperienced puppy. A child can be trained not to put anything into its mouth without permission (so I'm told by firm parents). Not so a dog, and usually it doesn't matter. If the plant disagrees with it, the dog will be sick and there the matter ends (if your reasonably sized dog happens to be indoors when it starts heaving – and it usually is – pick it up quickly and carry it out; they find it quite difficult to retch while being carried).

Slug pellets are lethal, however, and being sweet, a dog will go out of its way to eat them. If you see this happening, rush it straight to the vet, or give it a couple of doses of washing soda crystals put straight down its throat to make it sick. But you'll still have to syringe its mouth clean. I nearly lost Tulipa this way but spotted and acted on the trouble before the poison got into her bloodstream. Liquid slug killers are OK, once applied to the ground. Mercurial lawn dressings can be nasty and I never use them. Otherwise I've had no trouble with garden weedkillers, pesticides or fungicides. Rat poison must never be placed within their reach. It causes a slow and painful death.

Generally it is interesting to notice which plants a dog most enjoys eating in your garden. Mine like hairy bitter cress, a weed now at its lushest and good to include in salads. They're crazy for every sort of campanula, leaves, buds or flowers. Incidentally, I wish that rampion, *Campanula rapunculus*, was available in the seed trade, as it is said to be excellent salading.

Basically, dogs like to eat anything they see you eating – peaches, apples, pears, raspberries, lettuce, green peas, chicory, especially when blanched in the cellar, likewise seakale. They love nice crunchy tulip bulbs and crocuses, but steer well clear of daffodils. Very sensible. An ancient brother

and sister living together in our village got upset tummies after eating daffodil bulbs under the impression they were onions. They put the remainder of their meal down for Clara, the spaniel, but she wouldn't touch it.
11.2.88

THE SPRING IS SPRUNG

WINTER is very nearly at an end. Spring-like days were already with us in January, but there is nothing unusual about that. Indeed, the season is not unduly advanced. My first *Iris histrioïdes* blooms were not out till 2 February this year, whereas they usually manage it for January. Somehow these first spring days, coming as they do in winter, always take us unawares. We react, according to our natures: either accepting and enjoying the moment gratefully and without reservation, or shaking our heads and muttering that we shall pay for it later, which gives enjoyment of a different kind.

A friend on the telephone the other day remarked that I couldn't be gardening in this weather. 'Oh yes I can,' I said, 'and in the garden is where you should be too.' He thought not. I like home comforts but it's quite surprising how easily some people are put off; a grey sky with a hint of dampness in the air, and they'll keep the curtains drawn all day, metaphorically speaking.

Another fallacy that seems to be current is that the ground is waterlogged. It is nothing of the sort. I garden on clay and there are some sticky patches, true, but I have recently, in catching up on my autumn work, come across several places where cracks in the ground from last year's drought have not yet closed up. The rains we had last month would have flooded our valley in a normal year, but not in this. These rains, however inconvenient, are badly needed, and we should be on our guard against a spring drought.

Although there is a best moment for doing most garden tasks, it is often preferable to tackle each of them when it is in your mind than to delay, with the consequent likelihood of not doing it at all. I have been pruning my hydrangeas. Perhaps I should be wiser to leave it till the end of next month, but I am banking on nothing too serious in the way of frost coming along, and the advantage of getting this job behind you early is that you don't wreak nearly as much damage through knocking off unfolding buds as you would later.

Hydrangea pruning (except for a few oddments like *Hydrangea paniculata* and *H. cinerea*) consists entirely in thinning out old and tired branches to make room for new. If your bushes habitually suffer from frost damage, there will be no pruning to do; merely the removal of dead wood (or of the whole bush if you're going to be sensible about it). But prosperous bushes do need pruning, say every other year. Having done it to 'Madame Mouillère', the most popular white hortensia, I see that nothing I have left in is more than five years old. Every five years, in fact, the bush is entirely renewed. Up to that age, old branches are still capable of producing strong young shoots. They are about 18 inches long and dark-brown. The bush itself is 5 foot high and more across. If I wanted a larger shrub, I should do no pruning, but the quality of its blooms would fall off. I'm not out for whopping great heads but I do want whatever variety I grow to do itself justice. Another attention you should pay your hydrangeas now is by feeding and mulching them with bulky organics like farmyard manure, deep-litter chicken manure, garden compost, leaf mould and the like. The mulch will keep them happy through any drought that may develop and the food is necessary for what is, by nature, a greedy shrub. In about six weeks' time I shall add a boost of general inorganic fertiliser to their diet at 4 ounces to the square yard. Hydrangeas will make a fantastic display, this year, after last summer's baking, so they will need and deserve extra food and drink to make good this drain on their energies.

I tend to think of hydrangeas and rhododendrons in the

same breath. Both can be similarly used and abused, but their seasons are complementary. If you have a young rhododendron that looks a bit leggy or that could become so because its natural habit is inclined that way (as with the scented, June-flowering *Rhododendron discolor*) it is a good idea to remove the leading bud on every shoot all over the bush. This is a form of pruning. Gardeners do it automatically on flowering shoots, though they call it dead-heading. Most of the choicer rhododendrons don't flower when young – which is partly what makes them choice. You are not losing anything by removing its leading buds; you are simply stimulating the two or three dormant lateral buds just behind it into growth. Instead of one large new shoot, you get about three smaller ones. The result is a denser, more compact bush with a generous foundation of branches. In fact, by removing these terminal buds you will often stimulate an already leggy bush to make young shoots from its bare legs. The ideal moment for performing this task is just as the leaf buds are emerging from dormancy and beginning to expand; this may be at any time from March to June, according to variety.

Vines should be pruned quickly, now, if not already done; otherwise cuts made into old wood bleed most horribly, once the sap is rising, in March. It is well worth removing all the old leaves from epimediums and from Lenten roses (*Helle-borus orientalis* hybrids) now, so that you can enjoy their flowers unencumbered by sordid foliar appendages.
19.2.70

Discovery and Revelation

GARDENING is laced with epoch-making discoveries. I'm sure all readers will agree. One of my own recent discoveries is that you can move full-grown plants of parsley without killing

45

them. Well may you gasp because, of course, we all know from the word go that parsley has to be sown *in situ* and left undisturbed, apart from a little judicious thinning (I love doing things judiciously: it gives me a feeling of sterling worth), for the rest of its life.

Well, I'd used some last summer for bedding with tagetes (nothing so common as marigolds, mark you) and they had made colossal plants. It was 'Unwin's Bravour', in case you're interested, and gave me some excellently level results, unlike their 'Moss Curled', which I'm avoiding for the future; even one po-faced dud in a grouping can spoil the sample. At the end of the season, way had to be made for hyacinths and pollies; it seemed an awful shame to throw those beautiful, bright-green frilly creatures away, so we decided to move some of them. Their roots were enormous – long, white, fleshy fangs, that would have made a meal in themselves (if they hadn't first made a meal of us) – but looked most unpromising material for pushing around the garden. However, nothing succeeds like success, as I always tell my partner at bridge after we're landed in an impossible contract and are then presented with it by the defence.

It was years before I got around to the discovery that bizzy lizzy (busy lusy) of the kitchen windowsill, that scrawny object that should be known as skinny liz, becomes a transformed Cinderella if planted in a nice dank, dark spot in the garden for the summer. If you will but grow the seed strain importantly listed as *Impatiens holstii* hybrids,* which was the one I cut my teeth on, and be sure not to stint the water (a soaking wet summer with week upon week of driving rain is a great ally), it will build up into a lush 3 foot hedge, glistening with rude health and spangled all over from August till November with characteristic flat-faced flowers in an outrageous assortment of vivid pinks, mauves, magentas, scarlet and carmine. You would have to turn to a modern dress fabric to find a more riotous association and the curious thing is that it works. All you have to do is relax and enjoy yourself.

---

* Discontinued years ago, you might have guessed.

46

Of course gardening is not for enjoyment. No, no, indeed not. It was never intended to be. There is no virtue in enjoyment. The hard grind, the solid slog, these are the character-forming attributes of our – I nearly said hobby – of our mission.

What invisible worm eats the stylosas? Which of the devil's disciples devours the *Iris unguicularis* before we have time to cull their buds? You thought it was slugs, but have you proved it? Have you been into the garden with a powerful torch after dark on a wild winter's night to look? I knew you hadn't, but I have. I'm always telling people when they bring me their grievances to search out their enemies in the night garden at every season of the year, but they never take the slightest notice. I know they're not going to from the superior expression on their faces when I make the recommendation. *They'd rather not know.* They'd far rather moan to me about their wretched clematis shoots and buds being eaten to shreds by an unknown force than identify the said force and perhaps do something about it. Or if I tell them what the probable cause is and suggest a cure, 'I've done that,' comes the pat reply and a triumphant look as much as to say 'You just suggest something that I haven't tried' (I often suggest they should give up gardening).

But I am straying from the stylosas. The revelation that I am about to unfold. No, I think unfolding is reserved for miracles. Explode? I should enjoy exploding a revelation but that one's reserved for myths and theories. Reveal then? That's it; revealing a revelation is unexceptionable. We had guests coming to dinner and at the last moment I realised that I wanted to show off with some stylosas which I grow better than they do, so I rushed into the garden with my Space Beam torch, a bright-red, scientific, streamlined affair, and there it was, the culprit in the act of decapitating a bud. Not a slug at all but a bright-green caterpillar. Rather engaging, actually.

And do you know why it's a mistake to plant an ivy by your back door? I should be furious if you guessed because I was fooled, utterly. It is a beautiful green-and-cream variegated ivy with outsize leaves: *Hedera colchica* 'Dentata Variegata', no less. The back door leads into our kitchen, as is the way of back doors. It's nice to have it open in fine weather, so we have a gauze fly-screen (this was my civilised American brother-in-law's hygienic brainwave). In November, we took this down for the winter, but warm weather returned, the door was left open and in surged a vast army of bluebottles and wasps. They were just looking in after pollinating the ivy's blossom, for November is Ivy-Blossom Time.

I have scarcely the space, now, to disclose the secret love life of the violet, which must await a future thrilling instalment. But when I relate that a visitor told me of a young violet (*Viola cucullata*) in her garden which had never yet flowered but had seedlings all around it, you will appreciate that another crop of revelations may burst upon you at any moment.
21.2.74

TREE CARE

SEEING that trees are the largest and most important components in our gardens, it is surprising how little we know about them and how easy it is to care for them misguidedly. I have to include myself in this generalisation. If anything goes seriously wrong with an important or sizeable tree here, my instinct is to turn for help to the tree expert. Some experts are or seem extremely expensive and this tempts one to go to a freelancer or less than fully qualified arborist, which can be entirely successful; or it can be disastrous – I am thinking of my mulberry.

What led me into this subject was wound dressings, which are, admittedly, not nearly as important as the wounds themselves, but if they're not doing the job they're supposed to it's as well to know we're wasting our time and money.

I have had my suspicions about their efficacy for some time. Apropos of a pruning job, I wrote in this column in April 1979 of 'painting the wounds over with Arbrex like a good boy', which was the end of the paragraph and of the subject as printed after editing, but in the manuscript I had added in parenthesis '(One can never be dead certain that the wounds wouldn't have reacted just as well without being dressed, and then there'd have been no question of getting the paint on one's clothes)'.

When in the USA last summer I was told that experiments by Dr Alex Shigo, a leading expert on tree care and tree diseases, showed that wound dressings made no difference – a claim which considerably upsets orthodox opinion. On my writing to him he kindly supplied me with relevant literature.

In *Plant Disease* Vol. 66, 1982, of The American Phyto-pathological Society, he writes, 'There are many types of wound dressings. The common treatment for wounds has been to cover them with shellac or some asphalt or bituminous material. Why paint or dress a tree wound? The rationale has been to block out micro-organisms; or to keep moisture in; or to keep moisture out; or to apply chemicals in the dressing that will kill the wood-inhabiting micro-organisms. Anyone who knows anything about micro-organisms and their size knows the wound cannot be shielded from them. The moisture-in or moisture-out rationale is also unrealistic because dressings coat the surface of the wound. Experiments in which trees were dissected and micro-organisms isolated revealed that treated wounds did no better than untreated ones.' The relevant photographs of treated and untreated wounds on the same tree show that dressings do not prevent discoloured and decayed wood from developing. 'To be worthwhile,' he continues, 'a dressing would have to do better than the controls to justify the time it takes to treat the wounds and the cost of the dressing.' Quite so.

Now what about the actual pruning? In the first place, a very pertinent question is whether, for the time being, the tree needs messing about with at all. Hear Dr Shigo: 'The tree-care industry seldom gets credit or profit for examining trees and then stating that the best thing to do is to leave them alone for a while. I spend money gladly when after a medical exam I hear the doctor say all is well, keep doing whatever you are doing! Why can't we have such a system for monitoring healthy trees?' That seems a fair analogy and only goes to show how mean we are apropos of plants in expecting advice to be free unless it leads to action.

Much damage is done to a tree by removing its branches flush with the trunk. To leave a stub is also bad but the flush cut is worse. This isn't just because it leaves an unnecessarily large, open-wound scar but because you have cut back beyond the collar, which is located at the base of every branch and which is in most species visible as a bark ridge. If you are removing a branch you should do so as close as possible to this collar but on no account into or inside it since it is at the collar that new cells will be made to wall off the damage caused by your cut or, indeed, by any other kind of damage or wounding undergone by a branch.

This walling off, which Dr Shigo calls compartmentalisation, is a tree's main line of defence in the face of wounding or attack by disease-causing agents. Unlike humans and other animals, trees cannot restore injured and infected tissues by healing, that is to say by new replacement cells made in the same position. All the tree can do is to hive off the damaged area, setting a boundary beyond which the damage may not spread. It is not successful in thus localising trouble all the time but it is some of the time and the collar of a branch is the point at which this walling-off process is initiated.

When you look at a tree with a dead branch you can see, at the base of the dead tissue, a lump or callus which the tree has made, sealing itself off with a barrier of new tissue, from the dead. If you decide to prune away the dead branch you must beware undoing all the tree's good work by cutting back beyond its reparation work.

Dr Shigo is a pragmatist. He realises that the signals are not always clear and that in the real working world we can't get it right all the time; but perhaps eighty per cent of the time. That wouldn't be too disgraceful, but still involves knowing more than do most of us about how trees survive.
23.2.84

A Lack of Vision

Isn't it sad that other members of your family are so singularly lacking in the imagination and visionary projection with which you yourself are gifted? If only they would learn to trust you, the garden could be transformed.

Outside the window that my study looks out through is a 9 foot chestnut pole. It isn't quite straight but it has been knocked in as vertically as it will go and in the past year it has weathered nicely. I can visualise it as a column of honeysuckle; a particularly good form of our native *Lonicera periclymenum* that Valerie Finnis let me take cuttings of three years ago. The outside of the flower is dark, glossy red of a sumptuous richness in contrast to the white interior. She hadn't a name for it. Probably it is one of the many clones masquerading as 'Belgica' or 'Serotina'. I might call it 'Valerie', thus adding to the long list of plants already blessed with the kudos of being named after her. Happy honeysuckle.

But my miserable brother doesn't like the pole. He can't see that in a very few years it will have vanished beneath a fragrant mantle of blossom. When that has happened, I shall hear no more of the matter, not because he'll then see what a brilliant outcome my plan has had but because he'll have ceased to notice the pole.

Now we have to cut a yew hedge back to the bone, but he won't mind that. In fact he knows more about how it should be done than I do. But I remember the furore at Sissinghurst Castle and what the head gardeners endured when the yew alley there had to be given shock treatment. It had been extremely badly planted in the first place, not straight nor regularly, even, but, most seriously, leaving far too little lateral space for the hedge to grow into. Five feet across the base is a minimum. So, within thirty years the alley had almost disappeared.

Luckily yew responds extremely well to being cut hard back into old wood, allowing it thereafter to reclothe with young shoots nearer to the centre of the hedge. The new growth doesn't necessarily or even primarily come from the place where you made your cuts. Most of it comes from the centre but the point is that it comes. In a mere few years you'd never have guessed that there could have been such a fuss. But you should have heard it. Vita Sackville-West was weak when drastic action was called for and one wonders what would have happened if she'd been alive.

This problem is bound to crop up sooner or later where a path runs alongside a hedge because your annual hedge trimming can never go quite as far back as it did the year before, even if the girth increase is only an eighth of an inch a year. It is now seventy-five years since the hedge I have to take in hand was planted and it has bulged some 9 inches too far over the adjacent path. Realising that *il faut souffrir pour être belle*, I shan't mind the scars at all but there'll be plenty who will.

I long to see vegetation sprouting from four ancient cattle-drinking tanks in our garden. Built of handmade bricks with nicely moulded coping, they stand about 3 foot high and Lutyens worked them into the garden design. Until 1963, they were full of water, as intended, being interconnected and gravity fed from a distant pond. But that hard winter killed the supply pipe and the tanks have stood empty ever since, collecting bits of rubbish thrown in by visitors.

The one in our formally designed rose garden is a principal central feature. I should love to see a bamboo, perhaps *Phyllostachys nigra henonis*, making a fountain of growth out of it. I asked a young landscape architect friend what he thought of the idea. But although he was looking at the empty tank as we spoke he seemed unable to picture a bamboo in it. This surprised me.

However, one has to be practical as well as visionary and I fear that the bamboo would be too dry, in its raised position.

This happens to be one of the most difficult parts of the garden to reach with water and if you don't make that task easy it just doesn't get done. Perhaps I shall have to settle for a drought-resistant grass like *Stipa gigantea*, but that doesn't have attractive foliage; only beautiful inflorescences. The stems, I feel pretty certain, would get bent and broken by the public, which looks terrible, so I fear I shall have to await further inspiration. An agave would look splendid if only it were hardy.

Basically our garden doesn't call for big changes because it was so well designed initially but there was one small alteration that I made ten or twelve years ago which has turned out well. In our front lawn I replaced a perfectly uninteresting ball and saucer piece of yew topiary with that strange, almost grotesque, Chilean bamboo, *Chusquea culeou*. Just before he died, two years ago, my eldest brother, who had till then disliked it, recanted. He admitted that it had been a success after all. I grunted. One doesn't express feelings on such an occasion but I was pleased.

Any true gardener or arborist who instigates the planting of a tree must needs have an image of it in his mind as a full-grown specimen such as he hopes it will become, even though he probably won't live to see it. That shouldn't worry him, so long as he feels that he has set the wheels in motion. Posterity will be glad.

But sound plans like this are far outnumbered by the thoughtless mistakes we make when we plant trees and shrubs in the wrong place and they outgrow their comeliness. Such mistakes could often be forestalled by taking note of the behaviour of the plants in question where they have matured. Instead of immediately saying, 'I must plant a catalpa,' because of the ones you saw covered with blossom when you were honeymooning in Paris, take a look at the old hulks in Parliament Square in winter. Changing one's mind is a sign of strength.

26.2.87

MARCH

COURSES FOR CORPSES

MANY gardeners are debating what course to adopt towards the hideous trail of victims left by winter's little onslaught. I have to write 'little' because it would be lacking in proportion to set recent events on the same level of high tragedy as the misfortunes of Phèdre or the Duchess of Malfi. Yet I note a threatening bulge in the numbers of garden owners applying for tragedy-queen roles. In some cases it is hard to distinguish whether it is they who are dying (broken-hearted) or their plants.

Winter came in two bouts: three weeks in December and another nine days in January. A month is not long, but it was sharpish. Where I live, in East Sussex, we were terribly lucky, so I have to experience twinges of guilt at not joining the wake. Still, not everyone is agonised. One friend from Gloucestershire writes: 'With 34 degrees Fahrenheit of frost here we've had to revise our ideas of what is hardy, but the garden stood up to it pretty well on the whole and is looking really rather good, so I feel smug.' She has a right to.

And let's admit that the demise (or apparent demise) of some old friends can be something of a release. Plants don't always age beautifully; unawares a creeping boredom steals over us. After all, the whatever-it-is has been there a long time and has served us well. Then comes winter's magic touch and with a cry of joy we rush for axe, saw and spade without questioning whether the plant was as dead as it looked. I am reminded of an old Welsh friend's story of a farmer whose wife was being borne on her last journey. As the bearers went through a gateway they stumbled over uneven ground and bumped the coffin against the gatepost. There was an unmistakable movement within the box. The lady was not dead after all and, indeed, lived for several years afterwards.

But at last she died in earnest and as the procession reached the same spot the farmer said, 'Now, gently through the gateway.'

So when the pundits tell you that you must wait till July or June at earliest before deciding whether a tree or shrub is truly dead, they ignore the fact that you may want to make your own decision without waiting for Dame Nature's. And good luck to you. Or you may see the shrub as a peg to hang a few more plants on. My mother's old friend Averil Colby, writing from near Bristol, says, 'The snow and gales have killed my nice pittosporum (I don't know the variety) and although I have some seedlings coming on I must have something to cover the skeleton that the winter has left . . . It is about 12–15 feet high and well branched, and I wondered if I could put two clematis to cover it for this year?'

That's quite a task for a clematis to fulfil in a year but when you're in your eighties you want to condense the extract from time's allowance. I should be inclined to put my money on some *Cobaea scandens* while the clematis were gathering strength. A cobaea started now, in gentle heat, could easily put on 15 feet of growth by the autumn, given some nice soil to get away in.

But does anyone suppose that a 15 foot pittosporum has really given up that easily? I feel confident that within a few months it will be breaking into a mass of tiny shoots all over its more solid wood, at which stage the obviously dead outer portions on the tree can be shortened back.

Couldn't they be shortened back now? some gardeners will understandably be wondering, about some particularly mal-evolent garrya or eucalyptus covered with scorched foliage. After all one has got to live with one's plants and it's rather a trying exercise to have to avert your gaze from too long a list of eyesores. You may need to be led around blindfold.

Serves you right for growing too many evergreens.

On balance I think it is sensible to give a light trim to all afflicted bushes so as to be rid of their dead leaves. Hollies do at least have the grace to shed their frosted foliage forthwith. They're certainly not dead and for the time being we merely need to sweep up the mess before the wind scatters it. Dead holly leaves discovered when hand-weeding elicit a variety of unmusical responses.

The leaves of evergreen ceanothus remain on the bush for a long while. These ceanothus have limited powers of regeneration. At the best of times it's a toss-up what will happen when you cut back into their old wood. On occasions they surprise me by throwing up some vigorous shoots, but this cannot be depended upon.

Don't take much notice of the green revealed when you pare a sliver of bark from low on the main trunk. Green can remain here for many months on a specimen that has long been dead. Split bark in old wood can generally be taken as a death sign. You'll see a lot of this on your tender hebes. The odd branch may still be living. In such a forlorn case it isn't worth trying to save the plant, if you can replace it. Ceanothus are fast-growing, too, and dead-looking cistuses are better replaced forthwith – no questions asked.

> Thou shalt not kill
> But need not strive
> Officiously to keep alive.

4.3.82

THAT COLD DRAUGHTY CORNER

I HAVE an old friend who lives (at Weeks Farm, between Headcorn and Egerton) in a flat, bleak area of the Low Weald in Kent. The soil, a slightly alkaline, dour clay, alternately floods or bakes with cracks in which you could sprain your ankle. She is a great gardener but sometimes too independent, refusing to take my advice: for instance when she indulges self-sown buddleias and won't get rid of them.

One shrub that I have particularly disliked for years is *Elaeagnus × ebbingei*. It grew against the corner of her house, near the front door and just where I park my car, so I made a regular practice of backing into it. Then it got coral spot, a disease to which evergreen elaeagnus are particularly subject. The larger part of it died. But, alas, the surviving remains bid fair to make a full recovery. I backed into it with increased animus. Now, glory be, it has died and finally been extracted.

Pamela Milburne rang me last evening with the news but now wants advice on a replacement. Should she replant with the same again? (She has a warped sense of humour.) She can't bear to see nothing there. It protected her when she went in and out of the house. She doted on it . . . etc. I told her to dwell on the fact of a gap being an opportunity until I'd had a good think. I don't like snap recommendations.

Now I have to admit that in liking that wretched shrub, whilst it was healthy, she had a point or two. It was doing a job in a horrible situation, just off the north corner of her house. The wind cuts or whistles (or both) round that corner, she was always telling me, with dramatic emphasis. Well, but that is in the nature of corners. They are an open invitation to that sort of wind. But it is the coldest winds that do the most cutting, there. The elaeagnus put up with them for a number of years. Furthermore its blossom, in late autumn, is deliciously scented, as Pamela was never slow in reminding me. So I have been scratching my head.

I know we like evergreens for providing year-round shelter, but I think another evergreen would be a mistake. Either it would be as boring or more so than the elaeagnus, or it would show its dislike of this unfavourable spot by losing its leaves or by their becoming so brown and battered by winter's end (always a bad time for this class of plant), that you'd far rather there were no leaves at all. The only evergreen I thought might be a possible was *Sarcococca confusa*. Nothing much taller than 6 feet is wanted here. The sarcococca would never grow taller than that and, in these draughty conditions, might not achieve half the height. It does like shade and is pretty hardy, both points in its favour. And it had deliciously scented flowers (unless you get too close to them) in mid-winter. The almondy scent of elaeagnus is better, though.

How about a deciduous elaeagnus, then? Perhaps *E. angustifolia* Caspica Group, as *The Plant Finder* noncommittally lists the kind with silver-grey leaves of oval shape. I have this on a north-facing slope without protection, but the draughts are absent. I wouldn't mind Pamela experimenting with that; I should learn something myself without suffering from any disagreeable consequences.

A similar case in point would be *Betula tianschanica* 'Trost's Dwarf' (I wonder if Trost himself is a dwarf). It is a plant I don't know and one shouldn't really recommend without experience, but the Madrona Nursery's description is encouraging: 'A small dense bush with elegant, deeply cut, thread-like leaves. Gives a similar effect to cut-leaved Japanese maples but much hardier and easier to grow.' How about that? And they are a Kentish nursery at Lydd (very exposed but near the sea), with a most interesting list.

A shrub that you could not only cut back to tailor its size but which responded with a smile to regular cutting-back treatment, would be a good idea. So how about *Cornus alba* 'Elegantissima', which I originally had from Pamela? She could take a hardwood cutting from her own plant (I took half a dozen). It will put up with some shade (the site, after all, is not dark as it would be if overhung by trees); its white margined foliage is light and cheerful and its purplish-red stems in winter are a further asset. At the end of March you prune it as hard or lightly as the circumstances seem to demand. Of course, these dogwoods do like moisture; the north corner of a house can be very dry as rain-bearing winds come from the opposite direction and anyway the house itself probably mops up a good deal of the moisture available. Well, one could try (if, indeed, at eighty-eight she's in the mood for experimenting, but she's pretty sensible on that score and less impatient than many in their twenties).

Another shrub that responds well to similar treatment is the common elder. If you chose one of its cultivars entirely for foliage effect – and some of them have no pretensions as flowering shrubs – then the fact that cutting back prevents blossoming would be immaterial. I like *Sambucus nigra* 'Marginata'. Its leaflets are broadly margined in white (pale-yellow in the early stages). It shows up excellently in deeply shaded positions and loses none of its variegation in those curcumstances.

Pamela Milburne's is the first garden open to the public in the National Garden Scheme's yellow book, the new edition of which is now on sale. That will be for the crocuses, this Sunday, 8 March. Not only are they abundant in her orchard but so are scillas, *Anemone blanda* and suchlike early bulbs. The weather is a complete toss up at this time of year and crocuses will sulk if not coaxed open by early spring sunshine, but if the day is kind, wow! If not, you can have tea, discuss the weather and decide what you would plant on that difficult corner.

This garden is open again in June and July and shows the difference between a relaxed, intimate and personal style of gardening which everyone can apply to themselves, and the sort of gardens we more often visit on our National Trust tickets.

5.3.92

When Plants Take Over

It is quicker to destroy than to create and I was surprised what a mountain of cutting back I achieved in a couple of hours the other morning. My brother was the spur. He pointed out, so nicely and unarguably that I could not demur, that apart from our front path, it was impossible to turn to right or to left or move anywhere in our garden without being confronted by obstacles.

Around your feet, shrubs swell out so that a tottery visitor and supporting friend or relation are unable any longer to move side by side. At head level the blue rinse brigade, said my brother, had their hair nets tweaked off by overhanging boughs. Actually, blue rinses are rather out now (or have they merely moved down the scale?) and chestnut seems to be much commoner, while ladies who emerge from the privacy of their homes wearing hair nets deserve (just my opinion) to lose them. What's wrong with a head scarf? 'Wait till I tie my head on,' was one of my mother's favourite expressions before we went round the garden. Still, overhanging boughs and, even worse perhaps, bamboos, do drip like mad following rain, dew, fog or hoar frost – all rather commonly incidental in our climate.

First I tackled a bulging myrtle, *Myrtus communis tarentina*, which is an inferior variety of the common myrtle, itself one of the most delectable of all shrubs. *Tarentina* has the one merit of neat foliage, but in England it is generally shy or late flowering (October, and then most of its buds fail to develop). Our specimen was not particularly well sited but that happened before I was born.

Another inherited plant is *Hebe carnosula*, which is hardy and grows no more than a foot high, but gradually covers (very efficiently, I must say) a large area including, in our case, a substantial corner of lawn and more than half the width of a flagstone path. It has little ropes of grey-green foliage and its white flowers are an agreeable, though unimportant, bonus. It is one of those cunning self-layerers that roots as it goes, not just into the lawn but into the cracks between paving stones. I liked to see a great apron of it surging forwards, but most of that has now gone.

Corokia × *virgata*, another evergreen New Zealander, with minuscule spatulate leaves, grey on their undersides, has grown much larger than I expected. So many shrubs do. Dimensions given in books and catalogues never can square up with what actually happens, over the years, in your own garden. This is a quiet, sleepy plant. In May it covers itself, just for a week, with tiny, yellow, vanilla-scented stars, and later is spangled with pale-orange berries. Now perhaps 12 foot tall, its height is no problem. Cutting away its lower, forward-spreading branches has actually improved matters in several ways. I have ferns under it; they are happy. But I also have *Bergenia purpurascens*, which is distinctly thin and wan. Bergenias, in my experience, are more tolerant than loving of shade. Its winter leaf colour is this species' greatest asset and for that it needs an open situation. So I shall replace it with snowdrops – one of the expensive cultivars that I am slowly increasing by division, at this season, from an original singleton. And also, to flower in June, *Dactylorhiza foliosa*, a glamorous hardy orchid which will have sufficient head room now that the corokia is gradually changing its status from bush to tree.

In another trickily narrowed passageway, the problem is a self-sown *Erica mediterranea* (*E. erigena*), which put itself at the edge of the paving itself. I couldn't have moved without killing it, so I have compromised and merely reduced its bulk, as also that of its neighbour, *Hedera helix* 'Conglomerata' which is a bush ivy, with spikes of tight, non-climbing shoots that are upright in youth but gradually subside and loll. Much nicer lolling, but there we are; I have been firm.

About my *Ozothamnus ledifolius*, which I wrote of last October, I still don't know what to do. My brother, who dislikes both the shrub and cats, says that the one smells of the other. I corrected him and said the shrub smells of prunes but he wouldn't have it. 'I like prunes,' said he, 'and sometimes have them for breakfast; it can't smell of prunes.'

If I cut these ozothamnus back, they'll not flower for me next May and they'll look awful, whereas now they look marvellous. But the path is disappearing.

Some visitors hate what they see and don't see in my garden. One wrote last July, 'The long grass had not been cut, the plants were not named, the pear tree was covered in lichen, the tovara was moth-eaten; in fact I enquired from one of the gardeners if you had died recently.' Another, in September, wrote, 'The more times I see your garden the better it seems. It has a kind of insane passion about it. And I fear that it will never be possible to design such a garden – it has to be loved – to be breathed like the clay that became Adam.'

Comforting, though insanity is a little unhealthy so I must watch it. Anyway I hope my brother will notice what I have done more than what I haven't – yet.
11.3.82

STAKES ON THE FUTURE

MANY gardeners shy away from the very idea of needing to give their plants support. Rather than that, they will fill their borders with pygmies that have been dwarfened to the point of entirely losing their natural grace and personality.

This is quite unnecessary, even in a small-scale setting. All that's called for is a changed attitude. Any job, however menial, that calls for a little skill so that it can be well rather than badly accomplished, leaves you with a feeling of achievement. Support to plants must be discreet yet efficient and that's the sum of it.

It is best to anticipate how the plant is going to develop and what its needs will be and that requires experience, but experience is soon acquired. Once is enough. We need never be ashamed of a disaster so long as it is not repeated.

How have you supported that bowl of daffodils on your window ledge? If with one stick and a loop that bunches stems and leaves inwards, you deserve no marks. Any sort of bunching looks constrained. The outer blooms should lean outwards a little, without flopping; the central stems should remain upright. At the same time you need to enclose all of the daffodils' lank foliage up to the middle of or two-thirds up the leaf, so that it can only splay outwards at the top.

For a start, use a soil-based compost, not just peat or fibre.

The firmness of the soil will retain pieces of stick or cane in the position where you want them. These should be thin and unobtrusive. If cane is used, here or in the garden, remember that one end is always thicker than the other. Upturned pieces of cane look unbalanced, stupid. Push the broad end into the soil. For your tie, use thin string: two-ply fillis is ideal on an indoor job; five-ply for such as dahlias and heavier border plants. Fillis is soft, naturally pale, fawn-coloured hemp.

There is no need to cut a length of string from the reel or ball before you start. Make a clove hitch over the top of the first cane so as to leave a sufficient length of fillis at the free end to do the job. It does not usually need to be looped around every daffodil stem, just those on the perimeter. Take the string round a stem and back on itself before proceeding to the next stem or cane. Two or three canes should be enough in one bowl and you secure the fillis with a clove hitch to each cane as you come to it. Finally, back where you started, you complete the circle with a reef knot (a granny will slip). Get someone to show you how to make these two basic knots before you start and practise the clove hitch (a) around a table leg and (b) slipped over the top of any stick or stake. I find that Dutch students never need to be shown; it's like mother's milk to them, but English trainees are lost.

In a border, metal supports are favoured by some. They are easily pushed in or pulled out and they last for ever. But they *always* show. Another method, in the all-herbaceous border, that I don't think much of, is to stretch and attach to stakes, horizontal netting (black is the best colour), through which the plants will grow. This means that you can never thereafter move freely among your plants for whatever purpose (cutting, dead-heading) and that weeding is hell. Goose grass will make hay of this situation.

For thicker stemmed plants, use bamboo canes. Weather them for their first year, when they're pale and shiny, in the vegetable garden (tomatoes) or picking plot (helichrysums). Never truss a stem tightly to its cane. Short vibrations in the wind will destroy more quickly than no support. A little play must be allowed. Don't make more ties than are necessary. In most situations one should be enough for even a tall delphinium, if you delay inserting your canes until the stems are already 4 feet high. The spike itself should never need tying and the top of the cane should not reach higher than the base of the spike. If the spike is so weak and flabby that it collapses even then, you have a delphinium that's not worth growing.

When knocking in a stake or cane, *keep it upright*. Anything else looks terrible. Shorten the cane at the top to just above a joint, so that it won't split when knocked with a mallet. For this shortening, don't use anvil secateurs as they always split the cane.

Some perennials have stiff stems but are weak at the base, so that they tend to keel over. For such as *Eryngium* × *oliverianum*, *Asphodeline liburnica* and *Lychnis chalcedonica*, quite short pieces of cane and a low tie will suffice.

For many-stemmed plants like *Clematis recta*, monardas or alstroemerias, or a Michaelmas daisy like *Aster sedifolius* (*A. acris*), brushwood (alias peasticks) is more effective than canes. We use hornbeam because it is a by-product of the firewood we cut when coppicing. Birch is twiggy; hazel, cut a few years after coppicing, is best of all. You can bend its twigs over to the centre of the top of a plant colony without them snapping in two.

Length of brushwood used needs to anticipate the height to which the supported plants will eventually grow. One blunder that stared at me in the double herbaceous borders leading up to Battleston Hill at the RHS Gardens, Wisley, when I saw them last August, was that the length of brushwood was in many cases totally inadequate to the height of the plants, which had broken out of their supports. This is a mistake we all make when we're starting. The RHS trainees doing the job had not been properly supervised. They in their turn will go into the gardening world without knowing how to do the job properly or how to instruct others to do it and so yet another skill is lost.

19.3.87

COMING TO TERMS WITH RHODODENDRONS

MOST cultivated genera of flowering plants deserve our admiration here and there, even if cautiously accorded and hemmed about with personal prejudice. However, the rhododendron has succeeded in totally shutting off the minds of a considerable section of the gardening public. They neither want to see, nor even less to look at the things. Berlin-wall style, they blank them off. It isn't just that they can't grow them though that is frequently the case; they simply want to treat the rhododendron as a non-plant. Given such a diverse, showy and, in the main, hardy group of shrubs, there must be some serious psychological hang-up to account for this situation and when we look into the matter we find that the rhodophobe's opposite number, the rhodo-addict, is chiefly to blame. It is sad that humans should make themselves the chief obstacle to the appreciation of a beautiful flower.

The rhododendron ignoramus finds himself excluded (although he may be allowed, with a derisive sniff, to wallow in 'Cynthia' and 'Pink Pearl') and he resents this. Either he can join the exclusive band and bandy the magic jargon of Exbury and FCC forms, of 'Hawk Crest' and 'Rothschildiana', or he is in the wilderness. What, as an outsider, he sees of a cliquy élite can be discouraging. The rhododendron enthusiast is often an extraordinary phenomenon. Like the rider on horseback, he floats on a higher plane than the rest of us common mortals; the rhododendron has become his flower, created by divine ordinance to grace his woodland acres. And a pretty horrible mess those acres can make of a flower which includes many bright colours that need handling with discrimination and restraint. The very treatment that they so rarely receive.

Yet the rhododendron transcends its treatment by maniacs. I would say to those who live in a state of permanent repulsion, go back to square one. Make yourself look at all sorts of rhododendrons, which includes the azaleas, with unprejudiced eyes. Stop saying, 'I don't like rhododendrons.' By all means say, 'I don't like *that* rhododendron,' but go on from there to analyse what it is you don't like. Are you being reasonable for disliking it for that reason? A dull, heavy and oppressive leaf perhaps? All right, but then go on to look at other rhododendrons with different leaves and see if there are not some among them, at least at certain seasons, that are very beautiful; worth growing for themselves, in fact, as foliage shrubs and never mind the flowers.

Start looking at the different kinds of flower form and their arrangement in the truss. You could hardly deny that the bells of *Rhododendron williamsianum*, for instance, are other than elegant and that they show especially prettily among those little heart-shaped leaves, some green, some newly bronze.

'They're no good to me,' I can hear you saying, resentfully, adding, perhaps, in a spurt of defiance, 'and I'm glad I can't grow them.' I like gardeners to be spirited about not minding that their soil won't grow rhododendrons and I think it a rather feeble non-acceptance of the fact when they go to the lengths of creating a special raised peat bed wherein a clutch of calcifuge shrubs may be herded in defiance of nature. But if an alkaline soil prevents you from growing these shrubs, that is surely an excellent reason for visiting and admiring them in other gardens where they flourish. That gives us the chance to enjoy a wider range of plants. It is a puny sort of possessiveness to reject them because they won't grow for us.

If you can grow rhododendrons, however, and if you can persuade yourself that *some* of them are rather lovely, the next step is to learn how to accommodate a few in whatever sort of garden you have, so that they don't stick out like the proverbial sore thumb. The temptation always is to fall into the Surrey-suburban cliché of a bed planted entirely with rhododendrons, azaleas, some heathers on the carefully moulded promontories, a little clutch of 'Sky-rocket' conifers as exclamation marks to show that a trained designer has been at work, the fastigiate cherry 'Amanogawa' somewhere around and perhaps a double pink 'Kanzan' presiding over all.

Rhododendrons of most kinds will take their place easily among all sorts of other shrubs and herbaceous plants, not to mention bulbs. They don't have to be treated as special features any more than do roses. I've just seen a delightful photograph in an American publication of a group of *R. yakushimanum* growing in partial shade and interplanted with a drift of double white wood anemones (*Anemone nemorosa*). This is a slow-growing rhododendron, but there is no need, on that account, for close planting (just to show you've lots of money and can afford to buy a lot of plants). To have space to play with between your units can be as relaxed as having them all joined up, although joining up is what they will eventually do. This is a particularly beautiful species, its leaves for long covered with a glaucous bloom. The flowers, pink in bud and opening into a white truss, are marvellously shaped and presented. In this case, funds permitting, I think it probably is preferable to have a group, but in others, one is often enough. If you're afraid of its creating a dull spot in your border in summer, grow something through it like a climbing codonopsis or monkshood, that is itself summer-flowering and will not exceed what the rhododendron can cope with from a hanger-on. There'll be clematis suitable for this purpose too.

Discreet use of rhododendrons means that they'll never jump at you. I believe I have some fifty different kinds but it's amazing how many visitors think I grow none! Yes, I know that could be taken in two ways.

22.3.84

VISIT AN ENGLISH GARDEN

APRIL comes in this weekend and with it is renewed the characteristic English pastime of visiting gardens. 1979, indeed, is being promoted by the English Tourist Board and others as the year of the garden. There is no special reason for this year being singled out rather than another but it is always worth telling our overseas visitors that English gardens deserve a detour. None, however, will derive more pleasure and profit from visiting English (by which, of course, I mean British, but that is an ugly staccato word) gardens than the English themselves.

Every garden visited, whether new to us or unfamiliar, is an adventure and I shall make a few suggestions for enjoying your visit to the full. First, equip yourself with a notebook having waterproof covers: the Alwych range is excellent in this respect. Write in it your name and address and a plea to the finder to return it to its owner who will pay generous compensation. Of course, to save yourself the trouble of losing it you may prefer to do without the notebook but this would be a mistake. Looking through its entries will hold you in good stead as a mind-jogger for years to come. Furthermore there is nothing more encouraging to a garden owner nor more likely to start him or her conversing with you than to see, as a notebook clearly demonstrates, that you're serious about your subject. And you'll never enjoy a garden more than going round it with the owner and seeing it through his (or her) eyes.

But it is also most stimulating – and here comes my second piece of advice – to visit gardens with a congenial companion having similar passions to your own. True there is the danger that your voices may become so audible during your animated discussion of the scene that indiscretions may escape at a

71

fairly high decibel level, but perhaps you won't mind too much about that and anyway a spot of charm combined with a swift turn of subject works wonders if you find yourself in a tight corner.

Try and organise your thoughts and analyse the scene before you. 'I like this; I don't like that; why?' This is where discussion is so enormously helpful in its crystallising role. Do always look at a garden's settings and layout, giving yourself up to the general mood it is trying to evoke, before you put your nose to the ground, so to speak, and sniff out the plant contents in detail. It is great fun discovering what sort of people the owners must be from the ways they have revealed themselves through their 'art'.

Garden design is endlessly fascinating as you try to perceive how a certain effect was gained or why, on the contrary, it worries or jars on you. In striving to be informal, many gardeners make the curves that outline their beds or borders far too tight and numerous. Try and work out how you would reorganise them so that they made natural, reassuring sweeps that didn't draw attention to themselves. The same with paths, both in the materials used and in the direction they take. In their width, also. Is this in balance with the plantings they take you past? Sometimes, when you see a particular balance that strikes you as exactly right it is worth pacing it out and making a note of its proportions. Or a sketch, if you can sketch. I wish I could.

Never feel discouraged because the garden you are in seems so different in scale and contents to anything you can attempt in your own plot. In the first place because there nearly always are details of planting, say (and you should always make a memo of good plant associations), that you can apply to yourself and second because there should be no need for the stimulus of emulation in order to enjoy. I've no room for large conifers, for instance, in my own garden, but to visit a pinetum is as exciting, in its way, as mountain scenery to a man of the plains.

Do be good about respecting other people's property. I feel it necessary to mention this sorry subject again since receiving a letter from a reader who opens her garden to the public six days a week. 'In your *Country Life* article of 8 February you refer to *Primula vialii*, saying that it has a reputation for being short-lived. It certainly has a short life in this garden. I lost, by theft, at least six mature plants in full flower last year.' She is right in saying that such losses increase from year to year. No plea will touch the professional thief but, to quote: 'I caught several offenders last year (not unfortunately the primula thieves) and they were all highly respectable well-to-do members of society. I told one woman, who was stuffing a plant of golden thyme into her bag, that she was no better than a common thief, and she looked outraged. Another said that we had so many of the particular plant she had ruthlessly pulled up that she "did not think it would matter taking one".'

There are fairer ways of acquiring plants than this and it is notable how generous gardeners are to each other in the fostering of this passionate pursuit.
29.3.79

THE SNOUTS GO SHOOTING

AMONG the many excitements of spring are the young emergent shoots from hitherto dormant plants. This latent energy suddenly unleashed seems all the more powerful for being apparently static, so far as the eye can discern, yet change is apparent from day to day.

All those lacy, overlapping scales that enclose the huge, calf's head resting buds on *Gunnera manicata*, urge me to place my spectacles across their snouts. Then a leaf pokes out on one side, like a cocked ear. Probably it gets frosted, but on an established plant that really doesn't matter. There's a quiverful of potential leaves in reserve and they emerge, one after another, in the course of several months. It is not until July that a gunnera is in full fig.

I cut my *Arundo donax*, the giant reed grass, to the ground the other day. Their old shoots, 12 foot tall, were sprouting at every node but (as with the bamboo, *Pleioblastus auricomus*) much the handsomest growth is obtained by channelling a colony's entire energies into young shoots from the base. Some of these were already two or three inches up and I managed to snap them off. They are terribly brittle. I'm sure they would have cooked well or even been tender enough for a raw salad.

The dragon arum, *Dracunculus vulgaris*, puts on an amazing act each early spring. Its thick, sprouting shoots are pale-brown with darker, more or less horizontal striations. It's like an adder's tail disappearing underground. Yet in the aggregate, these perfectly conical shoots of different thicknesses put me in mind of a troglodyte village. There's more going on than meets the eye.

The thickest herbaceous shoots on any plant I grow are those of *Eremurus robustus*, a foxtail lily, 8 foot tall by May with a rope of pale-pink star flowers. The shoots are apt to emerge prematurely, especially in a year like this. We mound their crowns over with a dome of grit, so as to delay their emergence, but I doubt if they'd have been held back much even if I'd applied a daily renewed ice pack over them. It is a dramatic moment when these shoots erupt, and they all, within a day or two, do it simultaneously. The consequences are apt to be unhappy. Frost can destroy their succulent foliage but this year it was the wind. No sooner had their leaves partially expanded than they were subjected to such buffetings that they simply snapped off. This must have weakened the plants but they've survived more years than I have. In the long term, they win through.

Hostas can look pretty good, especially the glaucous *Hosta sieboldiana* types. And rheums, the ornamental rhubarbs, with rose-red, bulbous noses. It is a good moment for propagating them from the smaller buds, plus a shield of rhizome behind this, that lie behind the terminal, leading shoot.

Some plants have a natural aptitude for making a bouquet of their foliage. If you have allowed tulips to clump up, in a mixed border, over the years, all those bulbs together present a delightful bunch of leaves and shoots. The outer leaves hang outwards. The inner ones, supporting the flower buds, point upwards, prick-eared, while the buds themselves are strongly designed like rockets taking off. In many cases, the leaf surfaces have a glaucous bloom on them. With *Tulipa marjoletii*, the pointed leaves have undulating margins. Their scale is small but good things come in small parcels; they make their mark.

Then there are the alliums. Its young foliage is the main point of *Allium karataviense*, each bulb producing a pair of broad, glaucous, slightly mottled leaves. After that, the plant is never as good again, the flowers a tepid affair and by the time it flowers the leaves are fast waning. That goes for the majority of alliums. My group of *A. giganteum* looks wonderful now, with overlapping, long-leaved stars of intensely glaucous foliage only a few inches above ground-level. I have them just behind *Santolina pinnata neapolitana*, which I have pruned back to inconspicuous stumps. By June, *A. giganteum* will be carrying purple globes on 4 to 5 foot scapes (naked stems), but the foliage is withered and brown. You can cut it away before the floral display. I don't have to do that because the santolina has by then grown enough new foliage to perform a concealing role. The allium can be as sleazy with its underwear as it likes.

Before you start grumbling about your colchicums' dying foliage in May, feast your eyes on them now. What a wonderful gloss and what a rich shade of green they all have. Again, each corm presents a bouquet, and the bouquets *en masse* are skilfully bunched so that every leaf obtains its share of light. When they start yellowing, turn your back on them for another week or two, to give them a fair chance of building up their underground storage supplies; then cut them to the ground and interplant with a temporary filler to last the summer and autumn through and to make a background carpet to the colchicums' flowers in September. One or other variety of *Helichrysum petiolare* is ideal: fast growing, mat forming and not too tall.

The young leaves of *Veratrum nigrum*, pale-green and pleated, are almost too good to be true but I see that slugs are attacking mine already and soon, as usual, they'll be a reproach to my indolence. I should spend more time in the garden and less on writing. *V. album*, funnily enough, is not nearly so appealing to slugs and snails. Its buds expand weeks later and the leaves, from the first, are a much darker shade of green, but still very beautiful. It is my preferred species; the panicles of white stars show up so handsomely in the summer garden. But it is slow to propagate. If you can find stock at all, don't grumble at the price.

My last words shall be for the unfolding croziers of the more substantial ferns. They have an animal-like energy that makes some people a little uncomfortable. There is something distinctly reptilian about the young fronds of *Dryopteris wallichiana*, which is the most exciting fern in action that you could hope to meet in a cool temperate climate. Covered in dark-brown scales on emergence, the actual frond pinnae are palest, tenderest green.

29.3.90

APRIL

The Old Rose Garden

THE rose garden at Dixter is a gem of a construction by Lutyens, made around 1912 against an old cow house, or hovel, with a round, brick cattle-drinking tank as its focal point. Lutyens framed its other three sides with scalloped yew hedges. There are four beds set against these (but divided from their roots by vertical sheets of strong galvanised iron); the other six are island beds (divided by flagstone paving) two of them square, the others long but angled to points at one end. It is a restful and satisfying design.

Intending from the outset to make a rose garden, my parents planted two pendent beds with a mixture of vigorous Hybrid Perpetual and Bourbon roses, such as 'Candeur Lyonnaise' (which they brought with them from their first London garden; it dates from around 1905 and still has immense vigour), 'Madame Isaac Pereire' and 'Grüss an Teplitz' (a German admiral famous in the early years of the century). The other beds, again treated in pairs, were each planted with two varieties of Hybrid Tea rose. 'La Tosca' and 'Prince de Bulgarie' is one coupling that I just remember. It was entirely replaced by 'Madame Butterfly' in the early thirties at which time the square beds were given over to 'Shot Silk' and 'Betty Uprichard'.

From the time the garden gradually came under my direction, mixtures of varieties became increasingly indiscriminate. I loved propagating roses from cuttings and I loved to have them on their own roots, so I would either buy one plant and thereafter take cuttings from that, or else beg cuttings from the roses I admired that friends were growing.

It was only gradually that we came to appreciate the significance of replant disease and of how materially it affects rose growing. Getting rid of an old bush and replacing it with plants of my own raising was only partially successful. The majority of new ones did not survive. Some did and made fairly decent bushes in time. Others made excellent bushes, though following a slow start.

Seeing that my planting methods are piecemeal and that old bushes of fifty years' standing may grow side by side with young plants newly raised from cuttings, it does not at all suit me to change the soil in between replacing bushes. On the scale of a rose society's garden, this task can be mechanised, replacing the contents and soil of entire beds all in one operation. It is still an expensive exercise, but for the sake of the rose it is still gladly undertaken.

Not so in my garden. The rose garden is far from any other soil supply, its entrances are narrow; there is little space for manoeuvring machinery and the wholesale treatment – out with the old, in with the new – doesn't appeal to me anyway. Seeing that the soil is excellent for any other plant except for the rose, which has fouled its own patch, I do not see why I should be made a slave to this one flower, which occupies no greater a place in my affections than many another.

But what would suit a formally designed garden of this kind, other than roses? Something that would not be outrageously extravagant in terms of labour and outlay? Few things are impossible, but, to get me going, I needed the physical and emotional backup of a similarly minded confederate. Fergus Garrett, a friend during and since his college days, is now my head gardener. We're going places and it is exciting. The site is very sheltered and very hot in summer. Last year, we tried plugging gaps left by defunct roses with cannas – an elegant, easy and prolific one, *Canna indica* 'Purpurea.' It has narrow, purplish leaves, an upright habit to six or seven feet and small red flowers in considerable abundance. It revelled in the rose garden and was particularly striking with a margin between it and the paths of self-sown, purple-flowered *Verbena bonariensis*.

What we shall therefore now aim for is a summer garden of voluptuous luxuriance. The garden is cut off from other areas, so you will suddenly and unexpectedly be plunged into it. As you fight your way through an overhanging jungle on either side, your progress may sometimes be entirely blocked. But there are plenty of paths and alternative routes, so you can try again along one of these. There'll be no planting plan and I have as yet only unformulated ideas of what will be included, aside from cannas, the verbena, castor-oil plants (*Ricinus*), perhaps dahlias, *Melianthus major* (of course). There are a whole lot of seeds I ordered with this project in mind but quite what they were I forget. That can wait till we have the plants ready to put out. We'll need a lot of them, but then we have a lot of seed.

Lush-looking hardy plants can be included. John Treasure has given me a sucker off his colony of *Rhus glabra* 'Laciniata'. Cut to the ground annually, this shrub produces large, pinnate, elegantly dissected leaves. Beth Chatto has promised me seedlings from her *Paulownia* (but I've bought some seed in case she forgets). In contrast to anything pinnate, that has enormous, hairy heart-shaped leaves. Foliage is bound to be the dominating theme, because it is so much more imposing than flowers and remains in good order for several months. But I can add in an annual like the spider flower, *Cleome* 'Helen Campbell', whose palmate leaves are as handsome as its long-flowering, terminal heads of white blossom.

Yesterday, we had a grand exhumation of old rose bushes – I contemplate calling this 'The Old Rose Garden'. The rending noise of huge old roots reminded me of a hyena devouring a plank of wood. Friends of up to fifty years' standing, they have given me great pleasure in their time but now we're moving on. I have, for the time being at least, left room for a chink of sentimentality. A few rose bushes remain, including 'Candeur Lyonnaise' and 'Madame Isaac'. Also 'Madge', a blush white, deliciously scented polyanthus rose, which no one seems to be offering any longer. Also, and for much the same reason, 'Florence May Morse', a commendably long-flowering, straightforwardly red floribunda rose. And we've left *Rosa foliolosa*, which many rose

addicts find hard to recognise as a rose at all, with its lax
habit and very narrow leaflets. Small, single magenta flowers
is its floral contribution.

Come and see how we're progressing in five months' time.
1.4.93

Not Always as They Seem

A FRIEND in the nursery trade was asked to supply a plant of
Clematis heracleifolia 'Campanile'. A year later he was posted
a good-flowering specimen of this clematis from the same
customer who wrote, 'This plant was supplied by you as a
bush clematis to Mr R. and myself. It appears to be nothing
more or less than a weed, and we much regret that we paid
14/6d for such a plant. Can I have comments on it, please, as
we are most disappointed in such a plant.'

Now, *C. heracleifolia*, in any of its several cultivated and
natural varieties, has clusters of small, bell-shaped flowers of
much the same colouring and size as a hyacinth's. They are
non-climbing and 'Campanile' itself is a sub-shrub dying back
annually to a woody framework. It could accurately be
described as a bush clematis and this lady doubtless saw it
so described in some newspaper or magazine article. Possibly
she visualised a bush version of some large-flowered clematis
like 'Nelly Moser' or perhaps she saw a photograph of
'Campanile' but with nothing to give scale, and hence
imagined each flower to be 6 inches or so long. Another
clematis of which a similarly false impression is easily gained
from a close-up photograph is the bright yellow *C. tangutica*. I
have often been asked by visitors to my own garden to have an
example of the yellow clematis pointed out to them and
generally, when they see it in the flesh, they feel let down.

Close-ups can, indeed, be most deceptive. In a recent lecture to the Horticultural Club, Anthony Huxley showed a number of enormously enlarged close-up photographs of familiar wild flowers and it was quite impossible to guess what they were. The detail thus highlighted can be both interesting and informative. Sometimes, as with an enlarged head of yarrow (*Achillea millefolium*), a delightful pattern emerges such as might be used in fabric designs. Most often, however, these enlargements are fascinating but repulsive, in the way that one's own face looks coarsely repulsive when magnified in a concave mirror.

As far as buying plants is concerned, these deceptions arising from a picture or from a glowing but incomplete description served up by some journalist (like myself) in search of copy fodder, only go to underline the importance of checking up. The preferable way to do this is by seeing a plant in the flesh before you decide to acquire it; but a good substitute, if you can conjure up some sort of mental image from an accurate description, is to check up with the help of the RHS *Dictionary of Gardening*, wherein detailed plant and flower measurements are included.

Another rich field of deception is in written colour descriptions and, scarcely less, in pictorial colour representations. The only way to be accurate over written colour descriptions is by reference to a standard, namely the RHS Colour Chart. But few of us have the chart for reference and so descriptions usually fall back on pleasant colour adjectives like carmine, crimson, cerise and rose-red, whose interpretations can be all too various.

Pictures suffer mainly from deficiencies in colour photography and printing. Blues are particularly difficult. Thus a catalogue photograph of *Clematis montana rubens* will come out clear pink – just what we should like it to be, in fact. But this clematis actually has a strong blue element in its make-up which makes it pinky-mauve. The camera lies and the customer feels cheated on discovering that all the clematis he thought were going to be pink are really quite a long way from it. On the other hand the blue varieties of clematis, which are, admittedly, none of them true blue but with only a little mauve mixed in, come out a horrible dirty mauve in their photographs. In this case it is the nurseryman who is disgruntled because he knows that a blue clematis like 'Lasurstern' looks so much bluer in the flesh than on paper.

Sometimes the plant we behold with our very eyes gives an entirely false impression of itself, so that even seeing can't necessarily be synonymous with believing. Weeds can look like precious plants and vice versa. No weed is more adept at looking important during the resting season, when it is reduced to a dark-green rosette, than the willow-herb in one of its lesser manifestations (they are such an interbred lot that I have never been able to sort them out). Often they take on the guise of a sweet william. On the other hand I have a charming perennial at the front of my mixed border, at whose expense visitors are constantly making unkind jokes to the effect that if it grew in their gardens they would weed it out. This is *Crepis incana* and I must admit that when only its leaves are visible it does look rather like a dandelion or hawkweed. And it is one of that group, but without any disagreeable habits. Its flowers are pink and nobody fails to admire it in its flowering season. Only a little faith is required at other times in the year.

2.4.70

PLANTING FOR THE BLIND

As a part of the compassionate image in which many organisations like to present themselves, gardens for the blind are springing up all over the country. Knowing that I am interested in garden scents, a reader, who is at the head of a firm of chartered architects, wrote asking me if I had any suggestions to offer in this line that could be incorporated into a project he has undertaken; namely, to design a small section within a public garden in a West Country town, which will 'serve the special object of becoming a pleasant and attractive amenity for the blind and handicapped'.

How I loathe that word 'amenity' which has become so fashionable in the past twenty or thirty years. One has to accept it now, of course, even to use it oneself, though I try not to. To me, amenity horticulture embodies a sort of official approach to gardening which is the negation of spontaneous enjoyment. It is the dispensing of organised favours through a controlled budget to a pabulum-fed public. The stench of condescension wafts strongly on the air. When pleasure gardening becomes amenity horticulture it has earned the seal of official approval, the antiseptic kiss of death.

Gardens for the blind also smack of condescension, it seems to me. 'Look, the poor thing's blind,' you can imagine one do-gooder saying to another as they watch a visitor to the garden they have specially created moving hesitantly from plant to plant, pinching each of them and raising fingers to nose. Is this what blind people want? Has anyone asked *them*? How many gardens for the blind are instigated without any consultation of the prospective users?

I have not investigated this question myself so I can only hazard guesses on what's needed or wanted. It seems probable to me that blind (or in other ways disabled) people would generally like to be treated in the same way and by the same standards as the rest of us, in so far as this is possible. It is variety that spices our lives. For each pinch of lemon-scented verbena I would also offer the contrast of more astringent smells such as arise from plants like hydrangeas, erigerons, broad beans and primroses.

Many people disagree about scents and whether to like them or not. Do you recoil from the smell of a bruised *Clerodendrum bungei* (*C. foetidum*) leaf, or from *Iris foetidissima* or from the peanut butter odour of *Melianthus major*? I find them interesting and not unpleasing. I don't want the whiff of bad meat emitted by the dragon arum, *Dracunculus vulgaris*, all the time, but I like to know that it is there and why. It doesn't have to be sweet briar all the way.

What about smells like tansy, wormwood, marigolds (both pot and tagetes), yarrow (*Achillea filipendulina*)? They are very pungent but we should be the poorer without them, blind or not.

When I took a party of blind people round my own garden, it struck me that they were even more interested in the feel of plants than in their scents. Something like the Chilean bamboo, *Chusquea culeou*. Its ribbed canes are exceptionally short-jointed. It is intriguing to run your hand up one. A particular favourite with me in this respect is the fern *Blechnum chilense* (*B. tabulare*). There is a firm harshness of texture which makes their fronds particularly satisfying to grasp and then run through your hand.

In a different way, flowers communicate pleasure through the sense of touch. Something delicate and ephemeral like a hibiscus blossom or an ipomoea gives you a tender feeling of mortality on its behalf. Not that that helps the plant, but it helps you.

As regards gardens that the handicapped can enjoy, raised flower beds are the commonest solution. That's fine if the materials used for raising them are themselves discreet yet pleasant to look at, not abominable green plastic containers, such as I have seen. Another disadvantage in the raised bed is that it is so often used as a receptacle for cigarette ends and all sorts of other rubbish. Many plants grow tall enough to be appreciated at an easy level anyway, without special arrangements for giving them a lift.

The donors of an amenity generally require a motto, like 'a garden for the blind', on which they can focus (probably, also, a plaque commemorating their generosity). To tell them that what's needed is better attention given to the planting and maintenance of gardens already available would seldom meet their aspirations. Yet a garden of varied contents, well designed, planted and cared for so as to please us all, would probably suit the blind and disabled also, always excepting a few obvious misfits like barberries and prickly pears (though there is a satisfaction even in learning how to handle cacti without gloves on).

A second letter from my correspondent tells me that he has discarded the idea of raised flower beds as inappropriate, so that's fine. The gardens have just growed, over the years, and need a unifying design which he has suggested be achieved with a pergola. Which looks excellent in his plan. And perhaps it can be encouraged to drip with stalactites of wisteria and laburnum, both scented, as well as the inevitable roses. It will enclose the 'rather boring rose garden' that is already there. I can just see it! 7.4.83

Deep in the Border

As I write after sunset in glorious late March weather, two of us are in full spate on the Long Border, the mixed border in my garden which is 110 yards long and, for two thirds of its length, 15 feet deep. Late, you may well think, for a job that many gardeners would have tackled five months ago, but I don't believe we could have hit upon better conditions for an annual overhaul during that period than we have now. Without skimping or rushing anything that needs to be done, we can work on till six o'clock each day having the minimum of anxiety about our fun being spoilt by conditions on the morrow.

I only hope this weather lasts or is repeated over Easter, when so many gardeners will have the leisure and urge to set to in a similar way.

When you can do a job is a far more flexible affair than is generally suggested in books, broadcasts or the press. We are splitting and replanting in improved soil nearly all the patches of border phloxes, last upheaved four years ago. We could have done them at any time in the last six months. Some varieties are already six inches tall on their new growth, so we've got the hose out and watered them in. It was only a few days ago that the ground looked too sodden to be stepped on, let alone manipulated. In fact, however, once you break into it you find that it's in a lovely crumbly state and full of fat worms. Water will settle the soil round newly disturbed roots. The shoots will quickly recover from their daytime limpness.

Indeed, we could have delayed splitting the phloxes for another six weeks, had this been necessary. The great thing is to complete the operation once started as quickly as possible. Ours were only out of the ground for half to three-quarters of an hour. If the young shoots are too long to cope with such a disturbance as they would be in May, they can be pinched back, thereby reducing water losses by transpiration. The result will be several breaks from the stem that's left and a few, smaller, flower panicles instead of one big one. Only a slight disadvantage.

I was struck again by the marvellous lightening effect that the fibrous phlox roots have on a heavy clay soil. Other plants, with a few deep fang-like roots, can work no such transformation, and are apt to be unhappy in heavy ground. *Salvia nemorosa*, for instance. I've heard of several gardeners losing it during the winter and yet it is a tremendously hardy plant, adapted to Continental winters. With such plants it is a real help to leave their old growth over them through the winter. They'll never get sodden in the way that they can when everything has been cleared overhead.

I've done a kind of patching-up operation on my *Iris ochroleuca*, leaving some of the healthy shoots undisturbed to flower this year but replanting others that have strayed too far from the group's original outline, back into the centre, which had become bare. This bare, unproductive area is packed with old rhizomes through which nothing can penetrate. They only need digging out and the ground digging over.

How careful you have to be in handling the old dead stems on some plants. Phloxes and Michaelmas daisies can be knocked over like skittles but eryngiums, for instance, or peonies or japanese anemones or any herbaceous euphorbia must be cut carefully and individually. The moment you get impatient, giving a wrench or a tug, away breaks the fat young shoot at the old stem's base, so integral a unit do they form.

There are certain areas in my border that I scarcely ever disturb, other than skimming or prodding weeds off the surface. These are the places where plants like *Eryngium* × *oliverianum* can just sit and ruminate interminably, which is what they like to do, while others can self-sow and colonise. The snowdrops do this among the Japanese anemones; *Allium christophii*, with the largest globe heads, among *Sedum* 'Ruby Glow'. Forget-me-nots fill in among tulips that carry on year after year. Sweet violets in purple, mauve, pink and white make themselves very much at home and so does the summer-flowering *Viola cornuta* 'Alba'.

At winter's end you'll find a mantle of moss on the surface of undisturbed places such as these. A lot of it will peel off while you're weeding but in plant crowns it will remain. Many gardeners seem to worry about moss when there's no need to do so. Moss doesn't create a situation, it merely expresses one. That situation may in itself be harmful, as in a badly drained lawn, or it may simply indicate that, other competitors being in abeyance and the weather right for it, moss is enjoying itself. And why not? Nearly all mosses are pleasant to look at.

So when you read an advertisement for the latest moss killer don't be driven into thinking that your own moss is a disgrace and that positive action must be taken against it or else the world will want to know why not. Moss can be killed easily enough but if it's back again within six or nine months, give your shoulders a good shrug.
8.4.82

MY FIRST ORCHID

THERE must be an enormous number of adults who come to gardening without the faintest notion of how to set about it. They are at sea without a landmark in sight. It is very different for those of us who have been brought up to the idea and practice of gardening from their earliest childhood and it is hard for them to imagine how it must feel to be clueless. Now and again I do get an inkling and it happened to me the other day when I was given my first orchid.

I don't mean one of the hardy kinds such as grow wild in our woods but a real hothouse effort, albeit the best known of all, I dare say. *Cypripedium insigne* is what we knew it as for many years but as it is not a true lady's slipper it has inexorably to be restyled *Paphiopedilum insigne*. These paphiopedilums, then, are among the most popular of greenhouse orchids and they include, thanks to the hybridists' patient efforts, a whole range of incredibly bloated, coarse and vulgar creations of immense size and rubberised substance, but this particular old dear is still as loved as ever it was and remains serenely unspoilt. As a plant its appearance is unremarkable, not to say dull, consisting as it does of numerous dun-green strap leaves of stiffish texture growing obliquely on a low-domed plant. In early spring it should be covered with its beautifully marked flowers in shades of yellowish-green, dusky yellow and reddish-brown. They are borne singly on longish stems that extend well beyond the foliage and a well-flowered plant in your drawing-room is something to be proud of. If not well flowered you can still pick such blooms as there are and use them in flower arrangements.

This was how I saw them in my friend's house and when I exclaimed my pleasure she offered me a plant there and then. For a moment I hesitated being, you'll understand, a flowers-of-the-field kind of chap on the whole, but I do have a sneaking affection for cannas, dahlias, calceolarias even. And so, although I've held out against orchids for half a century, I capitulated gratefully, bearing my trophy home in triumph.

But then came the big question. How was I to make my exotic newcomer happy? It clearly wasn't altogether happy at the outset, since it hadn't borne a single flower, so it was no good telling myself that I must simply make it feel it was still in its old home. Some sort of positive action on my part was called for. Pending a decision on what this should be, I pulled seedlings of oxalis out from among its tufts. This little beast, with tiny, bright-green shamrock leaves and bright-yellow flowers, is a pest in so many greenhouses I know that I am quite determined it shall never get a hold in mine. Given the slightest chance it infests every pot; also your greenhouse staging, the floor beneath and even escapes into the garden.

I'll ask Maurice Mason how to grow it at the next RHS show, I decided. He's chairman of the orchid committee but nonetheless approachable on such an elementary question. However, he wasn't at the early March meeting and I wasn't at the next one. So I asked another friend who was staying with me but has his own glass (including the oxalis). He reckoned the plant looked starved and that its leaves were much too short. The next thing that happened was that I had an irresistibly juicy-looking mound of John Innes No. 3 potting compost (the strongest mix) on my bench, wherewith I was re-potting lilies, and I suddenly felt that, if I were an orchid, this would be the kind of sumptuous repast for which I yearned. So I turned it out of its 5 inch pot, tickled away all the soil from among its thick roots with the tip of a widger (carefully throwing the soil away where any lurking oxalis would be beleaguered) and repotted into a 6 inch clay pot.

Only then did I begin to read about orchids. 'Three parts loam fibre, 1 part of sphagnum moss, and 1 part of Osmunda fibre well mixed with finely broken crocks', the RHS *Dictionary* instructed. And '*P. insigne* is capable of with-standing a comparatively low temperature but better results are obtained if 55 degrees Fahrenheit is regarded as an approximate night temperature in winter.' That would ruin me. My greenhouse heating only comes on when the temperature drops to 35 degrees Fahrenheit. Then I read a discouraging article by Arthur Hellyer in the *Financial Times* under the ambiguous heading 'Trying Orchids'. 'Nearly all orchids need a very moist atmosphere which ordinary greenhouses are just not constructed to maintain.' And, 'Their needs are quite different from those of other plants and they do not mix well with the ordinary run of greenhouse favourites.' Mine will have to rub along with cacti, fuchsias and all the bedding plants I overwinter.

Never mind, I don't have to believe them. I have the greatest faith in John Innes composts for every kind of plant and I'm sure the atmosphere in my greenhouse is conducive to smiles of goodwill in every plant that enters it. Further news on the orchid front in a year's time.

15.4.76

MORAL AND IMMORAL SCENTS

LISTENING, the other evening, to Debussy's prelude, 'Les sons et les parfums tournent dans l'air du soir', I could not help wondering which scents? There was no need to ponder on the sounds; Debussy had rendered them voluptuously and, in doing so, he had really guided us pretty accurately on the odours, too: those heavy, swooning scents of a tropical evening, that make 'faint with too much sweet'.

It is a funny thing about these overloaded flower scents, that they smell so delicious when you catch an airborne gust, suddenly and unexpectedly, most probably when your mind was on other matters, yet when you go purposefully to seek them out, and bury your nose, like a moth's proboscis, into the heart of the flower, the scent goes bad on you. It becomes positively disagreeable. My one-time music teacher, Kenneth Stubbs, who was also an expert gardener, used to classify flower scent into those that are moral and those that are immoral. The distinction, when you come to think of it, is quite clear. Moral scents include all those warm, foody, daytime smells like coconut-scented gorse, clove carnations, vanilla *Azara microphylla*, mignonette, lupins, wallflowers, stocks and thyme.

The immoral kind reserve their main strength, appropriately, for evening and night-time. To give them their botanical names is to kill their magic. Reminiscing on frangipani-laden, tropical evenings is evocative enough, and circumstances would seldom require the precision of *Plumeria acutifolia*-laden evenings. But what nursery would supply a night-blowing cereus, on demand? Thornton's painting from the Temple of Flora shows a gorgeous white cactus bloom against the, perhaps too parochial, setting of an English church tower clock, with the hands pointing to midnight. Many of these night-expanding cacti are exceedingly fragrant. To get the equivalent of Thornton's one hundred-and-sixty-year-old cereus, today, one would probably need to ask for *Epiphyllum cooperi*.

Too often, there is no alternative to a botanical name; one must resign oneself. The summer-flowering *Eucharis* looks like a large, pure-white narcissus, except that its stamens form projections on the corona like the points on a tiara. In *Pamianthe peruviana*, the corona is much enlarged, while the petals themselves are narrow and spidery. Both are wonderfully fragrant, but are stove plants, alas, requiring a minimum winter temperature of 60 or 65 degrees Fahrenheit. However, the nearly related *Pancratium maritimum*, from the Mediterranean littoral, is very nearly hardly, and just as fragrant, flowering now. Bulbs are sometimes procurable, and if given a really well-drained and sunny position, as in a south-facing, raised border, would be worth trying outdoors anywhere in the south or east.

Stephanotis has usually been considered a stove-house climber, and it doubtless flowers most freely in stove conditions, but a friend in the next village has been surprisingly successful with it in his sun room, where a temperature of not less than 50 degrees Fahrenheit is maintained in his absence, and the plant has been flowering for the past month. He also goes in for gardenias and tuberoses in the same room. It is wise not to get too sentimental over a gardenia plant. This is an evergreen shrub that can and will grow very large in time, but is much freer flowering when young and still manageably small. Besides, there is a limit to the number of open gardenia blossoms that the human frame can tolerate at close quarters. Tuberoses (*Polianthes tuberosa*) are reasonably cheap, and the tubers, not lasting well after the first year, are best acquired afresh each early spring. They are ugly plants, with untidy, stringy foliage, and so might just as well be raised out of sight in a warm greenhouse and then picked when at their best. The scent is overwhelming but I agree that it is pleasant to be overwhelmed, now and again.

Datura suaveolens, the angel's trumpet, needs a lot of space, but you can cut this shrub quite hard back in spring, as you would an old fuchsia, and it will blossom on the young growth in summer and autumn. The foliage is coarse and so, truth to tell, are the large, drooping trumpet-flowers. They are, moreover, a dirty white. And yet, having said this, nobody (except, perhaps, the specialist in minutely exquisite alpine plants) could fail to be impressed and delighted by a well-grown specimen, laden with its funnels that expand at the mouth into five twisting, pointed segments. Given a sheltered, basking position, you can plant it in the herbaceous border for the summer, and get an added thrill from such exoticism in an English garden. There is a popular hose-in-hose variety with two layers of petals.

Many immoral scents are borne by perfectly hardy plants, including our own native butterfly orchids and wild honeysuckle. Of more topical interest, is *Osmanthus delavayi*, now at the height of its flowering. Each twig carries several scores of its pure-white, tubular flowers, so that a large bush in bloom is almost as impressive to see as to smell. But it is also a nice plant for its neat, evergreen foliage, and you can maintain a comely habit in it by lightly clipping the bush over immediately after flowering. It likes a sunny position and a good soil, otherwise it sulks and puts on little growth. Hard winters do set it back, but only temporarily and, given shelter, it flourishes even in north-east Scotland.

22.4.65

BEARING GIFTS

WHAT sort of gift, if any, should you take to hosts by whom you have been invited for the weekend or just a meal?

Increasingly it seems to have become a matter of obligation to take something, the standard formula being a bottle of wine. This is seldom fair either on the serious pleasures of wine drinking or on the discrimination of your hosts. The wine, anonymous at best, is a poor substitute for good drinking water (itself rarely untainted by nauseous chlorine). It quickly finds its way to the raffle in a local fund-raising charity, but even here, I find, wine is becoming a drug on the market. Winners would prefer a packet of Phostrogen plant food.

Food is a much better idea if you know in which direction your host's weaknesses lie. I love chocolates, especially mint or ginger chocolates, with my after-meal coffee, but no milk chocolate, please. I cannot abide its cloying sickliness. Belgian chocolates (especially the white-coated sort) are in a class apart; however sweet, they remain delectable. I also have a passion for black olives before a meal and so have many of my gift bearers. It is one of the endearing qualities in my younger friends that they have no inhibitions about eating as much of their gifts themselves as their host has the chance to. The likelihood therefore is that they will soon become quite discriminating about what they bring, especially as we freely discuss everything we eat and drink, wherever it came from. Too salty, too oily or too hard and unyielding an olive pleases nobody. In the event, it is rare to excel those from Sainsbury's delicatessen counter, which is where I buy them myself. My guests devour them with alacrity and their standards are set. But there are even better Greek olives about.

Should you take something that you have made or grown yourself? 'Here is a little piece of myself,' this gesture suggests, but it does include some pretty ropy samples of chutney, mint jelly and over-sweet marmalade. On the other hand a bookmarker embroidered in outlines of your favourite dog or cat is a special pleasure.

Often I take a bunch of flowers, if I know that flowers are appreciated (some people hate them cut) and that my contribution is likely to be different from what my hosts can pick from their own garden. This is, in fact, an innocuous way of showing off and it is especially welcome at mid-winter, with such as winter sweet and witch hazel, when flowers are scarce. In spring you would obviously take something as common as daffodils only to town friends without a garden. For anyone with a lively sense of smell, a bunch of scented flowers like lilies-of-the-valley or border carnations will be a treat.

Should you ply your hosts with plants and, if so, which will you choose? 'That plant you gave me has taken over my garden' is a familiar refrain more likely to loosen friendships than to bind them.

Often I look desperately at the plants potted in my frames, with the question 'What shall it be?' banging away in my head. Sometimes I give up in despair. At others I pick something out that seems utterly appropriate, only to find that, for the same reason of its being utterly appropriate, I have already presented it once or twice before. I have myself been the recipient of *Billardiera longiflora* from the same donor three times in as many years. And he is twenty years younger than me, which is comforting in a way.

Will the plants be wanted? is always a big question, because it's a waste if not and the plants will become a silent reproach to the recipient if nothing is done about them. I gave three quite nice little pot-grown plants, in flower, to show what they could do, to some dear friends a year ago, but it has to be admitted that they are not compulsive gardeners. I had occasion to call in three days later. My friends were out but the plants, now sadly wilted, were still sitting on the doorstep where I had given them. I took them to their pond and immersed them for a long drink. I've no idea and don't want to know if they were ever planted.

But some people must follow up their gift with remorseless enquiries after its health and progress, which isn't really fair when it was unsolicited and possibly less exciting than the donor imagined. 'How is the abutilon I gave you?' I'll be asked. Is it kinder to reply, 'Which abutilon?' with a blank look, or to say that it unfortunately perished. The latter has the risk of bringing a replacement on you.

Actually, far from feeling kind, the persistent pursuer sometimes makes me savage. When I was out one day, a visitor left me cuttings of *Rhododendron* 'Tally Ho', together with a long eulogy (which assumed that the variety was beyond my ken), not only of its flowers but of its lovely foliage and telling me how easily rooted it was. Maybe it would have been if I hadn't dropped the cuttings straight into the rubbish box. Months later he wrote with enquiries about his gift. Had I received it? Had the cuttings rooted? I was now cornered. The cuttings had not rooted, I told him. I intensely dislike all the hybrids of *R. griersonianum* for the harshness of their red colouring and additionally, in 'Tally Ho', the scrawny stemminess of its habit.

That seemed to settle the matter, but plant gifts are undoubtedly a hazard, at whichever end of the present you are. 23.4.87

MAY

SURVIVORS FROM THE ICE AGE

To be confronted day after day and for weeks and months on end by the same naggingly dead-looking shrubs that winter has left on our doorsteps can arouse an irresistible urge in the gardener's sorely tried bosom to sweep them all away and make a fresh start. Sometimes this is not a bad idea. If the chuck-outs were not really dead at all but merely playing possum, so much the worse for them: we shall be none the wiser. An established garden, no matter what its size, is always short of space for growing all the plants that we should like to grow, so that the gap left by a death can be snatched at almost with relief for the opportunity it affords of trying something new.

It is never worth struggling or waiting for a sickly evergreen ceanothus. If it looks doubtful, you may be sure it will soon look worse, and if it looks dead, it is dead. Powers of recuperation are not to be expected from this tribe. However, they are always worth replacing as they grow so fast and are the only evergreen, blue-flowered shrubs at our command. I have just lost four different kinds, including – 'Cascade' and 'Edinensis' – of whose hardiness without protection I was boasting in *Country Life* only a few months ago! The sole survivor has been the species *C. rigidus*, reputedly one of the more tender. My 12 foot plant, growing against a south-east wall, is thirteen years old, which is usually a dangerous age for these ceanothus, but it is bursting with promise of blossom. It is the earliest flowering of them all; in a precocious spring, the first sprays open at the end of March and the colour is an unusual and effective indigo. There is no more accommodating ceanothus for training against a wall, as its shoots tend naturally to lie flat against their backing. The foliage, too, is particularly neat and rather like a cotoneaster's.

Ceanothus are always pot grown and can be planted at any

101

season, but spring is the best time for the evergreens as they then have the chance to become well established before the possible ordeal of their first winter.

So it is, also, with the cistuses. Among these the only survivor here has been *C. × corbariensis*. A few others, like *C. × cyprius*, were lingering, but an elderly cistus, once crippled, will never make a worthwhile specimen again and should away to the bonfire. Many of the hybrids are sterile, but those which are not and, of course, the species, can quickly be brought back into circulation by gathering seed from the dead bushes' persistent seed pods, and sowing it now. I did this on 4 April, in a cold frame, with seed from Collingwood Ingram's beautiful *ladanifere × palhinha* crosses, and the resulting seedlings were large enough to handle and prick out exactly a fortnight later.

Another casualty to have received similar treatment is the red Australian Bottle Brush, *Callistemon citrinus*. This never sheds its seed pods. They cling tightly, like cylinders of grey beads, to the old stems on which they once flowered, and it may be years before they open up and release their dust-fine contents.

I sometimes find it hard not to be anthropomorphic about plants: this year my callistemon, on dying, has released its seed as never before, as though it knew this was its last chance of regeneration. Tapping the capsules over my outstretched palm immediately released thousands of seeds. I sowed them – much too thickly – and after ten days they are coming up like the sward on a pygmy lawn.

Callistemon belongs to the myrtle family, and I shall therefore not destroy my old plant but cut it down and hope that it will grow again from ground-level. This is the way our fifty-year-old myrtle (*Myrtus communis*) has always gladdened us, following a bad winter. The last time it was razed was in 1947. Since then it had assumed gigantic proportions – 15 feet by 15 feet – but all must be started over again. Still, providing next winter is not a repeat performance of the last, there is nothing to worry about and we shall lose only one year's blossom. This myrtle carries very handsome crops of purplish-black berries in the winter following a good ripening season, and self-sown seedlings often appear in the pavement cracks.

Eucalyptus is another member of the Myrtaceae and again it responds magnificently to being cut hard back – a fact of which we gardeners should take far more frequent advantage. Young pot-grown trees of the hardy *E. gunnii*, for instance, are very apt, except in the most protected positions, to blow over on reaching a height of 20 feet or so. But if a young, pot-grown plant is cut back to soil level immediately on planting, in spring, its roots are enabled to obtain a firm anchorage before the stem starts acting as a huge lever. It is just a question of steeling yourself to make that one snip with the secateurs.

I am delighted to find that *E. perriniana* has survived 25 degrees of frost. Shelter from cutting north and east winds is its main requirement. It is grown entirely for the weird beauty of its strings of disc-shaped, glaucous, juvenile foliage. I have just pruned my plant to a 4 foot stump, but although pruning must be regular and the plant grown as a shrub, not a tree, it is unnecessary to be as severe as I have been, unless your plant is rocking.

Trees of *E. gunnii* begin to flower and fruit when still quite young and the seed set in this country is viable. If you pick a branch, you will find it clothed in bone-hard seed capsules of various ages, just as in *Callistemon*. The way to extract their contents is by spreading out some ripe brown pods which have not already opened and lost their seed, in a sunny window. In a day or two the seed can be tapped out of them. It is very fine indeed, and should not be covered with soil after sowing.
2.5.63

ON WITH THE NEW

WHAT is one to do with the new plants that are coming in all the time? One must have them – some of them, anyway – but where to fit them in? I am certainly not one of those level-headed creatures that firmly refuses to acquire new plants because 'I haven't the space.' Always seize your chance and let the brooding on what to do with the acquisition take place afterwards.

It does help concentrate the mind if you then carry the new plant round the garden with you. I'm not going so far as to suggest you should ask it 'Where would you like to grow, dear?' because the plant, in strange surroundings, is unlikely to have any clear idea about this itself. But you can at least relate your vision (supposing you have one) of how it will look when grown to the various possible or impossible contexts passing before your eyes. I find it also helps to have someone with me. 'Come and help me find a place for . . .' I say. In the end it's usually I that finds the place but another pair of eyes tends to sharpen your own.

Shrubs, of course, are more difficult to position than bulbs or perennials. You'll often need to remove one shrub in order to make room for another. 'Where shall I plant my *Trochodendron*?' I rang Romke van de Kaa in Holland, to ask. He worked here from 1976 for three years and is a wizard for thinking of the right spot. Pause: then, 'You could get rid of the *Piptanthus*.' I changed the subject quickly.

Piptanthus nepalensis has grown in the same corner for thirty-five years. Once or twice I have changed the actual plant but it would never have occurred to me to get rid of it completely. It is a legume with rather large trifoliate leaves and clusters of substantial yellow pea flowers borne over a six weeks' period around May. Growth is rapid, to 6 or 7 feet, and the young stems are dark-green with hints of purple and a lovely glossy sheen on them like a dachshund's coat. But this shrub has one vicious habit: for no apparent reason and at any season of the year but especially in summer, old branches die. They are replaced by others but this dying back is a continuing nuisance.

However, *Piptanthus* does make a good wall shrub and not necessarily on a sunny wall. I had a space facing north-west where a long-toothed specimen of *Ceanothus dentatus floribundus* had been extracted last year. Its charms are of the obvious and flashy kind and I feel no compulsion to replace it. But a young piptanthus (I always have seedlings by me) could go there. The deed was done and *Trochodendron aralioïdes* stands in the old piptanthus's position.

Troc (for short) is the only member of the family Trochodendraceae. It comes from Japan and looks (to me at least) rather like an arborescent ivy. The flowers are borne in domed clusters in May and although they are green and have neither petals nor sepals they are charming, each with a circle of prominent yellow-tipped stamens. In its native haunts it will make a tree 60 to 80 feet high. I am prepared to cope with one tenth of this.

Richard, who works with me in the garden, generally has an eye for a plant that isn't earning its place and he's quick to point it out. We both gloomily contemplated *Camellia japonica* 'White Swan' syn. 'Alba Simplex', the other day. You had to peer into the centre of the bush to find an unspoilt flower. Admittedly there has been an extraordinary succession of night frosts this spring, but camellias have a way of rubbing in every real or imagined defect in the quality of our climate. If it isn't the frost that burns them it's the wind or it's simply old age and a case of the bloom dying on its feet instead of tumbling voluntarily to earth. And too often the leaves, although glossy, are like 'incredibly leathery plastic', as Tony Schilling put it when I invited him to join me in a hate session the other day.

I admit that a huge old camellia doing its stuff can be an impressive sight but it happens too rarely and we are too lenient about admitting to the camellia's faults. Besides, we all change. I remember how thrilled I was when my mother bought me this 'White Swan' from Waterer's, who had shown it at the RHS back in the late forties, I suppose. In 1976 it suffered badly from the drought and its growth has slowed down since. I had resolved to cut it hard back after flowering this spring (camellias respond well to this treatment) and to mulch it heavily.

Then Beth Chatto, after her recent visit, sent me a small plant of a purple-leaved *Sambucus nigra* which she loves and thinks I would and I certainly have a weakness for the elder tribe. Carrying it round the garden in my trug I suddenly thought: Why not get rid of 'White Swan' altogether? Last year (I mused) it delighted me by already being in flower in January. I should have that pleasure no longer. Never mind. There was something about the replacement of a camellia with an elder that appealed to me. Richard has done it and now points out the defects in my *Camellia* 'Magnoliiflora', which is flowering (and browning) with particular freedom this spring. We shall see.

Beth also sent me a piece of *Petasites japonicus giganteus*, which is one of those take-over perennials whose planting you are supposed to live bitterly to regret evermore. I have planted with joy and trepidation on the far side of our moat. It may be a thug but it is also beautiful and must not be disparaged.
3.5.84

SUBURBAN TREES AND SHRUBS

A FRIEND has written to my mother, 'I have just been out to buy a magnolia. Do I hear Christo exclaiming, "How suburban!"?' 'No, she does not,' is the answer to that one. I am sorry the garden centre she visited was unable to supply the *Magnolia denudata* she asked for, because it has more personality than *M. stellata*, which she bought instead, but I wouldn't be without either of them myself. Why should I dub them suburban? And anyway what are we getting at when we use this word in this context?

Clearly we mean to establish some kind of superiority for ourselves in matters of taste over those of our fellows who are obliged (or choose) to live in suburban communities. We imply that they, the suburban herd, are out to draw attention to themselves by making a splash with flowers of garish colouring which will be the envy of their neighbours, who will in their turn react by growing the same flowers with the same result *ad nauseam*. Come to think of it, there's something in that.

What of the plants themselves? I have made a suburban shortlist as follows: weeping willow, double pink cherry, flowering currant, forsythia, azalea, lilac, laburnum, hydrangea, double pink or red may. I would have included heathers, only they're not quite splashy enough. Perhaps dahlias and marigolds ought to go in. Apart from these, all are trees or shrubs and none are white. The suburban flower is always colourful.

Now we must ask what is wrong with any of these. Like other plants, several have faults. Weeping willows (I am looking out on coveys of them in new housing estates as I travel in the train towards London) are so confoundedly pretty; there is no resisting them. Many willows have weeping forms, but the one that is being universally planted today (for this is a recent fashion) is *Salix alba* 'Tristis', often listed as 'Vitellina Pendula'. Its young stems, young leaves and catkins are all of an entrancing greeny-yellow colouring in spring. Yet this is a terrifyingly unsuitable tree for a small garden. It grows fast and it grows vast and its greedy roots are a menace. When the penny drops, the craze will pass, I guess, and these willows will be confined, as heretofore, to suitable locations in large gardens and parks. For the small garden the weeping *S. purpurea* 'Pendula' is very suitable and charming, with stems of purple colouring, but it isn't a show-off tree like its candy-floss cousin.

I shouldn't dream of sneering at anyone for planting forsythia and I have several of my own, which I consider indispensable. And this is because they are so marvellous for cutting while in bud and forcing into flower in the house during the dreary months of January, February and most of March. Seen in other people's gardens in April, one looks forward to May. The trouble with forsythias is not so much their colouring nor their superabundance of blossom but the undistinguished or, more often, downright ugly shape of the bush on which they grow. There is really no help for this.

The currant, *Ribes sanguineum*, is not worth having in its commonest pale-pink form; the colouring is too indeterminate. But the bright carmine of 'Pulborough Scarlet' is excellent and shows the pendant racemes to advantage against their young unfurling leaves.

Double pink cherry suffers from being, nine times out of ten, the same old 'Kanzan'. When young or middle-aged, its habit is stiff and unpleasing, but in maturity 'Kanzan' becomes a fine tree, unless its sheer bulk forces the owner to get lopping. In summer it is a dull object.

So are lilacs, but I forgive them everything in their flowering season and I don't care how common and mauve the variety is: all are delectable. What could be prettier than pink or red may blossom on a small tree that is, by nature, a particularly pleasing shape? And there can never be too much laburnum for me. True it looks better against a blue sky than against a red-brick house, but that is a mere question of getting yourself into the right position on the right day.

As to the sort of azalea you are likely to meet in suburban gardens, so often it fails to get off the ground; it seems to lack the ebullience required by a suburban shrub. Hydrangeas have it. The hortensia in full career is a glorious splodger. Never mind setting; you must be inhuman not to be disarmed by its cheerful opulence.

Individually examined, suburban trees and shrubs come off pretty well, but there are such huge numbers of such few kinds. And the resulting sameness, though more concentrated and hence obvious in the suburbs, is scarcely less prevalent in towns, villages and on isolated properties throughout the country.

We must be prepared to fight to remain individuals, even in gardening. The friend I started by quoting is a mother with three smallish children; a shopping spree at the local garden centre can only be snatched occasionally. She wanted *Magnolia denudata* but there was no time to be other than contented to make do with *M. stellata*. Had she asked for *Forsythia ovata*, probably she would have had to make do with the more popular 'Lynwood' and an enquiry for their rarer relative *Abeliophyllum* would have elicited uncomprehending astonishment. That is how it goes. However, she surprised herself and, still more, her husband, by coming home additionally with a *M. grandiflora*. What could be more unexpected in a suburban garden than this doyen of the stately home or rat-ridden old rectory? Impulse buying does have its unorthodox side.

14.5.70

NODAL, INTERNODAL AND ALL THAT

LAST week, when describing how to make clematis cuttings, I wrote that you cut across the stem just above each node (or joint). Then I read Bernard Levin in *The Times* about the incomprehensible gibberish written in programme notes for concerts and recitals and my conscience smote me. Perhaps much of what I write is similarly incomprehensible. At least one candid friend says exactly that. But then, I tell myself, he's not interested in gardening and doesn't try to understand and anyway the only books on his few shelves are a set of Dickens, obviously a cheap job lot he's never opened, and a few digests.

Still, others have hinted that perhaps . . . And it certainly is off-putting if you're expected to rush to a dictionary or a glossary of botanical terms every time you sit down with a dog on your lap and a cuppa at your side thinking you'll have a nice comfy read from the old glossy. If node means joint, why the devil didn't I write joint straightaway and have done with those nodes? Thus I nagged at myself, but then sprang to the nodes' defence. First, node is shorter than joint but second, far more to the point, you can't make an adjective of joint to mean the same thing as nodal. A nodal cutting is one where the cut is made just below the node. A joint cutting, if it meant anything, would mean that you made it holding hands with your wife or apprentice. And jointal doesn't exist.

Neither can internodes be satisfactorily translated into interjoints. I didn't get as far as the internodes last week. They are, perhaps it will be no great surprise to learn, the stretch of stem linking node to node. The internodes on a clematis stem are often six or more inches long. A nodal cutting would consist of a node at the top, a stretch of internode and then another node at the bottom, below which the lower cut was made. This could be extravagant of material and a physically inconvenient unit to handle. But clematis are amenable to the internodal cuttings I described, in which the lower cut is made at any convenient spot across the internode. Roots can, in their case, be made as easily from the internodal as from the nodal cutting. Not only does this give you a cutting of a convenient length, but you can get twice as many cuttings made internodally as you can their nodal counterparts since each cutting in the former case includes only one node. You are with me?

Clematis are not exceptional in their capacity for making roots from the internodal cutting. Hydrangeas will and so, more surprisingly, will roses. Indeed, if we were only a little more adventurous and experimental we should probably find that a large proportion of the plants we root from cuttings would do so internodally. Mr Clapham, in a *Country Life* article, pointed out that fuchsias behave in this way and I had it from the girls at Sissinghurst – I beg their pardons, I mean the joint (or nodal) head lady gardeners (or lady head gardeners) at Sissinghurst Castle - that bedding verbenas root from internodal cuttings which is a great convenience when you are short of material.

Technical terms are undoubtedly useful and there is nothing aurally disagreeable about the words node and nodal though the propagator under whom I trained referred to noodle cuttings. Occasionally the technical term is actually sweet on the ear. I always think inflorescence, which describes the whole set-up of a flowering unit, is one of the most delightful words in the language, conjuring to my mind's eye a galaxy, a *feu d'artifice* of blossom. But more often the inventors of technical terms have no ear at all.

One of the ugliest words that has come into use of recent years, both as noun and adjective, is cultivar, shortened to CV. I frequently use it on this page myself since it so conveniently says what I mean, but I loathe the word as a word. A cultivar, short for cultivated variety, is a plant which has originated in cultivation and it is thus distinguished from variety, abbreviated to var., which is a natural group within a species, occurring in the wild. It always surprised me that when the word cultivar came into official usage, more than twenty years ago, one of its most enthusiastic champions was Mr John Gilmour UMH (you must know what that stands for), who is himself very musical and a gleeful singer of madrigals. 15.5.75

Camera Shy

THE editor and photographer from the best French gardening magazine are descending on me tomorrow, the choice of date being on account of my having alerted them that my plant of *Tropaeolum azureum*, in which they have a particular interest, was in flower. I must say a blue-flowered tropaeolum is quite something but my one tuber (in a pot in the greenhouse) has the most peculiar habit of growing and flowering only every other year. For eighteen months at a time it remains completely dormant. I have met this behaviour in no other plant.

Actually it is now nearly over and I had to warn my intending visitors that this is not a good time for photographing my garden. All is promise rather than fulfilment (the daffodils and osmanthus bushes, far from showing promise, are in the full tide of ostentatious decay). There must be some alpines, Monsieur suggested (on the telephone). Alpines are no help to a gardener with five or more acres. Primulas then? Only the remains of primroses that the sparrows and I hadn't eaten (they are awfully good in salads).

Anyway they're coming, so I looked around the garden to see what an outsider might see. Immediately, I fell to pulling weeds, which is always what happens when you begin to look at your own garden. I suppose he thought I was being modest, I ruminated, as I grovelled and stretched, chasing after ivy-leaved speedwells and hairy bitter cress, already running to seed; willow-herb, nipple wort and plantains (whose steadfast roots always require the tip of a sharp trowel), just setting out. But actually I'm not a modest person; he probably hadn't realised that. I can never see the point of modesty, which makes everything uniformly low-keyed and drab. If you're bad at a thing – mending the electric light or, more seriously, in my case, any sort of draughtsmanship – admit it like a man, but if you've done something rather well, like producing a blaze of floral colour in May, why pretend otherwise?

Anyway, the said blaze is notably lacking, apart from a rather sparse assortment of tulips and they, like the daffodils before them, are not nearly as numerous this year as last – I mean the ones that carry on year after year, not those that arrived fresh from the bulb field fattening grounds last autumn; they are only too predictably big and blowsy. It takes a year or two of ordinary garden fare to fine them down to acceptable dimensions.

Still, there are satisfactions, to me, anyway, though not to a photographer. An excellent set of young apricots, though the peaches were disobliging and hardly flowered at all. Although bullfinches were around earlier, they've not returned to eat the buds off that delicious September apple, 'Saint Everard', which is so good to pick straight off the tree.

There's tremendous promise on the Brunswick figs, which only perform well every third year, on average. Two or even three figlets are developing near the tip of each of last year's strong young shoots. People who insist on pruning their figs tight back against a wall don't realise what they're missing. There'll be a big drop, as always, of young fruit next month, regardless of whether you keep your tree well watered or not – that's my experience, anyway. But with luck many will remain to ripen in the latter half of August.

The brown and burnt-orange with carmine hints in *Euphorbia griffithii* 'Dixter' are looking good and I have this next to the rich evergreen Tasmanian, *Ozothamnus ledifolius*, whose own clustered flower buds are now dusky-orange. It is hard to analyse the expression of inner joy that seems to well up in this shrub. I'm not the only one that loves to contemplate it. Near by, the maidenhair fern, *Adiantum pedatum* 'Klondyke', is a work of the greatest artistry; a fragile, yellow-tinted shade of green. The twelve pinnae on each frond are set about an arc like fingers, while the individual pinnules are sharply angled, obviating any hint of muzziness.

What a good plant the white honesty is. It shows up so much better than the mauve and magenta kinds. My friend Pamela Milburne has an overlarge *Elaeagnus pungens* 'Maculata' (they always get outsize, sooner or later, unless they die first) from which she has removed the lowest branches so that you can see through and underneath it. All this area is a sea of white honesty blossom just now. On a more modest scale, I have some that have appointed themselves on either side of one of Waterer's old Knaphill azaleas, the albino, hose-in-hose 'Whitethroat', with very pale-green foliage. That's nice, or will be when the buds are fully open – not in time for the photographer.

My wisterias, *Wisteria sinensis*, are all bud so far, too, which gives me the pleasure of anticipation (sparrows have ignored them this year) but anticipation is of no use to a camera. From time to time I get fed up with wisteria, when it has been disbudded over a succession of years and I've been too idle to cotton it. In fact, I got rid of all ours – three large plants – at one stage, or at least I meant to but two of them, in fact, had layered themselves unbeknownst to me at a considerable distance from the main root. Years later it is from these layers, one of them growing through a vine, another through *Magnolia × soulangeana* 'Lennei', that the bountiful display will come. However, the French have abundant *glycine* of their own and anyway the display is not yet on.

Euphorbia mellifera, now 6 foot tall, is scenting the air with honey all around it, but is nothing to look at and neither is *Pittosporum tenuifolium* with its little maroon bells that smell so strongly of cocoa at night that it travels round two corners of our house and meets me in the porch. Someone should devise a way to photograph scents.

24.5.84

DEAD HEAD HUNTING

GRATEFULLY I seize upon the utterance of some fellow journalist when it provides me with a talking point, and now that I have Tony Venison within a hand's span of my predatory grasp, it is inevitable that he should be my occasional catalyst. I hope he will forgive me, because taking up a point made by a fellow professional invariably means disagreeing with him (to agree would be too flat-footed to warrant ink on paper). The reader (if he has not already signed off, Yours, DISGRUNTLED) will mutter something about these experts and will they ever agree? but that will give him a glowing sense of superiority, which is all to the good (unless it is his habitual state, in which case I offer my sympathy and condolences to his dependants).

The pearl before which I swinishly express a preference for truffles was this recent pronouncement: 'Dead-heading the daffodils, hyacinths and tulips takes more time than can be spared, but the quality of next spring's show depends on it.' I disagree. At the same time I do wish that some experimental station would settle the matter. A controlled experiment would not be difficult to set up but it would, I suppose, be considered unwarrantably expensive considering the (un)importance of its subject. And yet is it so unimportant that generations of us gardeners should, from the tender age at which we can first tweak a dead head from its stem till the latest moment when arthritis excuses us from stooping to hyacinth level – that we should spend all those hours upon a fruitless occupation when we might have been doing . . .? Yes, but doing what? There's the rub.

If a chap can come in from the garden ten minutes late for lunch and, sinking into his place in a state of all too obvious exhaustion, mutter, 'I've spent the last two hours and fifty minutes dead-heading the hyacinths,' no one can chide him for not having performed that queue of small household chores: sharpening the knives, gluing the table leg, even laying the table – which are expected of a man home for the weekend.

There is a kind of masochism about dead-heading. It may not qualify as hard work but it is sufficiently boring and repetitive to earn a thick slab (or should I say halo?) of virtue for its performer.

In my family we were trained to be good dead-headers from a tender age. Bribed, in fact. The orchard was stuffed with daffodils. All had to be removed, neatly stacked and subsequently borne in armfuls to the rubbish heap. It was not enough just to pull the heads off. That would have been far too easy and not in the least virtuous. Stem and all had to be picked and counted and we were offered a penny a hundred for our efforts: good money in those days when a penny was a penny (the other job commanding a stated fee was the trapping of black-beetles – a penny a beetle, I think it was, but that is not a very nice story. Younger readers, reared on DDT, probably don't know what a black-beetle is unless they've travelled on a French boat).

Now I wonder – and this would be another matter to be examined in the horticultural experiment of my dreams – whether the removal of the daffodil's flower stalk did not actually do the bulb harm, if it did it anything. After all the stalk is green: it is photosynthesising and might be expected to be making its contribution to the bulb's storage efforts.

Our overt reason for dead-heading is, as Tony Venison has clearly stated, for the good of the plant. We stopped it in our orchard of daffodils some thirty years since, and I cannot see that they have been any less prolific as a consequence. There is more to it than just the plant's benefit. After all, no one that I know of has ever suggested dead-heading the snowdrops, but why not? True, snowdrops manage to flower abundantly every year without being dead-headed, but that's not the point. Their heads are now heavy with seed and it must be very exhausting for the poor things. We should certainly organise their rescue, whether they like it or not. The only reason we don't is that we don't *see* their dead heads. They flop to the ground very shortly after flowering and are there forgotten.

Most of the time, then, dead-heading is purely for our own satisfaction, first as a method of getting dead heads out of our offended line of vision; second as a way of 'doing good'. Remember that, when you fetch the step ladder and set about the rhododendrons and lilacs.

25.5.72

A Study in Contrasts

You do not have to be a committed gardener in order to enjoy your garden.

I have a friend – I do not have to write about him over-reverently; he's younger than I am (though you'd never think it) – whose garden can be summed up in a few brisk brushstrokes. He calls his abode Broadlands and it must be conceded that it is a detached villa with an uninterrupted view from the back, of the South Downs. Nevertheless I think that, as a title, No. 477a Lewes Road West would better suit its hard-earned brand of anonymity.

The car-turning area in front of this house is readily enlarged (should your steering lock or aim not be too good) by running up on to a daisy lawn and this will afford you a closer view of the Leyland cypresses' progress. These were planted on the roadside boundary a few years ago after an unexpected gap had been created when a vehicle turned incontinently off the high road and plunged into my friend's front garden. 'A gap is an opportunity,' I probably told him (it is a favourite maxim). He took the opportunity to introduce Leyland cypresses to yet another front garden.

We must not ignore or run over the lawn's central feature which is a blue Atlantic cedar – *Cedrus atlantica* 'Glauca'. It stands 3 feet high and seems likely to remain at that height for the foreseeable future. However, the circle round it where a mower dare not trespass is dominated by splendid 4 to 5 foot samples of *Anthriscus sylvestris*, the cow parsley.

The side of a house where it comes nearest to your neighbour and draughts are strongest is always a problem area. Brilliantly, my friend harnesses the wind energy in this alley by hanging out his smalls to dry. Gauze modesty curtains in the sitting-room windows facing in that direction prevent the smalls from staring in. (I notice that this neighbour's house is up for sale.)

On the back garden front any outstanding headaches will soon be solved by a vigorous young horse chestnut. There is no more efficient ground-cover than a canopy of *Aesculus hippocastanum*. It will shortly engulf the patch where:

> Smelliest of veg the cabbage rump
> Is thick with blossom on its stump.

Insofar as he can spare his time for our hobby my friend is, I should say, a happy, carefree gardener.

Not so a lady who has just written me four typed sheets on the sort of gardener whom journalists like myself should be catering for. She is not a *Country Life* reader, I hasten to add.

She is typical, I gather, of millions who have tried hard to like gardening, joined a gardening class at one time (where, to her disgust, fellow classmates sucked up to the instructors by bringing them bits of esoteric plants for identification) and found that she loathed it more than ever.

Why garden? She forestalls the question. If you live in a detached house, something has to be done with the area between yourself and the nearest dwellings. So gardening is forced on you.

There is horrible lawn grass that insists on growing and has to be mown. She likes moss; she likes daisies, which hug the ground. Well, who's stopping her? The gardening equivalent of Mrs Grundy, I suppose.

My correspondent approves of evergreens which don't go bare and shed their leaves in the mischievous way of deciduous trees and shrubs each autumn, thus initiating a miserable clearing-up operation.

I did, in my brief reply, point out a fact that is surprisingly often missed about evergreens. They shed as many leaves in twelve months as their deciduous counterparts. The fact that they spread this shedding over the whole year instead of concentrating it into one season can be a considerable inconvenience, as I did not trouble to elaborate.

I suggested that an exterior decorator rather than a garden expert should be called in to advise. Artificial grass is available to reluctant gardeners and there is no need for paving to have cracks in which weeds can grow.

The gardening journalist does not want to resemble those school teachers who are always concentrating on the needs of the backward child, with the result that the bright kids are bored to sobs. We hope to be writing for those who, although admittedly a small minority, are committed gardeners and who love the time and trouble given to their plants.

Anyway the bored majority are constantly being catered for. They are numerous and they are a market. No market for long goes unsatisfied. Why, you can furnish a garden entirely with trouble-free, colourful accessories and never even begin to touch the plastic flower trade, if that is your wish.

It seems unnecessary for a small garden to make anyone miserable.

28.5.81

JUNE

IRRESISTIBLE COYNESS OF GAZANIAS

THE beginning of June seems an appropriate time to be writing of gazanias. Like all South African daisies – venidiums, ursinias, arctotis, dimorphothecas, felicias – they are the very essence of summer, radiant and fickle, gladdening and maddening by turns. Visitors to the RHS gardens at Wisley on a sunny day in summer or autumn will be entranced by their fabulous collection of gazanias,* near the alpine house. These have mostly been obtained by a process of selection of seedlings, made on the premises. Any of us can do the same, for gazanias are readily raised from seed, which can be obtained, initially, from one of several seed houses, and the plants will set seed in your own garden, thereafter.

Plants obtained from cuttings taken in the previous autumn, will come earlier into flower – about now, that is – and will be your method of perpetuating any particular variety that you have fallen in love with. But it is difficult to buy plants. With the exception of fuchsias, dahlias, and chrysanthemums, for which the public demand is terrific, nurseries do not generally find it worth marketing tender perennials that have to be sent out in May. The customer asks for one plant or two, and the expense is disproportionate.†

Gazanias are a bit of trouble. There is no disputing this, but I have been growing them for twenty years now, and plant out about ninety of them in a sunny bed, each early May (they will stand a few degrees of frost) and I can state from experience that once you have worked out the best routine, they take up very little time.

In any case the gazania personality is so strong that you

* Long since dispersed.
† Garden Centres have altered all this.

123

make yourself a willing slave. The plant is neat and clumpy, but the leaves vary greatly from plant to plant. Some are long, lanceolate and green; others may be quite short, pinnate and thickly white-felted. The latter, indeed, are often grown principally for foliage effect. Usually, of course, it is for the flowers. There is no basic gazania flower colouring. They may be cream, primrose-lemon or chrome-yellow; apricot, vivid or deep orange; brown, beige, purple or crushed strawberry-pink. And at the base of each ray there are markings in contrasting shades in which black predominates, but often including spots of startlingly brilliant green. You can't just glance at a gazania flower; you look, and blink and then look again with a crescendo of incredulous attention.

They are exceedingly fussy about weather and, even if the day is hot throughout, insist on strict Trades Union rules by shutting up at four o'clock. A closed or even a half-closed gazania flower is practically invisible, and distinctly depressing if you do happen to see it. There is no moodier flower, but when they do relax and bask, you will want to fling off your clothes and bask in sympathy.

No plant could be of easier cultivation, with the one rider of them not being hardy. They will grow happily in all soils, light and heavy, and are never attacked by pests or fungal diseases. Of course, their position must be open and sunny, but they will take any amount of wind and are unaffected by salt spray on the coast.

In autumn, you must think about propagating the varieties that are worth saving. Lifting and re-potting old plants doesn't work, but it is easy to take cuttings of non-flowering shoots. You pull them off with a heel and then trim this clean with a razor blade. If the leaves are long and floppy, you can shorten them by one third, also with the blade. Should the shoot have a flower bud, tweak it out.

You can get about nine cuttings into a $3^1/_2$ inch pot, using an open cutting compost, and this goes into a close frame. Bottom heat is unnecessary and a mist propagator is undesirable, since (as is the case with most hairy or woolly leaved perennials) the cuttings tend to rot away if kept excessively damp. Some of the outer leaves on each cutting are liable to die, and should be peeled off before their rotting spreads to the rest of the shoot. Give them air as soon as they can take it without flagging unduly.

I used to make my cuttings in the second week of September and pot them off individually about the end of the next month. However, this is space-consuming and I now find it even more satisfactory to make my cuttings in the last days of October. When they have rooted, in December, the pots are transferred to the open greenhouse bench, where they remain till March and the cuttings are only then potted off individually, into a cold frame, being ready for planting out six weeks later. If short of space in spring, you can plant them out direct from the pots in which they were rooted, but the plants take much longer to grow into nice fat specimens that way.

Whether grown in plastic or in clay pots, the roots of gazanias have a tiresome way of clinging tenaciously to the pot sides and bottom, and you are liable to leave much root behind, when turning them out. If you make sure that the entire ball of soil and roots is wringing wet, before you attempt the operation, the chances are that you will accomplish a painless extraction.

1.6.67

RAPE

THE vitality of yellow flowers gives them enormous importance in a landscape, when seen in quantity. They jump at you and twang the heartstrings, either with pleasure or, if the tune is wrong for you, with irritation.

Take a field of buttercups and forget, for the time being, to consider whether it is made up of *Ranunculus acris* (the field buttercup, rather tall and branching, my favourite, actually),

R. bulbosus (earliest on the scene and associated in my mind with the first flush of red clover) or *R. repens* (creeping buttercup, lover of wet places and fiendishly invasive in a garden). It may take you back to your childhood, awaking memories of swishing your feet through the flowers (as you would through leaves, in autumn, to make a lovely noise) and then admiring the yellowness of the pollen on your shoes. Or you may think: Bad land, poor feed unfit for cattle; fetch out the herbicides. Either way, the emotion will be strong. We find ourselves committed – those of us, at least, who still have eyes to see and emotions to be stirred.

Those fields of rape, now run to seed but lately describing a patchwork over the young green countryside (one that I love to see from the air – and there was a year, I suppose when subsidies were good, that the rape fields came right up to us and, standing on our roof, I could imagine that my garden no longer stopped at its normal boundaries but stretched to the horizon, probably beyond), how do they affect you? The hint of green in their solid presentation suggests a suppleness; their gusts of scent invade you unawares. The tender blue of a morning flax field is certainly touching but lacks the strength of rape, a strength which awakens disgust in those who will exclaim, 'That horrible rape; how I loathe it, and it ruins the honey. Did you know that it's the cause of all those pestilential pollen beetles that invade our summer gardens nowadays? They never used to.' Nothing is as it used to be.

I was reminded of rape in Turkey, on the return flight from where I am writing this piece. There, in the eastern parts of the country, you find innumerable outcrops of limestone rock, encrusted with lichens in shades of yellow, palest grey and rusty red. In every crack grows a trickle or bouquet of white arabis and yellow *Draba*. Don't ask me which species – we only had one of the ten volumes of Peter Davis's Turkish flora with us (they are heavy) and it did not include Cruciferae. But if you go to alpine garden societies' spring shows, you'll see cushions of similar drabas that have been cultivated with great skill under protected conditions and are now huge domes of yellow in large pots. This is a skill entirely divorced from what most of us aspire to in our gardens and it seems to have even less to do with nature when you see these plants in the wild. Each has its own personality yet all combine to enhance the rocks on which they grow with a pristine mantle. You approach your nose, expectantly, and what do you smell? Rape blossom. Delightful link between two members of the same great family of crucifers. Another piece in the jigsaw that has dropped into its place.

Kingcups (*Caltha palustris*, but a little different from ours with a few more, narrower petals, incurved, and a slightly larger bloom) appear in Turkey very shortly after snow melt, profiting from the wettest places. So brilliant are they in the landscape, that you can spot their patches from a great distance. They are no less eye-taking in parts of Scotland, where I especially feasted on them in the poor, peaty and undrained inland areas of the Isle of Lewis, kingcups being shortly followed by scarcely less abundant colonies of yellow flag iris.

Splashes of colour are especially welcome when they immediately follow upon the gloom of winter and it is yellow that predominates in earliest spring. Thus, it was the Lent lily, *Narcissus pseudonarcissus*, which inspired Wordsworth to write his best-known lyric. That is often flowering in March. Likewise coltsfoot, which deeply affected D.H. Lawrence. It is among our earliest wild flowers, transforming waste tips and neglected railway sidings with yellow daisies that respond and expand to the slightest hint of spring warmth.

We are often unaware of any foliage in these early flowers and, indeed, it is often absent or barely incipient. Forsythia has knock out impact, especially now that it has been bred to have the largest blooms on a densely compact bush. There is far more grace in the species *Forsythia suspensa* if only it has the space in which to grow freely into the large shrub it should be and without being senselessly hacked back into a shapeless blob, as is the fate of the majority of forsythias.

Where you can still find them in undisturbed meadowland, cowslips will make a stirring display. I photographed them in

Turkey, where the flower, instead of being pinched in at the mouth, is widely flared and makes a showier bloom. Another flower that engaged our affection, there, was a species of *Gagea*, which quickly spangled the ground with its stars, within days of a snowdrift's margins melting. Nothing aggressive about this, yet it created a natural garden, especially where joined by the pungent blue of *Scilla siberica*.

Dandelions are no less successful in Turkey than with us, and what a dazzle is theirs, when they open to spring sunshine. Most daisies do need sunshine to bring out their best qualities. White moon daisies scarcely open and close, but all those hawkbits, hawkweeds and hawksbeards remain quite drab till thoroughly warmed. In my orchard, they combine richly, through the first half of June with the moon daisies, but it is not till eleven in the morning that they have rubbed the sleep from their eyes, and then only if the sun has properly coaxed them.

Even in these days when so much of the countryside has been tamed, it is the wild flowers, whether or not we describe them as weeds, that make most of the big effects. One of the delights of high summer, especially on limy soils and right through our land to the north of Scotland, is the lady's bedstraw, *Galium verum*. Its rather tall sprays of yellow blossom take over so many sites, like ruined walls, on a Spartan diet, conveying the feel of sunshine even when it isn't there.

3.6.93

Which Plants are Poisonous?

Do you know which of the plants you grow in your garden are poisonous? Do you care? My own answers to these two questions are 'Only some' and 'Not much.' Till recently, that is, but I must admit to having become more poison-plant-conscious since New Year's Day when I acquired a dachshund pup whose chief idea, from the outset, has been to chew at absolutely everything. I see her with a twig of *Coronilla emerus*, the scorpion senna, in her mouth and a far-away chewing look in her eye, and my mind gets busy. Coronilla is a legume. Legumes include peas and beans and all sorts of fodder crops, so it's probably harmless. Then I remember laburnum, and my friend whose chickens got the staggers when they were pecking at the seeds under a laburnum tree, and I am tormented with doubt again. And so with every fresh morsel.

I have always found excessively tedious the stories that one mum will tell another (myself unluckily happening to be present) of how little Caroline was sick in the car, and how the sick got all over everything – but *everything*. Follows details of what everything and everyone consisted of. Gales of merriment. I shall have my revenge. Crocus (for Crocus is my angel's name) has twice made herself very sick indeed. She has sicked up everything, starting with her dinner and ending with some yellow bile – and not all in one go, mark you, but in stages, starting on the eiderdown and finishing on the Sumach rug, hand-embroidered, you know, and quite fabulous, worked by Christians, they tell me, in a heathen setting, but perhaps I've got it wrong and it's the other way about. Every time I thought I'd finished cleaning up, more was discovered, either by treading or by sitting in it! Ghastly at the time but killing when I think back.

Well, anyway, to cut a long story short (or is it the other way about?) I'm almost certain that the cause of the trouble was that she'd been nibbling yew twigs to pass the time while I was gardening. Fortunately, dogs are capable of being so thoroughly sick that they are none the worse for the ordeal, except for feeling hungry again when they ought to be feeling full and satisfied.

But it makes one a bit neurotic on their behalf, and I suppose it might be even worse with children. An outraged mother told Mrs Lindsay Drummond, who regularly opens her garden at Sissinghurst Place, to the public, that it was wicked of her to grow herb Christopher (*Actaea*) without warning visitors that its berries are poisonous. So it now carries a warning notice: 'This Plant is Poisonous; Eat it at Your Peril' or words to that effect. But if one plant, why not others? Where is it to stop?

Presumably, plants with bright, shiny berries are the most alluring to bauble-loving children. Our garden is repeatedly enveloped, each summer, in swags of black bryony, *Tamus communis*, a climbing herbaceous perennial that behaves rather like bindweed but carries ravishingly attractive garlands of gleaming red berries in autumn. I have always known it, since my earliest memories, and have always known that it was poisonous, but before that? Whether I was kept under constant scrutiny to make sure I didn't pop a berry in my mouth, I can't remember, strange to say. But we cannot hang notices on all our bryony plants to warn visitors and their children against them. Nor against bittersweet, *Solanum dulcamara*, which people will miscall deadly nightshade. This again comes up through other shrubs in various unlikely places and is charming with purple flowers and elliptical red berries.

It would be quicker, of course, to dig these weeds out, than to write notices for them all, but that's a grim thought, too. And what of our hundreds of yards of yew hedges? After all, children don't stop at berries. If they're sufficiently young and inexperienced, like my Crocus, they cram anything in. One might have a table of poisonous plants by the front gate. Visitors would be unable to recognise most of them in the flesh, but it might at least put them in a cautious mood from the start.

Not that one wants people to go round one's garden in that defensive frame of mind, but it's extraordinary how many of them, having paid their entrance money, seem to think they have no further responsibilities. Far from keeping an eye on their children, they lose sight of them completely. One sometimes feels that children should be admitted at double the normal price, rather than half. A few deaths by poisoning might even

130

be salutory, if the news got around, which it certainly would. But then the insurance companies might get tricky and then, again, I think of Crocus, and supposing it had been she. Almost certainly the really poisonous child would not get poisoned, anyway; it would be immune. One way and another I think most of us will continue to grow all the plants we want to (or that want us to), regardless, keeping our fingers crossed and refusing to meet trouble halfway.
10.6.71

FULL BORDERS WITHOUT CRUSHING

IT must be the hope and aim of every gardener that, by the time his deciduous shrubs and herbaceous plants are all in full leaf, his borders shall themselves look full and be without patches of bare earth. If he grows nothing but shrubs, and concentrates on those that provide an efficient ground-cover, this goal is fairly easily attained, but at the price of variety. To deny oneself the pleasures of herbaceous plants is stultifying and quite unnecessary. Many of them are no more troublesome than shrubs. It is true that they vanish from the scene in winter but there is a heightened and compensatory pleasure in the great surge of luxuriance that characterises their return each spring.

Then there are the fillers: annuals and tender perennials like dahlias that have to be bedded out anew each year. They will do their filling job in the end but become bad masters in the hands of unimaginative gardeners (often professional), with a tendency to elbow out the permanent plants. If you nod, you may find that the gaps in your borders become larger from one spring to the next and that increasing areas need to be bedded out.

Spring gaps are inevitable, except in safe borders, comprising the toughest of the tough. There are plenty of journalists writing for the safety-seeking no-trouble gardener without my adding myself to their number.

Winter losses were particularly widespread this year, not so much on account of the hardness of the winter, which was nothing exceptional, but because the autumn was so wet, and plants had to enter their dormant season, when they are least resilient, in a waterlogged condition. This was especially hard on the greys and on perennials like delphiniums on heavy, slug-infested soils.

What did you do about those delphinium gaps? Some of us planted them with more delphiniums. Others have gapped up with dahlias, which is as good a temporary measure as any, and gives us time to think. We may decide that we can, after all, get along quite nicely without delphiniums, for a few years at any rate, until we regain a hankering. We might plant up with shrubs or more reliable herbaceous plants in the autumn, or we might go on with dahlias.

I like some bold groups of dahlias in a border; they pull it together at a season when some together-pulling is particularly necessary. But they have certain disadvantages, among them the fact that they take a long time to fill their allotted space, but thereafter become so exuberant as to jeopardise their neighbours.

A friend has some large gaps in his shrub border, having lost a tree mallow – short-lived at the best of times – a deciduous ceanothus and a *Hebe* 'Midsummer Beauty'. It was a cruel half-year for hebes. Understandably he doesn't want to replace with any of these failures, and he reckons, very sensibly, that the neighbouring shrubs have enough vigour to fill in the gaps themselves, given a year or two. I asked him what the bits of paper on the ground were for and he said they were marking the positions for dahlias. Hm. An outcrop of dahlias in a shrubbery can look all right but I do just wonder if those gaps will be any smaller at the end of the season. It depends, of course, on the vigour of the dahlias he is using. If they are crushed by the shrubs, which are here the more important components, well and good, but if it works the other way round, then one must conclude that the filler has gone beyond its terms of reference.

This, however, is to take it for granted that, having set your course in spring, you are powerless to alter it in mid-season. Clearly that is nonsense. The gardener can interfere with and control his plants continually, and it is often desirable that he should. But he frequently evinces an inbuilt reluctance to busy himself in the borders at the height of summer. Spring is acknowledged as a work season and so is autumn, but in between, in the languid days, he expects the plants to get on with it and allow him to relax.

Perhaps his unconscious thoughts are harking back to the Garden of Eden, where Adam and Eve, as Milton describes their activities:

> After no more toil
> Of their sweet gard'ning labour than sufficed
> To recommend cool Zephyr, and made ease
> More easy, wholesome thirst and appetite
> More grateful, to their supper fruits they fell . . .

What did this sweet gardening labour consist of, one wonders? No more than dead-heading the dahlias and roses, perhaps. There was presumably no question, then, of having to prevent one plant from overpowering another, but here and now there is, so watch out!
12.6.69

SILLY SEASON

LITERALLY in my garden again, at last. There hasn't been much weather conducive to sitting outside, either for writing or relaxing, in this corner of the country since that marvellous fortnight in late April, but thank goodness for the rain, anyway. The hoses are temporarily out of sight.

I wrote a few weeks ago of how little there seemed to be in the garden to interest the French photographer and columnist who were to come the next day. In the event they boosted my morale no end. Some people are like that. Instead of having to point out to them the things they should be appreciating (or that you thought they should be, until cold superciliousness douched every remaining spark of optimism) they, on the contrary, see and enjoy all sorts of things that you hadn't noticed yourself. These new friends photographed a great many small details, like ferns growing in step risers, that they said could be applicable in the humblest gardens. It is a fact that you need seldom be overwhelmed by the size of a garden. Incidents within it of which you could make use can so easily be extracted. They appreciated my cooking, too, and I learned that I was wrong in supposing that broad beans are universally reviled as human food in France. In Paris, yes, but not in the south, where Philippe Bonduel comes from, and he proceeded to give me details of how they cook and serve them there. It is nice when people are enthusiastic about food. They make me feel less of a pig myself, or at least less bad about being a pig.

An American who came to lunch the other day predictably (only I chose not to think ahead in a rational way) left all the fatty meat on his plate from some lamb, best end of neck, which is a fatty joint. Therein lies half the pleasure in it. The flavour of the lean benefits from the fat and the fat itself comes out crisp yet juicy from the oven. He explained that he was on a diet and only ate red meat twice a week. I expect this was the third time.

It's difficult at the moment, and in this establishment, to find vegetables to go with meat. Bad organisation, I know. I haven't any spring cabbages because in my experience and in the conditions offered them at Dixter, it seems like infanticide to cut them when they're really needed. By the time they've hearted up we're in July, and somehow I can't muster much enthusiasm for cabbages in July or August, so I don't grow the spring-sown kinds either.

In the old days our kitchen garden always had some exceedingly pretty but fearsomely tough plants of a curly kale called 'Hungry Gap'. I don't find the name entirely appetising either. Some of my friends ask why I'm not eating spinach but what they mean by this is not what I do. They mean Swiss chard or spinach beet but that strikes me as a pretty mawkish vegetable, whichever part of its leaf you choose to eat. Real spinach is delicious but we've only just sown that and anyway it starts bolting almost as soon as it has made two or three leaves. Most of my friends seem to have the same experience, no matter which variety we grow or what the seedsman may boast of its long-holding qualities. How is it that I can go to Scotland in June and see wonderful plots of tall, lush spinach showing no inclination to bolt whatsoever?

In the event I've been picking desperately at a few purple-sprouting broccoli plants which have themselves been desperately trying to foil my attempts at preventing them from flowering. A number of them have got away from me – when a guest asks me what flowers they are I've served up I know it's time to desist. But there are still a few plants – even the pigeons have lost interest in them – that I have punched into a corner and keep plucking mercilessly while their attempts at resistance become increasingly feeble.

Because flowers come first here, we are always disgracefully late with our spring vegetable sowings. Sometimes this even seems to pay – parsnips are supposedly less prone to canker if sown late – but at others, not. If you don't sow your broad beans till June, they'll grow and flower well enough but the flowers don't set. That only leaves the bean tops to feast on. We did manage to sow three long rows of broad beans on 25 April this year, so I hope they'll come in with a prolific crop just when the house is full of guests or relations who are willing to get black fingernails shucking them for the freezer. Actually I do think it's worth opening up their bellies with a knife, in this case. If you try to give them the pea pod treatment you find yourself turning them round in a spiral, which is inefficient.

I visited a perfectly organised kitchen garden yesterday, 29

May, wherein the beans had been sown in series and those that dated back to an autumn sowing had made pods of just that size, some 4 inches long, when they are so delicious to cook and eat whole, pod and all. Horror was expressed at the very suggestion. It would be so wasteful. But why wasteful if you enjoy the result, I couldn't help wondering? There were droves of beans coming along for more conventional use (I wonder if they'll have to wait until they have thick jackets!).

I've been more fortunate with my salads in that a lettuce we sowed last July, named 'Suzan' and a fast developer, did not in fact develop in time to beat the winter – probably the drought retarded it despite a few waterings. But, pale and fragile though it looked, it survived into the spring and came on in May. Aphids were not slow in finding it, a rather fetching, pink-coloured species, but an awful nuisance to wash out thoroughly.

I did chicken in a tarragon mayonnaise one day, because the tarragon is so fresh and tasty just now, and decorated the dish with rows of borage flowers. At the four sides I had vivid red double nasturtiums. The double one doesn't set seed and has to over-winter under glass; hence its earliness. 'Municipal bedding,' my brother declared, and was the only one not to eat his nasturtium. But he may have found it hard to avoid the marigold petals scattered over the salad.

I've not used one of the notes I made for this article but the silly season grips me. I'm off to Scotland.

14.6.84

LUPINS

THAT brief fortnight when the lupins are in full blow is an occasion during the gardening year when I most fervently hope for a lull in the storms that constantly batter these windy islands. So far our luck holds out. The miracle which announces high summer's advent is once again being enacted. Lupins embody a number of satisfying antitheses. Sharp and pointed in outline they are yet so softly textured that one has to pat them. Meantime, the warmth of their summery fragrance is spiced with a certain spikiness. You might think that a mixture of lupins would look fussy, being made up of so many small flowers, themselves often in two colours, but it is not so. And this is because the lupin plant is itself a substantial unit so that you get a sense of fitness from seeing a bold splodge of blue spikes juxtaposed with another of carmine and that with primrose-yellow and this again with purple or with apricot. Wherever possible lupins should, it seems to me, be massed. They never look better than when seen as a vista of receding spikes flanking a straight and rather narrow path.

Mixed into a border, many of whose components will not bloom till considerably later, lupins present the gardener with a number of problems. Whether you cut them right down after flowering or whether you merely dead-head them, they will always look tatty. Subsidiary flower spikes in late summer amount to nothing much, while their foliage often becomes disfigured with mildew as the season advances. Here we have our lupins, together with a number of other early summer flowerers, gathered in just one part of the garden where they may all be enjoyed in their season but left in comparative neglect afterwards.

A good strain of seed gives wonderful results and I can see no point in going to the expensive trouble of buying plants in named varieties. There is no need to insist on plants or seed being of the Russell strain, because all lupins marketed are nowadays impregnated with this blood. The one drawback to the modern lupin is its tendency to die out, instead of remaining a true perennial. It is therefore a good plan to make a regular practice of sowing fresh seed each April and growing on young plants in a spare plot with which to fill gaps in the following autumn. By then, of course, these young plants will be quite large and will even have flowered a little, and lupins are reputedly bad movers, but providing the job is done with reasonable care no harm results.

If old beds of lupins are left for years without official renewal, we commonly hear the complaint that they have reverted, i.e., they have gone back to the wild state which is predominantly blue. In fact, of course, the lupins have gone in for a bit of unofficial self-renewal by self-sowing and this, if uncontrolled, will always result in an increasing proportion of smaller, blue-flowered types.

On a recent visit to the Brighton corporation's nurseries at Stanmer Park, I was impressed by what struck me at the time as one of the most laborious gardening practices I had witnessed for a long while. The soil there, on the South Downs, is chalky, and in these conditions lupins develop intense chlorosis. So that they may nevertheless get a display for their gardens, seed is first drilled in the open ground in the usual way. At this early stage the lupins seem able to tolerate the soil's high alkalinity, although a proportion were already looking pretty yellow. But from the seedling stage onwards the plants are grown in lime-free soil in deep, heavy wooden boxes. When on the point of flowering, boxes and plants are moved bodily to their flowering site several miles away and immediately the display is past the old plants are discarded and the boxes are replanted in the nursery with next year's stock.

One's first reaction is to exclaim, with much tongue-clicking, 'Just fancy! In this day and age . . .' But a little reflection serves to remind us how apt we are to get our values wrong in the name of that false god of labour-saving to whom almost every writer or speaker on gardening feels obliged to make obeisance before daring to give his recommendations. The people of Brighton are obviously deriving much pleasure from these lupins. Furthermore, the manner in which the plants have had to be grown because of the naturally chalky soil of those parts has been turned to advantage by allowing the site where they give their display to be used both before and afterwards for spring and for summer bedding. While we may not wish to emulate this practice in its entirety, it surely

contains a hint worth following. If we are going to sow some lupin seed every year, as I have suggested, it is only a step designedly to treat them as biennials. We can then plant as many groups and as large as we please in our borders, throw them out in mid-June when they have had their hour, and replace them with, say, Michaelmas daisies, or with early flowering chrysanthemums like the single mauve-pink 'Clara Curtis' or, again, with annuals like zinnias sown in the first week of May and grown on in pots. It is by such devices that an important border can be kept on a high plateau of interest and beauty over a period of four or five months, and who shall say that it is not worth the labour? It is a true saying that you get nothing for nothing and precious little for sixpence in this world.
20.6.63

SEATS AND SCENTS

IT is always interesting to notice the kind of seats that people put into their gardens, how numerous they are and where they place them.

If you open to the public you may be sure that any movable seat will be moved and, moreover, that it will never be returned to the spot it was moved from by the people who moved it. Probably they moved it to where there was a better view, and this is an all-important point very much to be taken into consideration. Seats should command the best view; on the other hand, they should never hog the view in the opposite direction. A bench will often be more modest and discreet than a seat with a back to it. If the bench's legs are set into the ground or into a concrete footing, that makes for a feeling of security and also renders it commendably immovable.

I sat on such a bench in a private garden recently. It was at

139

furthest remove from the house, so I was pleased to rest my legs and it commanded an excellent prospect. The only blot was the seat at the far end of the vista – a park-type seat with curved, horizontally slatted back. It was painted dazzling white. Except in a mainly architectural garden, that is a mistake. I took a photograph from my position on the bench and, when that was processed, there was the white seat looking as blatant as ever. Like at someone with a wall eye, you couldn't help looking at it.

I suppose the standard teak seat of institutional gardens will start to lose its popularity now that teak has been declared an endangered species. But it will be long in disappearing. I shan't be sad to see it go. Although never painted white, it is a heavy-looking, stodgy object. I remember sitting on one in the yellow garden at Crathes Castle (near Aberdeen). The dominant prospect, across a lawn, was of another exactly similar seat, staring at me. Whether occupied or not, there's an aggressive element in teak seats. They look far better if allowed to bleach and weather, but the rules are that they should be treated with preservative every year. The well-oiled look is hardly prepossessing.

There is another snag about teak seats. Nearly always they have been presented and inscribed to dear so-and-so who always sat here and enjoyed this view. Or they record the name of the patron who actually paid for the seat. The donor or his relations become terribly touchy about how *their* seat is treated, whether it has been oiled this year and why has it been moved? This can become a nightmare for anyone running an institutional or public garden. The seats pour in; there is a kind of vanity which ensures that the flow continues. A garden overstocked with seats is hideous. The only solution is to be firm and to cry halt. No more seats. This, of course, is unpopular. You need to be strong willed.

A garden without seats is unfriendly but they can easily be overdone. The English love to lounge about on lawns and grassy banks. I do myself. I like the smell of living turf beneath me; that basic planty smell. And the firm yet slightly yielding feel of the ground itself. Almost, when stretched out, you become a part of it. Mother earth, indeed. If there's springy heather to bounce on, so much the better, but I've not yet seen anyone make use of a heather garden in just that way.

A tree seat is fun, allowing you to face in any direction, according to the position of the sun. Tree seats are rarely obtrusive and generally look right, but you need the right sort of tree in the right position. I haven't that. The only possible candidate, position-wise, is a mulberry, but the stain from its falling fruits would make an unspeakable mess from July to October, at the height of the sitting-out season.

Wherever your seats may be, you should think of growing something nice to smell near by. We have two stone seats let into the retaining walls of our sunk garden. There are piers at either end of them on which to stand large pots in the summer. I like the pots to be showy but I also like to slip a mignonette seedling into each. Mignonette isn't showy but the least showy kind is the best smelling, warm and fruity on the air.

Another excellent ingredient is cherry pie – heliotrope. Seed-raised heliotrope is useless, with the minimum of scent. You need one of the old clones like 'Chatsworth' or 'Princess Marina'. Unfortunately they demand rather more winter greenhouse heat than I'm prepared to give them, so I have to buy if and where I can, which means that I am often without.

The famous Lutyens-designed seat at Sissinghurst looks handsome there, at the head of the moat walk. One only tires of seeing it copied all over the world. I feel that Lutyens himself would have come to wish he'd never designed it. I have a secret preference for the simple stone seat surrounded by box, in the white garden. The setting looks neat and cared for yet uncontrived. Box has its own inimitable smell which appeals to many people nostalgically. In fact they often grow quite repulsively lyrical about it as their eyes moisten while they think – aloud, of course – of granny with her rose basket on her arm, attending devotedly to the dead heads. Ah, they don't come like her, nowadays.

But there are better scents at hand. At my last visit, that single white stock which we see in many gardens, now, and in some places, like the Isle of Wight, it has naturalised on sea cliffs. A single plant wafts gusts of delicious scent.

Near by is *Rosa serafinii*, whose foliage is spicily scented. Equally, if flower colour didn't matter, you could grow sweet briar, with its stewed-apple scent, or *Rosa primula*, which smells of incense.

On our sitting-out terrace we have lemon-scented verbena, *Aloysia triphylla*, but that doesn't release its scent unless touched. I greatly prefer our old myrtle, *Myrtus communis*, and thank goodness it has at last recovered from the three hard winters that nearly killed it a few years ago. For the first time in six years it will flower freely this summer and we shall have its scent right through the house as well as on the terrace. 28.6.90

JULY

LABEL TALK

WHEN I was on my knees weeding, during our open hours, I heard a disgruntled male voice addressing me obliquely through his companions: 'If the plants were labelled we should know what we were looking at.' 'If I was writing labels I shouldn't be here weeding,' I replied. Silence.

The fact of the matter is that the only person who knows my garden intimately enough (a) to list the plants that need labelling and (b) to set the labels out, is myself. I have tried doing both and it is extremely time-consuming. There are many ways in which I prefer to spend my time; writing letters, articles and books, cooking, weeding, for instance. Or even just enjoying myself with friends. Why should I go through this annual grind, for annual it is in a highly mobile, chameleon garden? And expensive. Both in time and materials, the cost of labelling (though a figure is never put to it) is clearly considerable.

Names of plants that I have not yet learned go into my notebook, where I can refer to them in or out of the garden. The garden itself looks all the better for not being labelled – to my eyes, anyway. Last year I received a letter from a visitor who wrote that he and his friend's visit had been ruined by my garden's unlabelled condition. It seems odd, not to be able to enjoy your surroundings unless everything is docketed, but so it is in some cases. To generalise, I would say that the best-labelled gardens belong to owners whose vision is limited to the individual plant and to whom the scene means little. These are the collectors of plants. 'I have an important collection of grey-foliaged plants,' one such told me – a man, of course. Only men can be that pompous.

Labelling causes a variety of unpleasant side-effects in a garden of mixed borders like mine (they don't occur so much in tree and shrub gardens where the labels can be attached to their subjects and remain in position for many years). If the border is of any depth, the plant and label will be out of reach from its margin. The visitor then marches into the centre of the border to get his information. I do it myself in your garden, but I do not like to see tracks made to attractive plants in my own. John Treasure's way out of this one, at Burford House in Shropshire, is to place all labels at the border's margin. This certainly cuts out the trampling but it also increases the probability of name misapplication.

It is an endemic danger anyway, where there are mixed plantings that include bulbs, corms and tubers whose presence can only be hazarded at for half the year, by the label proclaiming them (in similar circumstances and as a warning to myself, I stick in short pieces of cane). The other day, in a garden where I was visiting, the label just in front of *Daphne tangutica* and the only one in sight, read *Cyclamen repandum*. If you run a plant sales department alongside your garden opening, your salesman may be mystified when asked, 'Do you have any of that *Cyclamen repandum* for sale?' Unless fully conversant with the garden's planting, he'll be quite unable to interpret that *Daphne tangutica* is the plant his customer is interested in.

In that same garden, I wanted to know the name of a tulip, unfamiliar to me, with red-and-green flowers. Persistently, in every patch, it was labelled 'Greenland'. Now 'Greenland' is a viridiflora tulip with pink-and-green flowers that I have grown and know well. It was there in quantity also, but unlabelled. Mistakes of this kind are easily made. No labelling is generally preferable to wrong labelling; the only exception is that which bears out the saying: 'A plant without a name is no good to a nurseryman.' I have a helianthemum that sells, descriptively, under the title 'Raven's Orange'. I was originally given it as a cutting from John Raven's garden at Docwra's Manor, near Cambridge. From time to time since then I've seen it correctly named in other gardens or selling centres, but I understand the nurseryman's reluctance to change a name with which he and his customers are familiar, especially when it sells the plant well, as does 'Raven's Orange'.

From the garden owner's viewpoint, labelling has a number of disadvantages besides that of visitors darting into borders to read them. A label may identify a long-coveted plant; farewell to plant and label. Anonymity is safer.

The pots of annuals, bedding plants, lilies and other bulbs that I stand outside my porch for display while they are looking their best, each of them has a small plastic label, usually including the date I sowed or potted them up or the number of bulbs used in the pot, as well as their identity. I push the label firmly in, near the rim of the pot, but at the end of every day (except Mondays, when we're closed) the label is lying loose on the soil surface. It's the same where I have labels in the borders, but in this case visitors not only don't stick the label back into the ground (which is often inconveniently hard) but leave it in front of the wrong plant. Nobody ever dreams of stopping to read a label at or near ground-level. It is always pulled out for inspection in an upright position. I write this without rancour; it is just a fact of life. There are, it has to be admitted, visitors who will pocket a label (unless, like hotel-room keys, it is inconveniently bulky), as being the least troublesome way of recording a plant name.

Even the 'best' of labelling detracts from the relaxed atmosphere of a garden. As an institution the National Trust feels a greater obligation to its members than do most private garden owners to their visitors who, they feel, will want to appreciate the magic of their gardens as they do themselves. Sissinghurst Castle is the most successfully organised garden that I know, but whenever I want to photograph a planting, there are two or three labels trying to spoil my picture. Naturally, when I remove them, I'm *very* careful to replace them firmly in the right spot afterwards, but I do not claim exoneration.

All that I have so far written has been anti-labelling. If only to save myself from a battery of protesting letters, let me conclude with the assurance that, from personal experience, I do feel grateful for being able to identify an unknown and attractive plant in a visited garden and I appreciate the effort made to inform me. I have made numerous efforts to label my garden in the past but an element of laziness has no doubt brought me to see the cons more clearly than the pros. I am delighted to give the name of any plant I'm asked about as I kneel at my weeding, preferably without the need to raise my head from what I'm doing. 'What's the name of that flower with pale-blue spikes?' I was asked. 'Veronica,' said I. The questioner was perfectly satisfied but another less easily fobbed off lady near by added, 'Yes, but *which* veronica?' 'Have you pencil and paper?' I enquired, difficult in my turn. 'No,' she said, 'but I've a good memory.' 'I'm not to know about that' (it was a Bank Holiday; perhaps I wasn't in the most genial of moods). Eventually she borrowed the necessaries – how glad I was to put her to the trouble – and with pedagogic exactitude I enunciated, '*V-e-r-o-n-i-c-a g-e-n-t-i-a-n-o-ï-d-e-s.*' 2.7.87

THE NEW VILLAGE GARDEN

THE suburbanisation of our villages is particularly noticeable in the south-east, where I live. Many of the reasons for this, we must accept. Farm labourers and other local workers – blacksmith, wheelright, baker and family butcher, for instance – are rarities. The population is now predominantly of retired people or of those in business who commute to local towns or to London for their daily bread.

They have money and they have social aspirations. Not for them the rough, cattle-proof thorn hedge that once divided their gardens from the road. Remnants of these hedges still exist along the lanes approaching my home but their days are numbered. Bedding out with dwarf marigolds, lobelias and dots of *Cineraria maritima* are fitted into a narrow strip at their base, rather than violets, primroses, stitchwort and periwinkle. Then comes a regularly mown strip before the footpath. This narrow strip may be gardened too, with spring bulbs. Not with small things like Lent lilies or crocuses (unless with a straight row of the yellow Dutch crocus) but with whopping great daffodils which are completely out of scale and out of tune with a rural setting.

One piece of hedge, significantly, was grubbed when its latest owners arrived and replaced with a smart, low-brick wall inside which brilliant blobs of hardy hybrid rhododendrons are now flaunting. The significance of this change is twofold. It could never have been risked, in the past, because straying cattle and sheep were a commonplace. And if they weren't straying they were being driven, and would have been delighted by the diversion of leaping into such a garden as I have described and taking a quick rhododendron snack (it is only the cattle which have become used to living among rhododendrons, where they are naturalised, that have learned to avoid them). Nowadays, almost all beasts are moved in trucks.

Dogs could be a problem to the 'friendly' open-plan concept, and they abound in my village, but are always waddling at the end of a short leash alongside their owners. Against cats there is no defence.

The other significance is that privacy is much less valued, today. The owners of a garden like to be able to look out and see who's passing and to be seen by passers-by. There'll be a hailing and well-metting and a general diminution of the tedium of having only your spouse for company, conversation with whom has long been reduced either to silence or to discussion of television or the neighbours.

So the gardens of these people have become public property. And it is hardly for us to say that because they are living in a country village they should avoid jarring elements like prize-winning daffodils or blobby azaleas and rhododendrons.

Tastes differ, as we were all taught at an early age but have never quite accepted. Blackthorn is lovely in an unkempt hedgerow but if I tell you to plant it in your garden as being appropriate to the countryside, you'll soon discover that it suckers like crazy and is a very sharp and uncomfortable shrub to handle.

Hawthorn is delightfully rural but the double pink-and-red forms are rather beautiful in their own way, and where shall we grow them if not in our gardens, even if we do live in the country? Must we move to suburbia if they are to become appropriate?

I adore laburnum, and in many parts of Scotland the huge old trees have become an integral part of the rural scene. Must I be dubbed as insensitive if I plant it in my country garden?

The change, I think, is irreversible. We must adapt and limit our preaching to others on how they should behave.

7.7.88

BEHIND THE SHORE LINE

A FEW weeks ago, when writing of the sample gardens concocted for the Chelsea Flower Show, I touched on the subject of shoreside plants such as would be suitable for a garden that was within a few yards of the sea and received the full blast of the weather. We have lots of coast in Britain and lots of weather so I feel stimulated to return in slightly more detail to this subject following a recent Sunday visit to Dungeness, that gravelly promontory that sticks out into the Channel in south-east Kent.

After watching a local boat coming in with its catch of fish, we walked back to the road which runs parallel with the shore a couple of hundred yards or less inland. Houses are scattered along this at fairly wide intervals with nothing but shingle between them and such wild plants as had succeeded in gaining a toe-hold.

There was no attempt at gardening by the locals, but

patches of colour outside a dwelling painted black with yellow window frames, attracted my attention. They were vivid pools of eschscholzias and there were cornflowers near them.

Approaching closer I realised that, scattered over the shingle surrounding the house, here was a real garden, with a varied assortment of happy plants. I called Beth Chatto, who was of our party, over to look and we were immediately fascinated by what had already been achieved in a very few years.

Native plants present or drawn from near by included seakale (*Crambe maritima*), which dominates just above the high-tide line. With its crimped purple and glaucous, cabbagy leaves and huge inflorescence, now in seed, it is a splendid plant. There were foxgloves, mulleins (*Verbascum thapsus*), horned poppy (*Glaucium flavum*), viper's bugloss (*Echium vulgare*), a biennial which always looks organised, with its central 2 foot spike surrounded by a ring of satellites, all in blue; sea campion (*Silene maritima*), making pools of white, and three species of stonecrop: vivid-yellow pools of *Sedum acre*, blush white *S. anglicum* and the invasive *S. album*. A bit of height was given by the burnet rose, *Rosa pimpinellifolia*, now covered in white blossom, and by common elder, which always looks exceedingly scruffy on its windward side, when growing near the sea, but gives important shelter (as does holly) to many smaller plants. Gorse, kept low and dense by grazing rabbits, might have been here but wasn't.

This gardener was clearly keen on herbs and many kinds were happily represented. The oils that give them their aroma are also a defence against desiccation by the elements, as also is the felt of hairs that clothes some of them. Notable, here, were glorious patches of lavender cotton (*Santolina chamae-cyparissus*) and of the curry plant, *Helichrysum italicum* (*angustifolium*). Both were densely covered with blossom buds. In an inland garden, these are a let-down, as their weight splays and deforms the shrub that carried them, but here their growth was too close and short-jointed for this to happen.

Lavender, too, was splendid and it looked as though rosemary, newly planted, was taking hold. Other successful herbs included fennel, lovage, marjoram, blue rue, sage, old man (*Artemisia abrotanum*) and absinth (*A. absinthium*).

By now we had been visited by a young man living two doors away, who makes films and is assistant to the owner of the black house with the yellow window frames. 'I expect you're wondering what we're doing,' I said to him. 'Oh I can see what you're doing all right,' said he, and encouraged us to carry on.

Two soft-wooded shrubs were here that you'd think too fragile for such a buffeting but are in fact noted for seaside resilience: tree lupin and tree mallow (*Lavatera olbia*). A third which might have been added is Spanish broom (*Spartium junceum*), with its delicious scent.

Bearded irises were growing well, but I shouldn't have bothered about them myself. Their fragile flowers are less suited to the elements than those of poppies which you don't expect to last, individually, for more than a day anyhow, and, besides, poppies carry them in far greater abundance over a longer period. Both species of our native scarlet field poppies were happily represented: *Papaver rhoeas* with globose seed heads and *P. dubium* in which the capsules are narrow and tapering.

I suppose I should have mentioned the cushions of sea pinks or thrift, *Armeria maritima*, earlier among the local natives. Equally happy were pinks (*Dianthus*) and, rather surprisingly, carnations, not even blown sideways but standing proudly. I should have expected rabbits to have devoured both as also stocks, but these naturalise happily on sea cliffs. So does red valerian, *Centranthus ruber*, but this isn't fussy and is as happy on shingle as on a chalk cliff face. The white kind is especially abundant at Dungeness. Another coloniser, not in this garden but a few yards along the road is toadflax, *Linaria vulgaris*. With its running rootstock I have to consider this a weed in most parts of my garden but it makes a lovely colony at the 15 inch level on beach, and is more compact, less weedy-looking, here, with its spikes of yellow snapdragons. The slightly taller *L. purpurea* does no less well and spreads by seeding, not by suckering. 'Canon Went' is the well-known pink variety of this normally purple-flowered species.

House leeks (*Sempervivum*) were growing in pots but would surely have thrived in the shingle floor, as did yuccas and phormiums.

Near the front door, *Erigeron glaucus*; what a super mat-forming daisy that is and I love its special smell – the plant, I mean, not the flowers but these, in my garden, have been crowded with butterflies including three migrant painted ladies from North Africa, pale in colour and worn-looking. The mauve or pinky-mauve erigeron flowers have a large green disc.

At this point the house owner, to whom, I fear, we hadn't given much thought up till then, emerged and was able to answer some of our questions. This turned out to be Derek Jarman, maker of feature films. The neighbours had told him it was useless to try gardening here. How wrong they were.
12.7.90

ABSENCE MAKES THE WEEDS GROW FASTER

IF you leave home for a few weeks in summer, you can only expect to find a great deal that clamours for attention on your return. Even with staff to help me, there's a lot of catching up.

They never get themselves into this sort of corner at Sissinghurst. Every Friday is devoted, ahead of the weekend, to tidying up. As public who just come and look, we take the result for granted. Until, that is, we start growing the plants that they are growing.

Take *Euryops chrysanthemoïdes*, which I first got to know in the Sissinghurst cottage garden, where all is red, orange and yellow. This is a half hardy bush with bright-green, pinnate leaves offsetting bright-yellow daisies. The flowers are borne continuously over many months and they always appeared fresh.

Then I grew it myself and realised that when the flowers go over, they look objectionable. On my return from Scotland, they looked awful. I pulled out my budding knife and set to there and then, making each cut at the base of the flower stalk so as not to leave a forest of beheaded stalks showing (a common fault in those who dead-head dahlias and chrysanthemums). I gathered the deads in my left hand, one hundred at a time and counted as I cut – three hundred and seventy deads in all, on four or five plants; big plants, as they survived last winter. I find that counting makes a job go quicker. I must have acquired that from my mother. If you tried to interrupt her thoughts when she was counting a job, 'two hundred and fifty-six, fifty-seven, fifty-eight . . .' she'd break out in a loud voice, till you shut up. Then only her lips moved, as she continued.

You should *always* carry a small, sharp pocket knife around with you. The officials look at it with curiosity when you're being scanned for metal at an airport, but I've never had it taken from me and it's surprising how often you'll want to whip it out.

Coming south through Yorkshire this time, I walked about a village at the foot of the Moors, where the gardens all seemed to be vying with one another. 'Is there a competition?', I asked one young woman. 'Not that I know,' she said, 'and if there was I shouldn't go in for it.'

I badly wanted to photograph some houseleeks in bloom on the top of one garden's stone boundary wall, but the best of them were looking inwards, as plants that know their place, should do. However, the owner appeared and gave me permission to come into the garden and photograph from her side. But there were some lupins in the way. 'Are you saving those for seed?' I asked her. 'I might be,' she said a little guardedly and hesitated. 'I've a knife on me,' I said quickly, to save her fetching secateurs. 'I'm a gardener, you see.' I had those seed heads off in a trice, handing them to her as I cut them. We talked a bit about her new greenhouse, full of tomatoes and lettuces, after that. So much more fun, chatting to strangers in their gardens than to have them come up to me in mine and tell me that I'm working hard – 'You *are* working hard' – or that it's never ending – 'It's never ending, isn't it? Like the Forth Bridge.'

I sharpen my knife at the end of doing the kitchen knives which, being larger, take longer. The little budding knife comes as a relief. It is great to have sharp knives; to work with blunt ones is a botch and a chore. I sometimes do that too.

Home return always brings some unwelcome discoveries. We have young rabbits in the garden -- the first time for a number of years. A woman wrote to me while I was away saying that she had a pair of mallard and swans on her pond and how was she to prevent them eating her waterlily leaves? I thought it rather a stupid question. After all, if we don't want that sort of livestock at large in the garden it isn't usually too difficult to discourage them. You can't really expect a good garden and a menagerie, all in the same plot.

But rabbits, deer and pigeons are different; not just uninvited but expensive to exclude. I used to shoot the rabbits with a .22 but I can't see too well out of my right eye, now, and to train myself to use my left eye and shoulder seems too complicated. Those around me are singularly unsporting, though Albert Croft knows where and how to set mole traps successfully. I suppose that's a kind of sport, pitting your wits against the enemy's. As far as that goes with the pigeons, they've won. The leaves on the young brassicas have been stripped to the midrib. Thank heavens they leave the root vegetables alone.

It's been so dry that the first sowings of spinach and turnips have been a failure but a second batch has now gone in. We've also sown Thompson & Morgan's Saladisi mixture that I count on holding me in good stead for nine months. Sugar Loaf chicory, too. Any time this month will do for these, for carrots and Florence fennel, if only they can be kept moist and growing lustily.

My chives want slashing to the ground with a knife. I haven't done that yet. A stout pruning knife is good for that job.

With campanulas – *Campanula portenschlagiana*, *C. poscharskyana*, *C. persicifolia*, now run to seed, you just grab all the flower stems and tug sharply so that they break off at the base. I enjoy the typically acrid campanula smell that is released as you do this. I notice it even when I bring the pots of chimney bell flowers, *C. pyramidalis*, into the house at the end of the month. Do this as the first blooms are opening and before the bees can pollinate them. They'll then last for weeks rather than days. Young pyramidalis seedlings for next year's flowering want potting up and then on until you have them in 10 inch pots by the end of August. The larger the pot the more stems will be carried for the display. Even a cottage living-room can do with one big plant. A 7 inch pot is not large enough for the full drama of the situation.

On my return, the lawns are utterly brown, which is unusual only in happening so early. My lawn policies are reprehensible. Mowing takes up a lot of noisy, smelly time that I prefer to be spent on flowers or vegetables. So I starve the turf and it demands less frequent cutting. As a consequence, it is much more susceptible to drought. I don't resent the price. An American visitor has just told me that spring in Massachusetts this year produced 25 inches of rain in two months. I prefer my drought and the sunny weather that produced it.
13.7.89

KEYHOLE SCENTS

ONCE again, correspondence sets off a train of thought, and once again it is on that fascinating and disputatious subject of scents. A friend writes, 'I've got a very strongly scented jasmine in bloom on the verandah and the scent comes into the dining-room through the keyhole! It is so strong that a little is enough.' There is an ambivalence about these very powerful scents, our reactions to them varying individually and also at different times as individuals.

A great deal undoubtedly depends on how strongly developed a sense of smell we start off with. Many women, in whom it is weak, apply far too strong a cosmetic scent to themselves; the men too, and increasingly nowadays, although they may call it after-shave lotion. The smell of it lingers in a room long after they have left but they are unaware, probably not noticing the scent on themselves at all after the first moment of applying it.

It is the same with flowers in a room, though sentiment and love of the flower may have much to do with what we will tolerate, here. As a boy I had a passion for cacti, and especially those with glamorous flowers. I was so thrilled with my white *Epiphyllum*, when its heavily night-scented blooms opened in the evening, that nothing would do but that I should sleep with it in my bedroom. When lilies of the valley are in flower, I still want them by my side, wherever I may be sitting, in a relaxed and receptive frame of mind.

Each scent is welcomed in its turn. July brings us *Lilium regale*. One bloom is enough to scent the whole of a large room, and so I usually restrict myself to the single bloom from a young seedling bulb. But even this is too much for my brother, who always comes to stay at regale time in early July. And especially if I mistakenly set the flower in our dining-room. He complains that its scent quarrels with the smell and taste of food. And he is right, so I am careful. It is only because I am so fond of the lily that I tolerate this clash of scents myself.

The odour of *L. auratum* is gloriously rank, and not to be borne nearer than the porch and even then your front door would need a Yale-type keyhole. But *L. formosanum* probably has the sweetest and most subtle of all lily scents – completely in abeyance by day, increasingly pervasive as evening draws on but always admissible to the politest and most sensitive company.

If you return to growing, and cut for indoor use the old-fashioned type of sweet pea that prevailed at the beginning of the century, you will be surprised what a powerful impression it makes; powerful and pleasing at closest range.

What of the balsam poplars? Following an article on scent that I wrote earlier in the year, a reader wrote specially drawing my attention to them and telling how much pleasure their unfolding buds gave him, his family and visitors both in the house and in the garden. He writes of their intriguing, almost exotic perfume that pervades the atmosphere. It does indeed, but I must say this is not for me. On a distant garden boundary, whence an occasional whiff reaches you when the wind is right, yes. But this is otherwise one of the most intrusive of keyhole scents. And should you happen to get any of it on your skin when handling the branches, you will be a long time losing it. Soap and water have little effect. Most poplars have a strongish personal odour. That of *Populus nigra* always takes me back to bug-hunting in my prep school days. Some of the most sought-after moth caterpillars that we used to collect fed on poplar. The balsam scent is possessed by a number of species, of which *P. trichocarpa* is possibly the most notable. It is not just in spring that you catch its pungent odour. Even in autumn it carries freely on the air.

Some keyhole scents have a disconcerting habit of going bad on you as the flowers fade. Delicious as hyacinths are, in their prime – and they are seldom, in fact, too strong to be enjoyed in the same room with you – the decomposing spike develops a villainous stench and must be removed betimes.

Tuberoses are similar. I do not often move in tuberose circles myself, because they need to be grown under heated glass and the plant itself is disappointingly shabby. But the waxy, white fragrant flowers were worn by Edwardian ladies and are still used a good deal in bouquets. In his novel *Nana*, Zola writes of how le comte Muffat, in the sweltering heat of Nana's theatre dressing room, was reminded (for scents are poignantly nostalgic) of a bunch of tuberoses that had withered in his room, once long ago, and had nearly killed him with their smell. 'Quand les tubéreuses se décomposent, elles ont une odeur humaine.' Such flowers (hawthorn blossom is another) are never even allowed by the nurses into hospitals!

15.7.71

Training a Critical Eye

The human faculty for turning the mind away from uncomfortable thoughts is oil in the wheels of life. And I suppose it's the same with the things around us that we choose not to see. The summer's accumulation of rubbish in a fireplace, for instance. Gradually there accumulates an assortment of spent matches, empty cigarette packets, apple cores, dabs of cotton wool, ends of threads, dead flowers and mouldy gourds from last year's growing – all passed unnoticed until some kind visitor purringly remarks that we'll be needing our fires again sooner than usual this year.

And it's the same in gardens. It is so much easier to spot other gardeners' rubbish, making, as it does, a fresh visual impression, than to come to grips with the eyesores we have got used to living with. In a well-organised herbaceous border that I have recently visited, I particularly admired and wanted to photograph some clumps of the 4 foot white form of *Campanula latifolia* – frequently dismissed for general garden usage as too coarse, and hence relegated to the woodland, but really very telling as a border plant. However, as soon as I examined the group through my view-finder, I realised that the picture was spoilt by the peasticks that were still all too visible.

Now peasticks have the great merit of being efficient and yet unobtrusive, but only if cut to the right length. The beginner uses them far too short. He is putting them in when the plants are still less than half grown, and fails to anticipate their needs when mature. The professional, on the other hand, won't be caught out like that. He is lavish with long pieces of brushwood, but with the consequences just described. If you can't gauge your various plants' exact needs at the time of supporting them, it is a simple matter to cut out protruding sticks just before flowering starts, but you must bring a critical eye to bear on the subject at the right moment.

A costly display of standard fuchsias that I saw in the gardens at Hampton Court last year was similarly marred by the supporting bamboo canes. Instead of cutting them down to the length required by the fuchsias, they were used full length as originally purchased. Consequently a canopy of fuchsias was surmounted by a forest of bright-yellow bamboo, standing 9 inches above them.

Labels, too, can make a hideous impression. I wanted to photograph an elegant group of the striped grass, *Glyceria maxima variegata*, the other day. But there was no getting away from its four-square plaque and, the plant being in the middle of a pond, I couldn't get at the label, temporarily to remove it. Anyway, I freely admit that this is an iniquitous practice, and that people who pull out labels will, nine times out of ten, either fail to push them back in again securely or put them back in the wrong place or both. In fact, photographers as a genus are a menace, trampling about where they should not tread, cluttering the place with their ugly apparatus. I only wish I could give up being one of them myself. But there is one good thing to be said for the camera man's eye: it is very far from blind. If you take photographs of plants in your own garden you are the more likely to become sensitive to visual features in it that jar.

On colour effects and juxtapositions the last word will never be said, because we all so much enjoy expressing our conflicting opinions. I recently saw a striking combination of *Lilium* 'Enchantment' and pink *Alstroemeria* Ligtu hybrids. My host seemed rather apologetic about it but, given its terms of reference – and it must be conceded that this lily, which was present in great quantities, is of a particularly brilliant and uncompromising colouring: orange with a dash of pink in it – the mixture was thoroughly effective and successful. 'They clash well,' as a one-time gardener of ours used to say. The fly in the ointment, however, was some pinkish-purple, self-sown foxgloves, in the vicinity, then at the tail-end of their flowering season but still capable of a perfectly vicious contribution.

I went home and found a similar lapse staring me in the face. How does one miss these things? A self-sown, apricot-orange primula leaning into a planting of pinky-mauve dimorphothecas. It took but a moment to yank the primula out, but I should have done so two or three weeks earlier.
27.7.67

On Making a Fuss

I WAS recently surprised that a South African reader should write to me expressly in order to ask why the 'ill odour' of *Melianthus major* (a native to his country) is never mentioned by English horticultural writers. At the back of his mind there seems to lurk a suspicion that, in order to present an unblemished picture of this foliage plant's visual splendour, a conspiracy of silence is maintained on its stench.

It is perfectly true that when *M. major* is touched it emits a rancid smell akin to peanut butter. I have frequently observed as much to friends and visitors to whom I have been showing my garden and I had no idea that I had retained a discreet silence on this flaw in my writings if, indeed, I have. But it does strike me as being of very minor import. 'Eat it up and don't make a fuss,' grown-ups used to say to us children, as we disgustedly prodded the skin on a baked rice pudding. The virtue of not making a fuss was instilled in us from an early age.

Smells affect different individuals in different ways and those of us who think a certain smell inoffensive or even pleasant have little sympathy for those on whom it reacts disagreeably. There are many who cannot abide the smell of rue. Now, I have every reason to dislike rue because it gives me the most uncomfortable skin allergies, but I positively like its smell. And I don't stop growing it because of my allergy. Knowing the origin of my trouble it is easy to wear gloves on the few critical occasions when the plant must be handled.

A number of composites have pungent smells that send shudders of disgust through their detractors: marigolds of the genus *Tagetes*, for instance; the golden yarrow, *Achillea filipendulina*; wormwood and sundry other artemisias. And I have another pet, this one of the Verbenaceae that used to be called *Clerodendron foetidum* but is now *Clerodendrum bungei*. This, too, smells rank when the leaves are bruised, though its mounded heads of carmine flowers, so popular with butterflies in autumn, are sweetly scented. I cannot say I am crazy about the sour smell of a bed of stinging nettles, probably because of other uncomfortable associations. If you like a plant in its principal features you can generally adapt yourself to what seemed, initially, displeasing in its aroma. The oily smell of zonal pelargoniums (bedding 'geraniums') used to repel me, and not, I think, because it was akin to the war gas, lewisite, but I like it now and I have likewise adapted myself to the sickliness of privet blossom as I have become increasingly engaged by the whole genus *Ligustrum*.

If you are given to making a fuss about small things, no one is likely to listen to you when something goes seriously wrong. So what is one to say about the drought? I recently gave a talk on 'Placing Your Plants' at Lady Birley's Charleston Festival, near me in Sussex. A reporter for a local newspaper rang me beforehand to say he would unfortunately not be able to attend (he wouldn't tell me why) but would I be talking about the drought and water restrictions? No, I said, that wasn't my subject at all. But he pressed the point. What were gardeners to do about the water shortage; what about the poor hydrangeas? Replying more coolly the harder he pressed I said that if gardeners had safeguarded themselves in no way, as by mulching, when the ground was still moist there was nothing they could do now.

All the same the drought does worry me a great deal more than I let on and I wonder whether gardeners who have not been submitted to its full blast, as we have in the south-east, realise just how serious it is. Our average rainfall in a year is 30 inches. So far, with more than six months gone, we have had less than 4 inches. These are desert conditions. Very likely we shall do some catching up in a soaking-wet tail-end, but that's of no help here and now.

We do, in fact, pump our own water and are better off than some, but the flowers come first, with me, and this leaves the fruit and vegetables in a sorry state. Not only did the fruiting canes shrivel on the raspberries before the crop could develop but next year's young canes are dying also.

And what are you to do when large shrubs and even trees suddenly become distressed? The larger the plant, the less likely is it to suffer in a dry spell, since its roots can search deep and wide for moisture, but when it does falter it is all the harder to rescue, for a little local treatment will be of no avail.

Still, it's a glorious summer and I cannot find it in me to wish it away. We may never see another such again. Day after day of cloudless skies; even brown lawns seem appropriate to such conditions. Let's not make too much fuss.
22.7.76

A Time for Yellow Daisies

THE yellow daisies which are so much of a feature in our summer and autumn gardens must be popular or we shouldn't see them there. I find them immensely vitalising and cheerful, myself, though you hear many voices raised in protest. We are told that they are brash; 'all that yellow' is said in a tone of superior disapproval as you might protest against 'all that starch' in a potato-rich diet.

There may be an unspoken feeling behind this that daisies – and yellow daisies, in particular – are beneath the notice of the connoisseur (defined as one who knows best). No true *aficionado* of euphorbias or species roses could be expected to say anything good of them. That in itself would be reason enough for leaping to their defence. But their own merits are an even better one.

If you have room in your garden to take the 6 foot *Inula magnifica* on board, do make sure that you get the right plant. There are inferior and smaller flowered daisies being passed off as this truly magnificent species (n.b. There is no such word as 'specie'. 'Species' is both singular and plural). Early blooms on an established plant will measure 6 inches across. The rays are finely spun and so long that they quiver individually in a light breeze. You notice this shimmering also in a long-needled pine such as *Pinus montezumae*.

The colour of this inula is bright, brassy yellow and it is a hefty clump former. *I. hookeri* is a softer shade and there is refinement in the way the needle rays in its softly furry buds unfold from a spiral into a full-blown daisy. In size this is no more than 3½ inches across but then the plant itself is only 3 feet tall. This has underground rhizomes and makes a colony which is apt to invade its neighbours. Some restraint needs to be exercised, either by chopping the colony back, in winter, at its perimeter, or by replanting it entirely, which has the advantage of reducing congestion.

There is some advantage in planting several invasive plants of comparable vigour together and allowing them to fight it out by infiltration. You can then stand back and just enjoy their interweaving antics. I have found that *I. hookeri* works well in harness with *Acanthus hungaricus*, whose 3 foot spikes of livid purple and off-white, hooded flowers make a strong contrast.

I have not grown it myself, but liked the look of *Inula glandulosa* (*I. orientalis*) as seen in the herbaceous borders at Threave, the National Trust for Scotland's garden and horticultural training college at Castle Douglas in Galloway. On a 3 to 4 foot plant, the deep orange-yellow, raggedy daisies seem large, being 5 to 6 inches across. A handsome plant but on the floppy side.

Elecampane, *I. helenium*, is tall but small-flowered and undistinguished; not worth growing unless you feel it must be included in your herb garden. But it's the sort of ingredient that gives a herb garden a bad name as a sentimental rather than a visually satisfying feature. Too many herbs look and behave like weeds.

Helianthus comprises the true sunflowers, while *Heliopsis* makes a sunflower-like impression. Annual sunflowers are fun, especially for children, given the speed at which they so satisfyingly grow, but they are absurdly coarse and it is their big, rough, unshapely leaves which make them so. Of the perennials, I find the double *Helianthus* 'Loddon Gold' vaguely depressing. As a plant it has little personality. The sturdy habit of 'Capenoch Star' is better. It grows to 5 feet, is self-supporting and carries plenty of nicely formed, anemone-centred daisies. But the leaves are boring.

It is above all for its foliage that you should grow *H. salicifolius*, which Miss Jekyll knew as *H. orgyalis*. Those narrow, down-curving leaves are densely arranged in a long brush, not unlike papyrus, and they look quite unlike anything else in a border. We need distinguished foliage plants like this. The small yellow daisies which open in late September are a bit of a let down, though Miss Jekyll tells how to make the most of them. She bent the stems forwards so that they covered and took the place of early flowering plants like *Gypsophila paniculata* that were by now in need of masking.

The trouble with *H. salicifolius* as a flowering plant is that it doesn't flower enough. On heavy soil it is, like *Crambe cordifolia*, easily killed by drowning in the dormant season.

Rudbeckias, the cone flowers, are annual, perennial, or something between the two. *Rudbeckia nitida* 'Autumn Sun' ('Herbstsonne') is wonderful if you can cope with the floppy habit of this 8 foot giant. Its green cones are framed by down-drooping, lemon-yellow rays. Like a number of other tall perennials, it is strongest in the stem if given a completely open position without neighbours to draw it up. *R. speciosa* 'Goldsturm' is by far the most popular perennial cone flower, though it is hard to pinpoint exactly what the true clone should be. Especially in America, where it self-sows like crazy. Black-centred, deep-yellow and 2 to 3 foot tall, this is a plant especially valuable for bringing light and life to shady (though not too dry) positions in August and September. Colonise it with bold ferns.

Annual rudbeckias have been much developed of recent years and I don't altogether fancy the developments, which sometimes result in over-dwarfed plants with insufficient energy. Admittedly the taller, handsomer kinds may need support. I have this year returned to 'Irish Eyes', alias 'Green Eyes', which is tallish at 3 feet, but a beautiful flower.

When I grow helichrysums for drying, I usually prefer the bronze and yellow shades, because they retain their colour more cleanly than pinks, reds and white. Thompson & Morgan offer separate colour strains and this is most useful. Unless you're bedding with them, grow the tall kinds, which have the boldest blooms. These are classed as *Helichrysum monstrosum*. But as a garden plant, making a spready, 3 foot bush, *H. bracteatum* 'Dargan Hill Monarch' is super. It has greyish leaves and a huge supply of its golden yellow, papery-textured daisies. Last year's plants came through the mild winter and are vast. They started flowering in early June and go on and on. Easily propagated from cuttings and over-wintered under glass, but seed makes a tempting alternative, though with some variation in the product.
27.7.89

AUGUST

CURRENT PREOCCUPATIONS

WE'VE been watering in earnest for the past ten days or more. Six thousand gallons a week seems to be the approximate rate. When I warned a friend who gardens on chalk – and chalk dries out twice as fast as my clay – that she, too, needed to be giving her plants water, she remarked resentfully that it seemed to have done nothing but rain so far this year. It did rain early on and everything grew like fury. That growth now needs sustaining. When the weather becomes settled in early July, as it did this year, it generally stays that way for the rest of the summer. Watering is quite hard work even with spray lines and sprinklers, but it's better to have to do it and be able to enjoy some sunshine than to be enduring the misery of wet, wind and weeds.

My weeds are doing very nicely, as it happens, and much of my time is spent chasing them up. The lesser willow-herbs are the ones I'm mainly concerned to extract before they self-sow, as they seed by the billion and every one germinates. Unless their stems are kinked near the bottom they pull out very easily just now, even if the ground is hard and dry. As autumn approaches, however, they make basal, overwintering leafy rosettes and then become tenacious, so that a levering trowel becomes a necessity if they're not to break off.

Incidentally I do wish the visiting public wouldn't try and help me by pulling the tops off my sow thistles and then dropping them on the ground. Not only is the pulled-off flower head quite capable of running to seed where it has been left lying, but the stump of the decapitated plant becomes much harder to locate; yet located it has to be and dug out properly, if it is not, hydra-like, to start into growth all over again with numbers of side shoots instead of a single central one. I don't think the aforesaid visitors are really trying to be helpful at all.

Probably just showing off to a friend. 'I know sow thistles when I see them,' their gesture implies, 'and it is an insult to my sensibilities to find them in a garden that I have paid to see.'

Weeding in a methodical way is most enjoyable, but if I have it in mind to tackle a certain area, I have to approach it with three-quarters-closed eyes (just wide enough not to walk into a pond or anything silly), otherwise I shall be distracted by other weeds or tidying jobs *en route* and shall never reach my destination. It's the same when my trug is full and needs taking to the rubbish heap or wherever it's to be emptied. Distractions on the way there or back may prevent me from ever returning. So I'm most reluctant to empty the trug at all. I take the largest one I have and fill it to overflowing till it's so heavy I can hardly move it. I know I should do better to bring a barrow to the scene of operations, but then there are manifold distractions *en route* to fetching that.

Of course weeding is much more than just that. As I come to them I'm cutting all my early-summer-flowering cranesbills to the ground, even if the clumps have fresh shoots at the centre. Within a week they'll have refurnished and some, like *Geranium sylvaticum* 'Album' and *G. himalayense* 'Plenum', will carry a small but worthwhile second crop of blossom.

Foxgloves become derelict before they've finished flowering. A rope of seedpods crowned by a short spike of still-opening flowers looks unbalanced and gawky. In any case a large proportion of your self-sown plants turn out to be the wrong colour for where they are. All such need radical treatment.

Border phloxes can be mischievous. The trouble here is that every root you break makes a new plant. Many such will be outside the margins of your official group and unless dealt with can easily outgrow and smother the neighbours through which they're shooting.

My pink-and-grey 'Versicolor' fuchsias are being an awful nuisance. I decided last year that the old clumps had become tired and woody after twenty or more undisturbed years, so the Dutch girls who were helping me at the time lifted them all – quite a task as they're very woody and deep rooted –

170

threw away most and just replanted a few. What's happened is that some roots, the deepest, were inevitably left behind. Fuchsias grow from root cuttings but the variegated kinds revert to plain green; in this case to straight *Fuchsia magellanica*, which is a very dull plant. I've now lots of it coming up all round the struggling, weaker variegated bits. I could move the fuchsias to another site but I want them where they are. Very vexing.

More intriguing is what's happened, just behind the fuchsias, in the spot where I dug out a plant, on its own roots, of the Bourbon rose 'Variegata di Bologna', three or four years ago. It used to get mildew badly and I wearied of this. In its place, a new rose appeared last year, grew strongly to 4 feet and flowered for the first time this summer. Instead of being variegated pale-pink and carmine, it was pure crimson throughout. Again a self-struck root cutting of the old plant has developed and again it has reverted to the type-plant from which 'Variegata di Bologna' originally sported.

2.8.79

IN SEARCH OF ORIGINALITY

ONE of the visiting public asked me to recommend any clematis that would thrive in a hot, dry garden in the South of France. Not knowing the area, I felt incapable of giving advice. Clematis like plenty of moisture in the growing season and to be cool at their roots. Most come from climates having abundant summer rainfall. All I could say was, take a look at gardens in the neighbourhood and see which clematis, if any, are thriving in them. Grow those.

I might have said why bother to grow clematis at all? You could be growing exciting climbers like bougainvilleas and bignonias (*Campsis grandiflora et al.*), which we find difficult

171

but which would bask and revel in the extra heat. Why not garden with your given conditions instead of against them? Yet that is perversely the way we so often carry on.

This is largely a matter of sentiment. We want to grow the plants we were familiar with at home or in our youth. British expatriates in East Africa, I remember from forty years ago, all wanted to grow roses. Seeing that there is no winter in equatorial regions, the roses have no resting season. They exhaust themselves by flowering non-stop throughout the year and within a short time, fresh stock had to be imported from temperate climes.

Despised cannas, on the other hand, grew and flowered prodigiously. If they needed a rest, they could be lifted and allowed to dry out on the soil surface, for a while. I haven't seen cannas in their native West Indies and Central America, but plants such as these and dahlias which form a fleshy rootstock, whether rhizome, bulb or tuber, are not merely providing for uncongenial growing conditions but, by so doing, actually need them. The tulips and irises of the Middle East are geared to a summer baking. Doubtless some similar condition (though not the subsequent blanket of winter snow which many bulbs receive) affects dahlias and cannas.

Be that as it may, I fell for cannas in Kenya where I just the once saw a big planting of different varieties in groups on either side of a stream and beneath the dappled shade of trees. Their normally horrible bedded treatment at the hands of parks departments is quite unnecessary and puts most gardeners off them. But is it climatically sensible to grow them in England at all? I think so. Their leaves will look splendid whatever happens and the flowers will be a bonanza if the summer obliges.

Life would be humdrum did we not live on the borderlines of what is sensible and what is stupid. No one can yet tell us, in advance, what kind of a summer we are going to have but it is as great a shame to miss out on all the flowers that will benefit from a corker as it would be assinine to grow nothing but. Thanks to heat and drought, it's a bad season with me for rust on the antirrhinums and red spider on the primrose plants but it's super for zinnias (on which I laid a tiny bet), tithonias (first cousins of zinnias) and petunias. Next year (*pace* the greenhouse effect pundits) it may be the other way about with the lovers of cool, moist conditions coming to the top. We have to hedge our bets.

But to take one's gardening traditions abroad is dubious practice. Box hedging is almost worshipped in New England, where a special society exists for its promotion, yet it is grown under duress and needs special protection against snow in winter.

Australian gardeners, I am told, are only just coming round to a greater appreciation of their amazing native flora while in the more populated areas of New Zealand you can travel for many miles seeing only plants of European, Asiatic and American origin. No doubt this is an exaggeration (I hope to be able to assess with my own eyes, later this year) but certainly their native plants, so widely cultivated in Britain, are far less regarded at home.

We most of us have a tendency to take what's native for granted and there's an element of snobbery in this. The exotic has greater appeal. The wildlife enthusiast would like us to grow nothing but native plants as these provide food for the whole range of native fauna, which are in need of protection. This would provide a rather unstimulating diet, seeing that, for geological and climatic reasons, our native flora is singularly restricted, and anyway, some of our fauna are sufficiently adaptable to be able to thrive on exotic food. Cabbage white caterpillars appear to be as fond of nasturtiums as of brassicas. Elephant hawk moths can be successfully reared on fuchsias and death's heads on potatoes. But if we had a flora like Turkey's or New Zealand's I should revel in making a garden feature of it.

Probably not of it alone. Not having a pigeonhole mind, I do enjoy combining plants experimentally which could never have got together in nature. And that is possibly a less unnatural way to carry on than planting all the roses in one place, all the hostas in another, the ferns in a fernery, the shrubs in a shrubbery, the bedding plants in beds for them alone.

Meantime the botanical gardens, in which there is only a limited horticultural driving force and design is at a discount (most botanical gardens are a visual mess, though packed with interesting detail) – these places are justifying themselves by educating us. Their plants are arranged by continents. Thus we can discover what grows in other parts of the world (supposing it doesn't object to growing in ours) without being obliged to visit them. There's a lot of it about, as we say of the current epidemic.

Gardening fashions are epidemic. They are largely controlled by officials trying to do a good job but lacking inspiration. Bureaucracy is the enemy of inspiration and individuality. It is in private gardens that we must seek and shall sometimes find these qualities. And what a joy that is, but it has little to do with fashion or with the worship of ancestral practices, with nostalgia or with a desire to educate or even to emulate. It is that intangible something which immediately proclaims that behind the scenes there is an original whose guiding hand has created something ephemeral, yes, but with the magic of a sunset.

This is unlikely to be achieved by trying to grow clematis in conditions that they loathe.

3.8.89

THOSE WELCOME INTRUDERS

THERE are certain plants that will always arouse differences among gardeners as to whether they should be regarded as weeds or not. Of these, the teazle, the thorn-apple and henbane are outstanding for their proud, architectural bearing and for the magnificence of the skeletons they leave us at the end of the growing season. This material is just the thing for dried winter arrangements in the house, yet one seldom sees them used.

Teazles (*Dipsacus sylvestris*) are the commonest. They are in full flower now, and will be found, mainly, in the clearings left by coppiced woodland or else by stream and dyke sides. The seedlings that will flower next year are also in evidence, forming a low rosette of dark-green leaves with stumpy prickles on their upper surfaces. If you are going to transplant some of these into your garden, always choose the very smallest, since teazles are tap-rooted and hence bad movers. But failing this, seeds are available (as they are of henbane and of thorn-apple) commercially, and they germinate as easily as foxgloves.

In its second year the plant sends up a central spike to about 7 feet, and there is a pair of side branches at every joint. Also a pair of long green leaves of oil-smooth texture, deeply grooved along the mid-rib, so that water collects in a reservoir where they join at the base and clasp the stem. It is rare indeed to find this reservoir empty, for as long as the leaves stay fresh and green. Even in periods of drought, a night dew falling on the foliage is enough to replenish supplies. One imagines that the device must be of some use to the plant, though quite how, I should not care to say.

The teazle heads are conical, surrounded by a fringe of spiny, whisker-like bracts. The flowers are mauve, and the thing that has always astonished me about them is the order in which they open. A band of mauve appears first around the centre of the cone; then divides into two narrower bands which travel in opposite directions, the last flowers to open being those at the very top and at the bottom of the cone. We are familiar with spikes of flowers that open from the bottom upwards (or occasionally, as in *Liatris spicata*, from the top downwards) and with flowers arranged in discs that open from the outside inwards, but this two-directional effort is really quite eccentric.

Throughout their flowering, they are besieged by bees, and on a memorable occasion I saw a grove of teazles in one of our woods that was attended by scores of peacock butterflies. In winter, their seed heads become a favourite feeding perch for goldfinches: there is no prettier way in which this delightful bird can display itself. So, one way and another, there is good reason for always allowing a few teazles at strategic points in the garden. There will be plenty of unwanted seedlings, but they are easily decapitated and will never come again.

Henbane, *Hyoscyamus niger*, is another tap-rooted biennial that must be moved from wherever you first spot a seedling in your garden to wherever you want it to be, at the earliest moment. It is a pale plant in its first year, the leaves margined with a few, large, jagged teeth and clothed in silky hairs. It starts opening its rather cup-shaped, five-lobed flowers at the end of the following May, and continues to carry them, one or two at a time, at the tips of its ever extending branches, right into August. They are an inch across, deep-purple at the throat but otherwise dusky-yellow, overlaid with a very fine reticulation of purple veins. Not showy, but a thing to look into.

But the plant itself is impressive and becomes increasingly so as it grows to about 4 foot tall by nearly as much across, its branches taking on sinuous curves like the tentacles of an octopus. The plant is as wicked as it looks, being highly poisonous, but I cannot imagine anyone being tempted to eat any part of it. As the leaves die off, the plant's most attractive feature, its seed pods, becomes apparent in all its singular grace. Shaped like a shuttlecock (the persistent calyx forms the feathers), they make chains, with one-inch links, along the top sides of branches that may be anything up to 3 feet long.

Henbane grows wild, most usually, in shingly places near the sea. On attempting to tame it, you will discover that its seeds germinate extremely unevenly, sometimes over a period of years. Once you have got your first established plant you are all right. Then you can distribute its seeds all over the garden, by the thousand. Sooner or later, a few will germinate and, as long as you can recognise them, you are well away.

The thorn-apple, *Datura stramonium*, is similarly unpredictable. It belongs to the same nightshade family and is even more poisonous, but is an annual, and will grow well only in warm summers. Its flowers are very like a white nicotiana's opening at night and sweetly scented. Again, however, its claim to fame rests in its seed capsules, which are the size and shape of a hen's egg and covered with thick prickles. From below the central capsule two opposite branches arise, each terminating in another capsule, from below which two further branches sprout, repeating the process until autumn ends all. The resulting skeleton is a branching candelabrum of fascinating outline.

6.8.64

RECHARGING YOUR BATTERIES

FOR his health of mind, it is absolutely essential that every gardener should uproot himself from his own patch, now and again, to go and see how other people are doing it, what their problems and interests are, how they approach the subject of gardening and with what result. In this way he keeps himself and his subject in perspective. He gets new ideas for what he would like to grow and how to grow it and he can better assess what, from his own point of view, is worth doing and what seems a waste of effort.

As we all realise, the two great categories into which gardening divides are that in which design plays the major role and that in which the plants and their well-being come first. We cannot help leaning towards one or the other facet, and the tendency nowadays among serious gardeners is for the plantsman to dominate. This is not unnatural, because there are so many fascinating plants at our disposal, whereas design of every sort has for long been stumbling and groping in a most unhappy state of uncertainty. My own garden was designed by Lutyens and by my father, both architects, so that some of their interest in the complete picture as against the details of content has inevitably rubbed off on me. Nevertheless my main obsession is with plants.

And yet I always feel outrageously ignorant when I visit

other plantsmen's gardens. If I am asked what are my special interests, I can only make the feeble reply of 'Everything,' whereas if I could only announce boldly, 'Rhododendrons,' or, 'Epiphytic orchids,' it would make life so much easier for my host and cicerone, who would know at once where to pigeonhole me. The trouble, of course, about wide interests is that they scarcely ever go deep, and this is where my (and perhaps your) ignorance shows up. Finding myself with an enthusiast for all the daisy bushes (*Olearia*), for instance, I realise that my acquaintance with a mere eight or ten of them is too inadequate for my company to be much of a stimulus. Worse still, I find that the names by which I know my little covey have either been changed or are, at best, under grave suspicion.

Better than to be asked one's speciality is to be posed a lead-directing question. Thus, when I am asked if I am not mainly concerned with herbaceous plants, I quickly scan the horizons of my interlocutor's garden and, seeing a heavy preponderance of shrubs, answer, 'Yes.' Then nobody is disappointed if we find ourselves on different wavelengths.

Is it possible, I sometimes wonder, to be a true plantsman and at the same time to attach sufficient importance to the arrangement of your plant material in its setting, to achieve a satisfactory scenic effect? I doubt it. On frequent occasions I have been led to the back of an enormous bush, behind which a wee treasure was cowering against a wall. The said treasure needed the bush to protect it against the prevailing winds, otherwise it would have surely died. I should have felt inclined to let it die, and to remove the monster bush from a position where it looked wholly out of place; then to replace with material that would look well and do well, though it might not be rare.

However, it is often feasible to grow rare plants in such a way that they do fit in with their surroundings. It is more difficult and requires more planning and forethought; that is all. The plantsman's garden may include a great deal of worthless stuff from the horticultural viewpoint, as would a botanic garden, but there will also be some real gems that will be completely new to you and which you can translate into the terms of a more flattering setting.

Always visit a garden armed with a notebook (with water-proof covers); and do not be content with just recording a plant's name. That will not be enough to summon it again before the inward eye. Make notes on its appearance. Then, within the next twenty-four hours, read through your notes and make sure that you can recollect each item described therein. This is most important. Most of us, if we leave the reading over for more than a day, will have lost the capacity for retaining that mental image of the plant where it was seen, and our written description will then be almost meaningless. Some gardeners transcribe their notes into a more legible and permanent book, but this is time-consuming and I do not find it necessary myself.
11.8.66

TIME TO STAKE THE LETTUCES

MY lettuces have bolted and are in imminent danger of being blown crooked by summer gales. I could stake them, or grub them. The third alternative is to head them back and use the resulting sprouts as leaf salading. That's never as good as a succulent, well-hearted lettuce, however.

Another use for sprouting lettuces and the one I put them to yesterday was in soup. This was such a success that I shall dilate a little. Cooked lettuce has always seemed a disappointment to me; tired, limp and discoloured. So, taking the idea for sorrel soup quoted by Jane Grigson in her book on vegetable recipes (Margaret Costa's Green Soup), I made the soup first, sweating diced potatoes and chopped onion in butter and then cooking them in chicken stock. Then blended the raw lettuce leaves with the above for a few seconds per batch in the whizzer. The soup was now chilled and I added chopped parsley (I always grow the plain-leaved, aromatic kind) and cream at the last moment. Besides retaining its flavour and texture the lettuce remained a beautiful bright-green.

A lettuce salad (laced with rocket) is something that I enjoy every day, as an American friend visiting me for a couple of weeks was surprised to discover. They are in general much keener on salads in the US than are we. Up till the end of July, that paragon 'Little Gem' – it has no peer – served me generously. It is classified as a cos but does not closely resemble the normal cos style, having a much broader, thicker mid-rib, of miraculously crunchy yet melting consistency between the molars.

But I have always had and continue to have disappointing results from later sowings. A half-row sown on 11 June is in now, but is literally half-hearted. A visitor from Cornwall sharing my enthusiasm for 'Little Gem', claims to have no such difficulty. I feel a bit sore about that and must continue to try harder (as school reports love to enjoin), I suppose. Meantime our end-of-July sowing was of 'Suzan', which is pale and flabby but does heart up reliably from a late sowing in the open. What a year it is for slugs, though. Not surprising, really, seeing that we seem to have some rain practically every day.

There are plenty of large and small white butterflies on the wing (though other butterflies have been pretty scant, to date), so there'll be trouble on the brassicas of another kind. Calabrese F 1 'Mercedes' has been a useful crop to date from a sowing on 31 March in a cold frame, later potted individually and then planted out when the weather had warmed up. In a moist year like this, calabrese has considerable stamina, provided you don't let it flower.

But caterpillars lurking in the heads are a problem, being of much the same shade of green as the edible flower buds. The recommended salt water dip prior to cooking won't extract many; they are too firmly wedged among the network of stalks. If you can leave your gathered calabrese in a colander until after dark, and then switch a light on them, you'll find that the caterpillars have come out to the surface to feed and are quite easily picked off. Whether this works when the calabrese is put in an artificially darkened spot for a time, during broad daylight, I haven't yet tested. Some people are much more squeamish about finding the odd corpse in their cooked vegetables than others. One doesn't want to cause unnecessary distress.

Black fly, that is to say the black aphid most typically found on broad beans in summer (on spindleberry shoots in spring), have been particularly numerous this year. Let this not be overlooked by those who imagine that a hard winter kills off the pests. Most pests have their own arrangements for surviving the winter; hard weather does not take them by surprise (neither does it the parasites and predators that live on them, fortunately).

We had to spray the broad beans. The commendably prolific variety 'Express', sown at the very end of April, has been a great success, again. Its pods are short but numerous and nearly always well filled with few of those gaps caused by incomplete fertilisation.

So far my nasturtiums have not been attacked. Black aphids always seem to be worst on them in London and perhaps in other cities. I don't know why that should be. But globe artichokes and the cardoons that I grow for ornament in the Long Border, have been afflicted and again we had to spray. Even though it is the base of the bracts that you eat in an artichoke, yet a mass of cooked aphids in the outer layers is an unattractive proposition, besides which the aphids attract ants, which love to 'milk' them, and you find you have brought hordes of these active insects into the kitchen unless you took earlier action by spraying.

Artichokes have been in exceedingly short supply so far this year; few of them survived the winter. The offsets with which we did succeed in establishing a new bed were only ready for transplanting a month later than usual, last spring, so that they have not started cropping yet, but I have high hopes of an autumn glut.

Artichoke gluttons who garden in a cold area where winter losses are the norm should pot up some single-crown offsets during the next month (reduce the leaves on these by half to

minimise transplanting losses). They will be well rooted by winter's onset and can be overwintered under cold glass or, at the most, under glass where only a few degrees of frost are allowed. Harden the plants off next spring and plant them out in May.
15.8.65

SHUN THE INVISIBLE WORM

AUGUST is a testing time in herbaceous and mixed borders. It becomes clear, as the month progresses, whether we are going to witness a rapid and early disintegration, with unfettered colonies of mustard-yellow sunflowers and golden rod taking charge of the autumn scene, or whether a plan has been at work which will allow the border to develop and 'to set budding more, and still more, later flowers for the bees'. The countryside tends to look its worst at this time of year, with masses of tired, dusty, caterpillar-riddled foliage. The more reason, it seems to me, that our gardens should be gay oases, now, of all times.

It is a good moment for taking a long, critical look at the perennial borders and deciding which passengers are really too frumpish to be endured any longer. I decided yesterday against a large clump of *Iris sibirica*. This is an excellent plant in a marshy spot near water, but in the border its season is too brief and, after flowering, its foliage becomes so obtrusive that it flops over and envelops all those neighbouring plants which one would prefer to be flopping over and enveloping it. So the irises have gone and have left a huge hole which is only waiting for the rain to stop and this article to be finished before I fill it with plants of the delightful single rubellum chrysanthemum, 'Clara Curtis', with scores of scented pinky-mauve daisies throughout September. Of all the plants to which one might propose a move from the open ground at this unlikely season, chrysanthemums are the most co-operative. The only danger is in their branching panicles of flower buds being so distressingly brittle and needing to be handled with velvet paws.

Herbaceous phloxes have been magnificent this year. They are not always the easiest of plants to grow successfully, but there is nothing to touch them in the late summer border (except dahlias, perhaps). It is easy enough to get your cool background shades and interesting shapes in the August border, but you really do need heavy splodges of colour to set these off. For this reason I don't mind phloxes of the most screaming pinks, mauves and magentas, as many of the old-fashioned sorts are. All this will tone in perfectly happily, as long as you keep those mustard-yellows I was mentioning, at bay.

The names of most of my phloxes are unknown to me. Much the safest way of introducing a fresh variety of phlox into your garden is by begging a piece from an obviously flourishing clump in some other garden but, naturally enough, it will usually come to you without a name. I have always been unlucky with phloxes I have bought in. The charms of a modern variety seen on a show stand leave one more clueless than with most plants as to its garden-worthiness. It should, but may not, be self-supporting and its flowers should be able to stand up to a reasonable degree of adverse weather without bleaching or bruising too badly or being prematurely knocked off by heavy rain.

But the greatest hazard when acquiring a new phlox is that you may be introducing the dreaded phlox eelworm with it. There will be no joy in phloxes for you where this pest is present. It is a microscopic creature which inhabits the stems and leaves of phloxes. When these disappear, the eelworms remain in a resting state in the soil around infected plants, and reinvade young tissues on their reappearance in spring. Although you can never see the eelworms you can soon learn to recognise their presence by the plant's peculiar reaction to eelworm attacks. The young phlox shoots and foliage become puckered and distorted and – an infallible sign

– some of the leaves on stunted shoots become reduced from their normal oval shape to a mere green thread.

There is only one course of action: the infected group must be dug out and burnt and no more phlox must be planted on this site for three or four years. There is a saving factor in this tale of destruction, however. The eelworm never invades the plant's roots, and as phloxes can be propagated very readily from root cuttings, you can take 2 inch lengths of root even from an infected plant, wash them, and prick them out in pots or boxes of clean soil, just covering their tops. This can be done at any time of the year but most usually in winter, and the resulting young plants will have a clean bill of health.

Some years ago Mrs Fish gave me cuttings from her Cotswold garden at East Lambrook Manor of *Phlox paniculata*, which is the wild type and principal parent of most of our herbaceous phlox cultivars. It is a wonderful garden plant and smothered just now with delicate mauve blossoms on airy panicles of a lightness and grace which have been quite lost in the course of hybridisation. Its only drawback is in growing, on my soil, 5 foot tall, and needing to be staked. However, my original group of this phlox is growing in a windy situation and when, about two months ago, it was still only 2–3 feet tall but on the verge of being blown sideways, I decapitated the top 6 inches of every stem. This is a good policy with many herbaceous plants which are required to be self-supporting and not too tall. They flower two or three weeks later from side-shoots and at a much reduced level.

My main planting of this phlox, growing unreduced to its full height, has annoyingly grown taller at the front of the group (which can be viewed only from one side) than at the back. Thus it is sloping away from the beholder and the back of the group remains invisible. The way to prevent a recurrence of this trouble is, when overhauling in the autumn, to lift and immediately replant the front of a group (without splitting it) while leaving the back undisturbed. This operation is a form of root pruning and will just sufficiently reduce the stature of the plants so treated in the following season.

29.8.63

Cultivating a Catholic Taste

THEY say you can't argue on matters of taste or that one man's preference is not as valid as another's. And yet, where flowers are in question, it is strange and interesting how an individual's tastes will always change and develop in one direction – if they do not remain forever static, that is. Would a devotee of wild gladioli and of the dwarf or small-flowered hybrids ever desert them in preference for the heavy, showy spikes of the grandiflora types? Transfer his affection from miniature daffodils and *Narcissus* species to the thick-stemmed, broad-leaved cultivars with waxy overlapping segments and enormous frilly cups or trumpets, all of unparalleled symmetry and muscular hybrid vigour? Or from single dahlias and other unpretentious dahlia oddments like the banded 'Giraffe' or the purple-fern-leaved 'Bishop of Llandaff', to the massive structure of the 'Giant Decoratives'?

No. A change of taste will always be in the opposite direction, away from the gaudy and towards something simpler, more informal and relaxed. It is yet another 'back to nature' manifestation; a reaction against the trappings and panoply of civilization, and the splendours of man's works as epitomised, for instance, in the modern marigold, so uniform in height and dwarf compactness of habit; so uniform, too, in its brilliant unwinking colouring, with an unremitting succession for at least four months of enormous, crinkly double globes, guaranteed to maintain their display in every sort of weather. They are the nearest approach to artificial flowers that real flowers have yet achieved. Who can wonder at their great and ever-increasing popularity or at the peons of praise heard on every side from gardening journalists and advertisers alike?

Any kind of revulsion or rebellion on the gardener's part is at his peril and is likely to land him in a mess. I recently saw a group of orange marigolds of the type I have just been lauding next to a group of gazanias. Now, the latter have brilliant colouring too. They are much more varied and each flower is so subtle that it invites a closer examination. But there we were on a dullish, windy day, like nineteen out of twenty days at any time this summer, and the gazanias, with rolled-up petals, were scarcely visible. Even if they had been fully expanded one could hardly have hoped that they would have held a candle to their neighbours.

And what happens, in the rarefied world of rhododendron addicts, when a devotee turns in disgust from the indestructible hybrids of never failing reliability to the species from which their development began? It is true (at least, many of us think it is true) that the species have qualities of elegance and charm that tend to be lost in the hybrids but the price of returning to their cultivation is a collection of invalids. The chances are that they will flower only in alternate years or at rarer intervals; that their blooms, when they come, will be excessively susceptible to frost damage and that the plants themselves will be habitually teetering on the brink of annihilation by frost, wind, sun scorch or drought. 'Roll out the hybrids' is an understandable reaction.

And yet, every once in a while, you meet with a success – your own or (more likely) someone else's. And standing, for instance, before the specimen of *Rhododendron hodgsonii* cradled in its sanctuary of hard-won shelter at Inverewe in north-west Scotland, you will sway before it with glazed eyes in an ecstasy of gloating appreciation, and murmur, 'This is it,' or, 'Here we are,' or something equally banal, but knowing that you have arrived.

The basis of good gardening must always be a love of plants and this love, when found, shines out for what it is and communicates with other plant lovers. Naturally you are likeliest to find it in private gardens, but it is quite frequently discoverable in public gardening too. You will unexpectedly come across an unstereotyped use of colour associations or plant juxtapositions or a varied and exciting use of plants themselves, as by Mr S.M. Gault in Regent's Park. But then in another part you will all too frequently come upon a motley and undigested jumble of tender greenhouse plants, bedded out for the summer months, many of them good of their kind and yet planted without a first thought of how to show them to advantage but with just the one idea of colour (and also, no doubt, of getting the greenhouses and frames emptied).

There is really nothing wrong with the ever popular rhododendron hybrids, with hortensia as against lacecap hydrangeas. Even the less strenuous African marigolds have acceptable manifestations. Tastes that can embrace them all are most to be admired and a realisation that sympathetic treatment and proper care for the well-being of plants are what ultimately count.

29.8.68

SEPTEMBER

The Anatomy of Pears

There is something very special about the pear. Its feminine nature has always been recognised. The sloping shoulders must in part be responsible, but its luscious softness (so different from the crisp apple) even more so. Rose Macaulay wrote a book called *Personal Pleasures* from which I most clearly remember the joy she describes of settling into a hot bath. If I were to write a similar book, the peeling of a ripe pear would come high in my rating.

It is extraordinary what a fine job a silver knife, without any edge to speak of, can make of this operation. But there are preliminaries. First you have to decide whether the pear is ripe. This is by no means easy. The look of it helps, of course, and if there is a high preponderance of yellow over green or of yellow underlying the brown (as in 'Conference'), you are likely to be safe from an underripe fruit. Crisp pear is anathema, bearing a horrid affinity to raw turnip.

My father was mad about pears (many of my friends' fathers were, I have discovered) and he abhorred 'the gardener's thumb', as he called it, that dented bruise insensitively pushed into and at the same time ruining any soft fruit like a pear or peach. His own method of testing a pear's ripeness was to position both thumbs at the top of the fruit so that they almost touched and then to move them gently towards each other. If the pear's skin wrinkled as a result of this movement, it was ripe. This works well unless your pears have been stored too warm or dry, in which case their skins wrinkle before they are ripe. Our apple shed is a good place for storing fruit in the normal way but it has been much too warm of recent months and I shall take the pears to the far cooler cellar. For they must be picked before ripe even if, as with Williams, the interval is only a week or two.

Having decided that the pear is not unripe there is, additionally, the worry of whether it may not have gone over the top and be sleepy. Pears, as I have already suggested, can be extraordinarily deceptive, even deceitful. They may retain some green in the skin and yet be sleepy. The quick way to find out would obviously be to cut the fruit in half as a first ruthless gesture. To me this would be quite unthinkable, showing an insulting lack of confidence in this exquisite fruit.

No, having decided that the fruit is, at the least, ripe, we must first pull out its stalk. It resists a little, then comes with a satisfying plop. Now we are at the climax of joy through anticipation: the peeling begins. With one hand, say the left, our pear is slowly rotated. The blade pointing forward, the other hand guides the knife round the first circuit, the narrow sliver of shoulder. Then, suddenly we are on the flat. The blade takes an almost vertical position and half its length comes into use or even three-quarters at a time, on a long calabash-type pear, as we make our next circuit, at the completion of which most of the pear is already peeled, juice is dripping freely and the rotating hand has to take a firm grasp on itself and on its prize if the latter is not to slither ungracefully and prematurely on to the plate. The lowest portion of the pear is peeled with the butt of the knife leading and then it is done. There lies our nude. But our hands are dripping, tacky and altogether disgusting. Either we lick them and then wipe on a napkin, which will make as obtrusive a brown stain on linen, in its way, as blackcurrant would make purple, or we rush for the nearest tap, opening any intervening door with bottom, elbow or forehead, or we are truly civilised and have a finger bowl ready to hand. Next a fork spears the pear's flank while we slice it in half (moment of truth) and then in quarters. A slight scrunching during this operation denotes resistance not so much by the core as by the gritty little stone cells that are peculiar to pears, some more than others. The core of a pear is actually very small and can be neatly extracted without wastage but not forgetting the string that links core with stalk plug.

It only remains to eat.

I have been led back to the pear by Edward Bunyard's *The Anatomy of Dessert*, published in 1933 but recently lent me by a friend. He had a true gourmet's appreciation of the fruit but was also an expert grower and nurseryman. His first paragraph: 'I begin with a confession. After thirty years of tasting Pears I am still unfurnished with a vocabulary to describe their flavour,' leads you into a most delightful dissertation. 'I have heard it said by an Englishman that the matter is really very simple; there are but two classes of Pears – those that taste of hairwash and those that do not,' he continues.

Thereafter the varieties worth growing in this country are described in their seasons: 'The pear should have such a texture as leads to silent consumption, and I therefore exclude from my pages all those notoriously crisp and glassy in flesh. Among the thousands of pears which exist it is easy to avoid the primitive varieties which have not learned the art of being fondant.'

It looks as though my subject will have to spill into next week. Meantime whip off your Williams if you have not yet done so.

2.9.76

EDIBLE TOADSTOOLS FROM THE GARDEN

THIS should be a good year for mushrooms. A friend from Wester Ross was remarking, the other day, that in Scotland the best mushroom seasons usually occur, funnily enough, after a dry summer. But I have noticed exactly the same down here in the south-east. In the years that are soggy, no matter how mild, mushroom activity is at a low ebb, but when a dry summer is followed by a good soaking, mushrooms are on the move.

Your first intimation of the fact is usually in some known spot in your garden: on a lawn, perhaps, and you then sally forth to the marshes or to some other of the few spots where permanent pasture still remains undisturbed by ploughing – but always go unprepared on the first occasion. Nothing frightens a mushroom back underground so easily as the sight of an approaching basket.

Wild mushrooms being so much scarcer than heretofore, there are strong reasons for turning to other species of edible fungi for their interesting flavours. Naturally, as flavouring, we have for most of the year to rely on cultivated mushrooms, which are a dependable product, but their very marketability and longevity are the result (as with so much market produce, from chrysanthemums to lettuces) of a coarseness of texture that can only detract from their welcome into a sensitive and discerning mouth.

There is a quite wide variety of delicious fungi – call them toadstools, if you want to be rude – growing in and around most of our gardens, and their seasons should keep our kitchens supplied from June till November. Last evening I gathered half a dozen young specimens of the blusher, *Amanita rubescens*, together with the first mushrooms of the season, and was thus able to compare their flavours, grilled and eaten with a tender rump steak. Now, some fungi, notably the shaggy ink cap, *Coprinus comatus*, both smell and taste like a wan version of a mushroom, but the blusher, while not as strong-tasting as a mushroom, is quite distinct and individual. As you cannot describe a flavour except by comparing it with another, I can only in this case rather lamely insist that *A. rubescens* tastes very good indeed.

It grows in our garden under some birch trees on a dry, grassy bank, and its extended season, from June to December, even, together with a propensity for cropping at the slightest provocation, are two of its great merits. On the same birch bank we also find its relative the fly agaric, *Amanita muscaria* which, together with the death cap, *A. phalloides*, are two of the few deadly poisonous fungi. You want to be sure of your species.

On this subject I shall quote that great fungus authority, John Ramsbottom (in *Mushrooms and Toadstools*): 'It is worth noting that deaths among English people have not been caused by eating toadstools intentionally but what were thought to be mushrooms.' Those, in fact, who have taken an intelligent interest in identifying a variety of fungi with a view to eating the edible ones, have come to no harm.

You want a good book of reference to look your specimens up in, before you have become familiar with them. *Collins' Guide to Mushrooms and Toadstools* is, on the whole, excellent, with clear descriptions and abundance of coloured illustrations. Now and again it lets you down by its omissions. Having hunted in vain with a view to tracking down a species of mushroom (*Agaricus*) that grows at the foot of our yew hedges, I had to conclude that it was one of those that was brushed aside with the remark: 'Several other . . . species of *Agaricus* are occasionally found in woods.' This is annoying but exceptional.

My own method, when looking up a toadstool, is first to make sure that it tallies in all respects with the book description and then to see in what points it unquestionably differs from poisonous species within the same genus. The strongest inducement to eating toadstools is when you see other people happily doing so, without ill effects, as on the Continent. My chief encouragement came initially from an adventurous elder brother. To see him eat and yet survive was too tempting, altogether.

Perhaps the best of the toadstools I commonly meet in this garden (though its appearances are all too erratic) is the parasol mushroom, *Lepiota procera*, and also the equally tasty and very similar shaggy parasol, *L. rhacodes*. The former used to occur by the swing in our orchard but now I have to look for it among nettles in the foundations of a ruined oast. With a cap 6 to 8 inches across, this makes substantial and meaty eating.

Late in the autumn we get blewits (a species of *Tricholoma*) by our front gate, again in association with and on either side of a yew hedge. These are tough of texture and make rather dull eating, but the mauvy colouring of the fungus is attractive.

That pest of gardens and old orchards, the honey fungus, *Armillaria mellea*, will doubtless be appearing as clusters of golden brown toadstools towards the end of the month. It is a terrible scourge, killing a wide range of herbaceous plants, shrubs and trees, and the idea of eating my enemy rather appeals to my baser instincts, for it is edible, but the book disconcertingly remarks that 'some find it too rich'. One always wonders just what richness means, in connection with food. As children we were warned off pork and goose as being too rich; likewise mince pies, to which my grandmother was over-partial. 'Granny has eaten too many mince pies,' my mother would tell us, to explain her non-appearance, and we were fascinated. How many honey fungi would be too many, I wonder?

7.9.67

WHICH WAY THE WORM TURNS

THERE is such a wealth of material worth including in our gardens, that it is constantly necessary to harden one's heart against the more dubious components and, with a stern, disinheriting finger pointed in their direction, to order them off the premises. If I mention some that happen to be the reader's favourites, let me hasten to reassure him that this is, in part, a personal matter. But neither shall I damn at hazard, for these plants all have faults and deficiencies. The question is whether or not we are prepared to put up with them. For a time, yes, but sooner or later the worm turns.

I believe I have never mentioned *Tradescantia* in these notes. The various cultivars of *T. virginiana* have long been hardy and reliable favourites in the herbaceous border. Their popular names – spider wort or Moses in the bulrushes – are both suggestive of a flower placed in the centre of radiating, rush-like foliage. The flower is three-petalled, roughly triangular, and there are some striking colour forms in the blue and magenta range. At its best, say in the early coolth of a June morning, this plant can be good, but it too soon goes to pieces. The flowers crumple in the midday sun; the leaves grow lank, the stems start leaning; seedlings spring up in all directions, their tops snapping off as you try to pull them out. The whole apparatus is a mess. Away with it.

There are good and bad magentas. Those of the tradescantia are good; those of *Liatris* have too much blue in them and are bad but that is not all. A plant may be striking but what if it hits you unpleasantly? That is surely not reason enough for growing it, unless we are masochists. The great talking point in respect of this composite is that its spikes of flower heads open from the top downwards. Thus, when the bottom of the spike is flowering, the top, which is the most visible part, is dead and brown. It is a hideous arrangement and jars against nature's chime. End of liatris.

The main reason for not growing *Echinops* is that they are nowhere near so good as *Eryngium*. The two genera are unrelated but give a sufficiently similar impression as border plants to be frequently confused. *Echinops* is the globe thistle and another member of the Compositae. Its prickly green foliage is distinguished for being exceptionally undistinguished. The globular blue or grey flower heads are quite pretty but never succeed in redeeming the coarseness of the plant as a whole. It is this coarseness in a number of herbaceous plants that is apt to give the whole genre a bad name, but it is easily avoided and is quite absent in all the eryngiums, the sea hollies.

The general run of Michaelmas daisies in the most popular and highly developed *Aster novi-belgii* class are all coarse plants. The more compact, bushy and self-supporting they are as plants, the less distinction have they in their habit. Thus, an old variety like the 6 foot-tall 'Climax', has an open pyramidal structure, with wide, well-spaced branches at the base of the panicle, and this is pleasing, although we may need to stake it. But when we've said that a modern cultivar is bushy we've said the lot. The bush is formless. All we're left with is the flower. That can be very beautiful, in September, but don't forget the months of boring bushiness that preceded it.

The modern erigerons are a doubtful crew. In one way or another, they seldom come up to our expectations as easy border plants. Planted in autumn, they die; planted in spring, they die (with me, anyway). One should not have slugs in one's garden, I know. Having cleared this hurdle, we find that the plants are just as floppy as the old kinds like 'Quakeress'. And we pay for a long flowering season in the coin of a short life.

I am glad that pyrethrums dislike my clay soil. Except for a brief fortnight at the start of their flowering season and only then if supported, they are a sorry sight. Perennial scabious (*Scabiosa caucasica*) cultivars look best in nursery rows. When we approvingly exclaim that a plant like this has such a long season, we should also pause to consider how much it is contributing at any one moment. Heucheras and heucherellas, again, are plants for lining out and re-setting every year. In a border they become woody, weedy and hopelessly costive.

Have you met the Virginian poke weed, *Phytolacca americana*? In the world of herbs it has the same coarse quaintness as *Leycesteria formosa* among the shrubs. The stems are thick, rising quickly to 10 feet or so; the leaves are large and flabby. The whole plant gradually becomes suffused with bucolic, purplish tints. The spikes of insignificant white flowers are succeeded by a dense conglomerate of purple berries. The seeds are poisonous, the roots are poisonous, the plant smells foetid but the young shoots have been eaten as a vegetable without dire results. I am sure you can't wait; it is easily raised from seed.

10.9.70

The Ginger Group

STEM ginger matured in syrup is delicious. None of those small fancy jars for me. You're paying more for presentation than for the contents. I buy it – or rather a friend buys it in Edinburgh for me – by the gallon. It is deliciously mellow and tender, none of those hot, stringy bits. The longer you keep ginger the more it mellows.

Nothing suits it better as a companion than banana. I don't know whether this was an original discovery on my part but certainly I came to it without outside suggestion. Perhaps it is a discovery that has been renewed over and over again, though not for all that long as ginger comes from the spicy east, bananas from the west. But it is the happiest of marriages, the banana's smoothness (slightly overripe for preference) affectionately interwining with the ginger's playful bite. Add a slice of Dundee cake; and cream, of course, with an Islay Malt whisky to wash them down and there's my simple supper of content, when on my own. You can keep your baked beans and your sardines on toast.

It is the fleshy rhizome of the ginger plant, *Zingiber* (I like *Zingiber*; the more you try it over the better it sounds) *officinale*, that we eat. It isn't hardy, so we have to allow others, over whom we have no control, to make the preparations for us (crystallised ginger is yummy, too). The near relations that we *can* grow in our gardens we do so (merely) for appearance's sake. A feast for the eye.

Best are the hedychiums, though I fell for the nearly related alpinias when in the States one autumn, but I fear they are even less amenable to our climate than the hedychiums. Some of these, and not necessarily the most insignificant, are reliable hardy plants in the south, standing the test of that succession of hard winters which is still recent history.

The easiest is *Hedychium densiflorum*. It makes a colony of 3 foot stems clothed with foliage in two distinct ranks. This is an immediately eye-catching arrangement. The leaves themselves, as in all hedychiums, resemble a canna's. The flowers, borne in dense terminal spikes in August, are biscuit-coloured. They do not last many days in bloom (a fault that can be levelled at all hedychiums) but there is a succession. The clone 'Assam Orange', introduced by Kingdon Ward, is to be preferred, being a brighter, more arresting colour. It ripens seed quite freely and is easily raised from this, though the seedlings will no longer have any right to the clonal title, while they may be less (or more) orange than the parent. None of which will greatly concern those of us who enjoy the expectation aroused from raising plants from seed.

It was Tony Schilling who introduced the currently most exciting clone within this species and named it 'Stephen', after his son. Tony has been fossicking around Nepal for many years, in between running the gardens at Wakehurst Place in Sussex (and this is where you should visit to see what hedychiums are capable of). 'Stephen' is one of a number of his introductions. You'd think it was another species (perhaps it is, I ignorantly but rebelliously suggest). The flowers are double the normal size, cream-coloured and sweetly scented. The hedychium scent is distinctly gingery.

I am hoping that mine may set some seed but it should be added that hedychiums are easily increased by division of their rhizomes just as growth is being renewed, in not too early spring. They like moist, rich soil. Every rhizome section will make a new plant even if dormant and showing no signs of life at the time you're splitting it. If dormant like this, pot the bits up in moist peat (or put them all into one deep box) and keep them in a warm, close frame until they are rooting (and shooting) strongly. Then pot into a normal compost and harden off. Never disturb your plants in autumn, as they are becoming dormant.

The most exciting hardy hedychium that I have seen is *H. coccineum* 'Tara' (Tara being the name of Tony Schilling's daughter). The flowers, on a foot-long spike, are borne in clusters of three, these three opening in succession (I have a cluster in my left hand as I write). They have an orchidaceous look, the colour soft orange (not bright enough to frighten those who are normally scared of orange flowers), but the long, protruding stamen on each bloom is a slightly deeper shade. The scent is delightful.

Another one that is coming into bloom at the turn of August–September is *H. spicatum*, which I had more than twenty years ago from Hilda Davenport-Jones as *H. spicatum acuminatum*. It is a tough plant with cream-white flowers. Nice but not extra special. I also have *H. greenei*, which can be treated as a foliage plant for bedding, its leaves being dark-green above and bronze-red beneath. The flowers are red but in the open it makes a terminal bulbil instead of a flower spike.

The only widely known hedychium for many years was *H. gardnerianum* and an extremely handsome plant it is both in leaf and flower. The latter is a good definite shade of yellow with red stamens. The sweet, gingery night scent is so strong as to be overpowering at close quarters (but it is a pleasure to be overpowered, on occasions).

This species makes dramatic colonies in Cornish gardens but in most areas it flowers too late to be treated as a garden plant. Rather we should grow it in pots, give it the benefit of cold glass protection through the summer months and bring it into the house (the larger the room the better) when it flowers in autumn.

In the same family Zingiberaceae, both *Cautleya* and *Roscoea* include good garden plants. *C. spicata* 'Robusta' has recognisably ginger-like foliage while its spikes of yellow flowers are set off by deep red bracts. I remember it looking particularly good in Alan Bloom's Norfolk garden, years ago, but I didn't make a success of it. Fat, moist soil would seem to be the recipe for success.

Roscoeas look rather like orchids. I particularly enjoy the clumps of pale yellow *R. cautleoïdes* as they grow it at Sissinghurst Castle above and among a mat of purple *Campanula portenschlagiana* (*C. muralis*). The purple ros-

coeas, as in *R. purpurea*, fail to increase my pulse rate. I never thought much of them at Wye College when I was there but they may be a wow if done full justice.
14.9.89

HELICOPTEROUS FLOWERS

ONE of my most regular pen pals, Mrs Xipolitidis from Prestatyn, writes a moan about the performance of her 'Huldine' clematis. She had earlier in the season spent hours twining its young shoots over their tall shrub-rose supports and had thought what a grand sight it would be looking up through all those flowers. The translucence of 'Huldine' is, indeed, one of its great charms, because it pretends to be white, when seen full-face with the light behind you, but get the light from the opposite direction or look at its flowers from behind, and you appreciate their delicate mauve reverse.

Anyway, all ended in tears, as often happens with this capricious clematis: a gale, an inextricable tangle, and no 'Huldine' to be seen. It must be there, somewhere and perhaps visible from a helicopter but Mrs X can see nothing from below. She's quite tiny anyway, as I've learnt from previous correspondence, but I doubt whether an extra foot or two in stature would help her much. '*So* what next do I do?' she asks, and shows herself ready to throw 'Huldine' out altogether. This would be a pity; I should certainly move it around until I found the right place; it is often tricky to identify the spot where a clematis can be expected to display itself to best advantage, and the empirical method by trial and error is nothing to be ashamed of.

Also, in the case of 'Huldine', you may have to try several places before you find the one where it will flower freely rather than make masses of leafy but unproductive shoots, as is often its tiresome way.

The question, however, of not tolerating plants that insist on displaying their charms to the sky and to the sky (including helicopters in it) alone is perhaps worth pursuing. Many clematis do just that; it's not their fault but ours for siting them badly. A professional flower photographer told me recently that she'd never yet seen an exciting example, worth photographing, of *Clematis montana* growing over a tree. I can believe her, and yet this is one of the most widely recommended uses for this most vigorous of all clematis.

What so often happens is that the clematis, instead of billowing out of the side of the tree in a cascade of pink or white blossom, runs up the middle of the apple, pear, cherry or whatever and does all its stuff on the high platform of the tree's crown, where no one with their feet on the ground can see anything even at the price of a crick in the neck. You would do far better by erecting a flag-pole in your garden with long nails knocked into it at intervals for the clematis to catch hold of. Then you would see every flower on it. A dead tree would work as well for a time, but dead trees generally have rotten roots and the additional wind-resistance caused by the climber usually brings the whole edifice down sooner rather than later.

A tree whose blossom I grew tired of never being able to see to advantage was *Paulownia tomentosa*. 'Surely the paulownia should be flowering by now,' I would tell myself each spring and sometimes it was, but it was always a case of me reminding the paulownia, never the other way about. I would look at it against a stony blue-grey sky and its foxglove funnels were almost exactly the same shade. Against a clear sky they just looked dirty. Perhaps from a helicopter they looked delightful against spring green but that wasn't good enough. The paulownia went.

So did a very different plant, *Rudbeckia* 'Herbstsonne'. I have a tenderness for this unpractical herbaceous perennial, now at the height of its season. One of the cone flowers, the central dome is green while the rays are fresh yellow, rather cool. It runs up to 8 feet and at the back of my mixed border I always had to give it stout support. And then what? The only place from where it ever looked anything was from my upstairs bedroom window. As I spend little time looking out of this the rudbeckia had to go but I must in fairness add that one sometimes sees this plant in an open situation and without stakes, swaying over a little so that its flowers can be admired and yet without collapsing.

Another autumn flowerer that has now, in my garden, grown too tall for proper enjoyment is *Clerodendrum bungei*. Given hard winters or an exposed situation, this handsome, suckering shrub gets cut to the ground annually and if it loses all its old wood it seldom flowers in time to beat the frosts. So I tend not to prune mine at all. The result, after several mild winters, is that it has run up to 12 feet and at that height its domes of pink flowers and carmine buds are less significant than the sweet scent coming off them. This is a popular plant with butterflies, of which I'm happy to note there is a prolific autumn hatch, including red admirals and even a few painted ladies.
20.9.73

BLUE BEAUTY QUEENS THE WATERS

THERE is something about blue waterlilies that has always thrilled me; the unexpectedness of their colouring, the exoticism of their tropical habitats and the proud stance in presentation, not floating but inches above water level.

In a diary that I've lately stumbled upon, kept while on leave in Uganda in 1946, I record being paddled across to an island leper colony on Lake Bunyonyi (near Kabale) and noted that we passed 'through lovely blue waterlilies, which I found it hard to resist picking'.

When I first visited Wisley, not long after, I was told that the two square pools (still extant), near to the laboratory building, were heated and had contained tropical waterlilies, but I think that must have been before the war, because I never saw them so used. But my imagination was fired. Everyone has daydreams of how they would spend a windfall fortune. Mine was no more ambitious than to install an outdoor heated pool in which blue waterlilies could blow.

Last year, as I recorded in this column on 7 November, I saw them still flowering in *unheated* pools in October, in such centres as Cleveland (Ohio), Boston and New York City, where they were treated as annuals. Their winters are fierce but summer temperatures keep the water quite warm enough for tropical waterlilies to feel they are at home.

On my return I told Nick Mills about it, with envy and yearning in my voice. Nick is a vet, and he has had quite a lot to do with tropical fish and aquaria. His mind started working on the problem and he made a series of drawings to show how I could achieve my object, with his help. He supplied me with a small electrical immersion heater, with a thermostat, and a black, heavy plastic circular container, in which to grow the lily with its own local heat supply, the heater being plunged into the soil close to its roots.

Cap in hand, I begged for co-operation from a botanical garden with houses for tropical plants, and in April became the proud, if anxious, possessor of three dormant rhizomes of *Nymphaea* 'Blue Beauty'.

It was still horribly cold in the open and I was in a twit over how to make them happy. The container, filled three parts with rotted turf from our turf heap, topped up with water and planted with the rhizomes, was stood in a window of our old day nursery when we were children, and the heater connected to the power supply. Meantime, an underground cable was laid in the garden from the nearest power supply to a terminal beneath a paving slab on the brink of our octagonal sunk garden pool.

Indoors, my blue beauties were none too happy. They made leaves but these never developed properly. There was continual trouble from algae focused around the heater. They built into a suppurating froth, which smelled and looked most unattractive and had to be skimmed away every few days.

In mid-June the weather warmed up at last and we made the big transfer. The tank was incredibly heavy, but it was moved and submerged in the sunk garden pool a few feet from its margin.

From that day the waterlilies never looked back. The large leaves that they quickly made soon covered all traces of container, bright-green immersion heater and electricity supply. At the end of July, the first two buds expanded. The other, hardy, waterlilies in the pool are pink. The contrast was idyllic. There has been a succession of blue beauties, one or (usually) two at a time, ever since.

I was enraptured and expected the visiting public, who are always magnetised by any piece of water, to be enraptured likewise. Not so. Most noticed nothing. One woman marched up to the water's edge and stared at the lily. After a time she uttered, 'Are there any fish?' and that was all. The most I've overheard is, 'Did you see the blue waterlily?' and a very flat, 'Yes,' by way of reply. Not 'Yes, isn't it gorgeous?' or anything even faintly enthusiastic. Trust the British to cut you down to life size.

I suppose I must make a few admissions in case you come and wonder what the fuss is about. 'Blue Beauty' opens for short hours; only from eleven to three on warm, sunny days and its colour isn't pure but the sort of mauve-tinged blue that always looks particularly and quite unnecessarily nasty when you try to photograph it.

The leaves have been severely attacked and punctured like a colander all over by the waterlily beetle, adults and larvae, which far prefer them to the leaves of hardy varieties. I am in a quandary over control, except to brush and pat them off with a fly swat attached to the end of a walking stick, but instead of drowning and sinking helplessly, they soon climbed aboard their edible raft, again.

Currently, there are no fish in this pool. I did have koi carp, but they multiplied incontinently making the water foul, green and disturbed so that no underwater vegetation that I wanted could survive. We emptied the pool and got rid of the fish to a new lake that needed stocking. There were close on two hundred of them.

The peace of the last two years has been blissful, and the water has remained quite remarkably clear. There is, after all, plenty of wild life in and around it from frogs and newts (including the big-crested kind) down to whirligigs, water boatmen, dragonfly larvae (I've watched a dragonfly oviposit-ing) and all sorts of smaller creatures that I know not but know are there. Since fish are absent, I could spray with malathion or derris (probably less effective), so the literature tells me, but what of all the trusting wild fauna that has come to me and is keeping the pond clean?

Perhaps I should have a few fish after all and feed them with beetle meals. But I hesitate. There may be beetle predators and parasites at this moment building up to epidemic numbers and about to wipe out my enemies. It would be nice to know. 25.9.86

More Haste Less Speed

A FEATURE article that I wrote some months ago on 'Coarse Plants for Bold Gardeners' aroused a good deal of interest among readers (one of whom so persistently refers to my 'Bold Plants for Coarse Gardeners' that I have got the title thoroughly mixed up in my own mind). In many cases, however, it turns out to be the wrong sort of interest, making its appeal on a 'get rich quick' basis.

You have a bank beneath the shade of large elms that has recently been 'cleared' of nettles. You want to colonise this area with suitable coarse plants. They must need very little upkeep and they must be able to battle with the nettles. You have little or no time for gardening yourself and you do not want anything that has to be raised from seed.

That is the general pattern of my correspondents' hopes, fears and requirements. And, after all, I did write, 'Coarse plants occupy a lot of space: they are economical in numbers. They cover the ground so efficiently in summer that their winter absence does not give weeds time to recover their breath.' That is all very well but one has to remember that the weeds got there first. They are the squatters in occupation and are not so easily dislodged. Those nettles, for instance, that have been 'cleared'. All this means is that they have been trashed and their tops removed to a bonfire. But the ground is still full of their roots and rhizomes and new shoots will form a dense carpet within a week. And even if the roots have been dug out or the plants have been killed with a nettle-destroying weedkiller, the ground is full of their seeds, and lusty young seedlings will be making a dense carpet within a month. And that is just one weed among many, each with its own plot to thwart your yearning desire for its final riddance.

Then what is the use, you will wonder, of these coarse plants I am recommending if they cannot after all cope with the very situation for which I was designing them? Take my *Gunnera manicata* for an instance. I have just measured up a couple of plants in my garden. One that I planted about fifteen years ago in a sunny position has leaves 6 feet across on a plant 24 feet across. Nothing but a little weak grass is growing underneath it. The other, original plant, dating back forty years is in shade. It has leaves 7 feet across on a 30 foot-wide plant but, being in shade, its leaves have splayed out and a few nettles and brambles are growing around its crown. Nothing of much consequence, however.

All this is very pleasantly labour-saving, but what if you were starting from scratch? First you must find a nursery dealing in gunneras; a water plant specialist is your best bet. The plant, you read, must have deep, moist, rich soil but you probably don't take much notice of this. You must, the catalogue also tells you, fold the plant's old leaves over the crown, in late autumn, to protect it from frost. However, you are not much of a gardener and certainly not in late autumn, when it is wet and nasty underfoot and anyway your young plants' leaves are too small to be folded over in the way described. You may make the further mistake of planting in autumn instead of in spring or of planting in spring before the last late frosts have taken their toll, and the first toll they'll take is from your gunnera's young leaves. This is of no consequence in a mature plant, because it can put up a succession of leaves until the frosts get tired of trying. But it is more than likely that you will lose the first two or three gunneras you plant, simply because you hadn't realised that they required all the care and solicitude of anxious parenthood to get them established.

Long before you have an established gunnera, you will have grown tired of trying. It isn't really difficult, not even time-consuming to get this plant under way, but you must remember to look after it in the right way at the right time, and this is just what the man whose thoughts and business are elsewhere is least likely to do.

Perhaps the gunnera is a slightly extreme case but only slightly. Most ground-cover – for that is what we are really discussing – needs considerable attention for the first two or three years. The ground needs thorough preparation for a start and all perennial weeds like docks, nettles, convolvulus, couch grass and thistles must be completely eliminated before anything is planted. Otherwise your ground-cover will be smothered and killed long before it has had a chance to cover the ground. And, once planted, you must still control the annual weeds, for a couple of years at least. Weedkillers will help you, but they must be intelligently applied, and that may well involve doing the job yourself.

My conclusion on ground-cover is that it does indeed save labour in the long run but is used successfully only by the dedicated gardener who has the time and is prepared to take the trouble to do the job properly. Those who most yearn for a labour-saving garden are those who are least likely to take the necessary steps to acquire one. Theirs will be the disappointments.
30.9.71

OCTOBER

DEATH OF A HIBISCUS

THE most glamorous of the mallow family are included in the genus *Hibiscus*. Our guide in the gardens of the Isola Madre, Lake Maggiore, pointed to one such gorgeous beauty and told us that each bloom lasted for only a day. Members of the party fingered its satiny red petals and reflected with cosy wistfulness on the transitoriness of existence. But this was a variety of the tender *H. rosa-sinensis*. Even in Italy it can be stood outside, in pots, only in the summer. Yet anyone who has become familiar with it as a large shrub or small tree in sub-tropical gardens, is unlikely to acknowledge the claims to its title or to his notice of the modest-flowered hardy hibiscus.

It is wisest to judge the many cultivated varieties of *H. syriacus* on their own merits and without reference to their gaudy cousins. We are considering, now, a hardy shrub that blooms in late summer and early autumn. The flowers are like small hollyhocks, bluish-purple, pink or white, often with a telling maroon blotch at the throat. They may be single or double. Left to itself, the shrub will make a fairly character-less, sprawling specimen, 8 to 10 feet high by as much across, but it can easily be returned to compact orderliness by a severe pruning into old wood, in spring. On the Continent, where it is largely used for hedging or trained as a standard to give height in formal bedding layouts, all the previous year's shoots are shortened back annually, in spring, just as one would treat the common buddleia. As the shrub flowers along shoots made in the current season, nothing is lost as the price of neatness. In this country, however, with our cooler summers, a similar treatment postpones the flowering season too far into autumn, and in a bad year you might easily get no blossom at all.

So we generally leave our *H. syriacus* unpruned. By the same token, this shrub is never so successful as in the stuffy conditions and extra summer heat of a large town: notably in London. And there is another factor biasing it to town rather than to country planting. Year after year our double hibiscus puts on a mass of fat, promising buds, and everyone congratulates us on the magnificent show we are about to enjoy. But no sooner do they start to unfold, than a fungus (botrytis, no doubt) attacks them and they turn mouldy. The sulphur-laden atmosphere of industrial towns is uncongenial to moulds, and so the London and Birmingham hibiscus is automatically protected. Country dwellers should stick to single-flowered varieties.

Our double hibiscus is 'Lady Stanley', alias 'Elegantissimus'. We have had it more than thirty years and it takes up a good deal of space in our mixed border, but has never been a success. Now, quite suddenly, it appears to be dying, and the joyful question arises of which of the many clamouring shrubs awaiting a final home to replace it with.

How often it must happen that a gardener orders or strikes or grows a seed of a shrub or, worse still, a tree, without any idea of where to place it! Sometimes one such can hang about in a pot or a spare piece of ground, for years, before a solution presents itself. A sudden, unsolicited gap can be a godsend. The only worry, of course, is why the shrub that is to be replaced died, and whether its replacement may not succumb to the same cause. It is tempting to pass the matter off glibly with an 'Oh, it died of old age.' But there is no such cause, in plants. The commonest of the many possibilities are, I would say, cold, drought, waterlogging, ants, moles and the honey fungus, *Armillaria mellea*.

After last year's winter, we know a good deal more about the effects of cold than we could have guessed at before. One lesson is that a shrub can apparently recover from the ordeal in the following season, only to give up the ghost in the second year. That has been many gardeners' experience this year, although last winter was mercifully open. Drought, too, can have a delayed effect, especially on mature shrubs. Water-logging is a trouble to which we are very prone on a soil that closely overlies an impermeable mixture of silt and clay. The

214

excessively wet autumn of 1960 was particularly lethal, and lilacs were the most notable casualties.

Ants' nests can be sufficiently disturbing to kill sizeable shrubs as well as herbaceous and rock plants. Unless you can dig the nest out, so as to include the queen, it may be hard to get rid of. Some people find the Japanese ant-killing fluid most effective while others have no success with it. Moles kill by lifting herbaceous plants and small or newly planted shrubs, so that their roots retain no contact with the soil. The notion that *Euphorbia lathyrus*, the caper spurge, deters them is quite unfounded. You are merely introducing one more weed into your garden. Much best is it to call in your local rat and mice exterminators.

The honey fungus will be revealing its identity just about now, by throwing up clusters of large honey-coloured toadstools at the base of the tree or shrub it has killed. This is the culprit I most strongly suspect in the case of my hibiscus and, of course, it may infect anything else I plant on that site. All the same, I should be annoyed if the hibiscus recovered after all.

1.10.64

ALL SWEETNESS AND LIGHT

DURING the summer, a friend at Kew suggested I should give a talk to their 'Mutual Improvement Society' on 'Pet Hates'. Just imagine talking for an hour on the plants one disliked most. Very depressing all round. I demurred. Today I receive a letter from an old friend and one-time co-student, now Editor of *The Garden*, suggesting an article on 'Plants I have Seen Quite Enough of', or something on those lines. The same tack, you see. Again I am jibbing.

How comes it that I should have acquired this reputation for

being a great hater, I want to know? There are few plants I
don't love, if I can have them on my own terms. True I don't
always wholly approve of the things other people do to them
but I can hardly expect them all to have the same tastes as
myself. She continues: 'One I should consign to the compost
heap is that yellow *Helichrysum petiolare* (I have seen it
labelled Lloyd's variety – but I hope it's nothing to do with
you), which seems to have flooded into institutional gardens
in the last few years. I could write quite a lot about that one!'
Now isn't that brutal? Elspeth obviously knew the plant was
one of my favourites and under cover of pretending that it
couldn't be, delivered this treacherous stab. I am deeply
wounded.

The yellow form of *H. petiolare*, so far unofficially but
appropriately called 'Limelight', has a magical luminescence.
Unlike the silver-leaved fraternity which go spotty in off-grey
and green when it rains, 'Limelight' is at its most radiant
when wet. I have it interplanted with the sombre-leaved,
purple-flowered heliotrope called 'Marine', and the favourable
comments on this brilliant association have not all originated
from me. It is true that if 'Limelight' (like so many another
yellow-leaved plant) is allowed to become dry and heated, its
foliage readily bakes to, first, a hectic, jaundiced shade and
then to brown. But badly cultivated plants can hardly be
blamed for looking ill. Perhaps the institution she had in mind
was situated near Wisley?

Elspeth concludes with another back-hander: 'But no doubt
you have other ideas – the only request I want to make is that
you do not go on too long about heathers!' Me go on about
heathers; why should I? Those scruffy, depersonalised objects
that you see religiously herded into the front garden of every
suburban dwelling, doing their gallant bit as fashionable
ground-cover, condemn themselves in these inappropriate
surroundings without need of any comment from me.

There's nothing wrong with heathers that moorland and
wide open spaces can't put right. There's nothing wrong with
hybrid tea roses once they've been severed from the hideous
bushes they grow on and brought into the artificial setting – a

hospital ward or mayoral reception, let us say – to which they properly belong.

Not that the 'I adore all the *old* roses' brigade have got much more to boast about. A week of glory followed by a diseased mess for eleven months. Definitely shrubs to be visited (if you can hit that glorious week) but not to own. I'm very glad there are masochists around to grow them and far be it from me to dissuade.

The same with bearded irises. I can't see too many of them in their prime, especially if someone has been obliging enough to dead-head their faded blooms just before my arrival. Theirs are the ideal flower and foliage for a formal garden setting. But as for actually looking after them, not to mention looking at them in their forty-nine weeks' off-season, I've had enough of all that, speaking for myself. There are more amusing forms of gardening. I'd far rather grow annuals and biennials, which I can sweep aside when they go off and grow another batch if and when the mood takes me.

Entrenched eyesores are pointless. Lavenders, too frequently, are another case in point to which I plead guilty. Odd plants, one here one there, go down to shab disease and once that happens a hedge never looks the same again.

I do think fashions make us overplay a theme, but that was always so. The reaction is inevitable. Thus, at one time we never heard a word against bergenias. They had everything: flowers, leaves, autumn and winter colour, a ground-covering, weed-suppressing habit, architectural thrust and style, a history of being loved by Gertrude Jekyll. What more could be asked of any plant? Then some nasty, insinuating kill-joy suggested that the leaves were not so beautiful after all; coarse and leathery, in fact. That flowering is shy unless the plants are frequently re-set – finis to no-troubledom. That dead leaves don't remove themselves but remain as a reproach. And so on. Even hostas can be overdone, especially when rhymed with toasters.

But some of my friends rule a whole genus out of court, which is ridiculous. Calceolarias and marigolds (*Tageks*), for instance. Both beautiful genera when the artful hybridiser hasn't made his usual blunder of aiming at the largest impossible blooms on the shortest of plants. I'm not a hater, you see. I love all plants – in their right place and not over-IMPROVED.

6.10.77

PERSPECTIVE ON GARDENING

THE fact that I am on home territory for forty-nine weeks in the year probably means that I am more receptive to impressions when I go away. At any rate I hope so, otherwise one's outlook would become dangerously limited and intro-spective. My last sally took me to the Mainland, the largest island of the Orkney group. Not much scope for a horticultur-ist there, you might think, but you would be wrong.

Because it is potentially so fertile, Orkney has been continuously inhabited for a very long time – five thousand years at least – and man denuded the islands of their natural scrub covering at a pretty early stage. They are bare and windswept, except where efforts have been made to restore some shelter. I was recommended to visit one such oasis, a quarter-acre lying in a slight dip on a cruelly exposed moorland slope. Its owner, a retired Orcadian, has always lived in Orkney and Shetland. He loves plants, but not the flowers that most of us go in for. Dahlias and floribunda roses would look wholly out of keeping with the surroundings anyway.

Edwin Harold (I'm afraid I never gave him my name) was walking back to his low cottage, scythe in hand, across a brilliant-green lawn, when I approached. I explained that I was a gardener (I hope I didn't say horticulturist – it is so easy to turn pompous under stress) and had been told of his garden and might I look round? 'Yes, you can go round,' he said, with a wave of the hand. We then got talking. Had his lawn once been heath like the rest of the surroundings? I asked. 'When I came here it was all dockens,' he told me, but before that, yes, it would have been heath. All the scrub surrounding us, now some 8 or 10 feet high, had been planted by him, and so the oasis had developed. 'I'll just go in; I might have left the kettle on – and then I'll go round with you.' I suspect, in fact, that he went in to switch on his waterworks because at the bottom of his garden was a stream and this he had diverted most cunningly and efficiently to drive a dynamo which had originally supplied him with electricity. Now he was on the mains and the dynamo only did occasional battery charging for a radio. It always amazes me how the Scots seem able as a natural part of their heritage to turn their hand to any sort of works, including the building or extension of their own homes.

Mr Harold put me several wistful enquiries on what it must be like to garden in Sussex and I agreed that there was far more scope but on the other hand the north had its own attraction, which was why I was there. 'I suppose you can grow all sorts of lovely fruits in Sussex,' he mused. There was an irony in this which struck home. Not a fruit have we gathered this year from apples, pears, plums, cherries, peaches, apricots or blackcurrants. The bullfinches stripped the flower and growth buds off the lot of them last winter and spring. Only where we had netted was there a harvest. So wasn't he really better off for not even having made the attempt?

I don't believe he'd ever seen a bullfinch in his life. But then that again, I further reflected, was a deprivation in its way. Even the most hardened trappers must be struck by the beauty of this bird from time to time. I pointed to an old nest in his elder scrub and asked him who had tenanted it. A hooded crow. It was my turn to be envious; we never see them at Dixter and they are such fine birds. For two years Mr Harold had robbed the nest and not allowed a family to be raised but this year, clearly, he had sickened. They had brought off three young. His satisfaction was evident. We agreed that the crow family were an intelligent lot but mention of the magpie drew another blank. He didn't think he'd ever seen one in Orkney.

Edwin Harold is considered naughty by serious botanists because he tries to establish aliens such as 'London Pride' in the wilds of Orkney. I don't think they need worry. His current protégé in this line is the pinky-mauve-flowered balsam, *Impatiens glandulifera*, whose seeds are carried by water. It has, I told him, taken over the banks of many Sussex streams and rivers. I think he was aware of this potential but I don't think he realised that in Orkney, where it was only coming into full flower in mid-September, it would never ripen its seeds. His plants were 2 feet tall at most and had been given his special care. In Sussex the naturalised plants grow to 6 feet without encouragement.

He was most successful with plants that keep their heads down and that can cope with rough grass: the common montbretia, for instance, and *Lilium pyrenaicum*. I have again and again noticed in the north how this lily builds into prosperous clumps under apparently wild conditions. 'But it doesn't flower for very long.' Summer is short in Orkney. The wild screaming of departing terns was a reminder that autumn was well advanced. Perhaps for soft southerners like myself Orkney is only for visiting in its short season, but the vigour of its year-round inhabitants suggests that we are a poor lot, however lush our gardens.

9.10.75

HURRAH FOR VULGARITY

THERE are some gardeners in whose company I feel vulgar. They will expect you to fall on your knees with a magnifying glass to worship before the shrine of a spikelet of tiny green flowers with feathered margins, yet will themselves turn away disgusted from a huge, opulent quilt of hortensia hydrangeas.

I'm not against tiny flowers and I don't mind what colour they are but if they're not to be appreciated without magnification I feel they were never intended for me. I am prepared to leave them to the company of their insect pollinators.

Some people cheat. They take close-up photographs of tiny flowers and then blow them up on screen or printed page for our admiration. 'How clever!' we exclaim, or are intended to exclaim. But it is the artist whom we are to admire more than the flower itself, which is seen out of context and doesn't really look like that to the naked eye at all. I have bought a close-up lens for my camera on several occasions, but I have always lost it and now conclude that I don't want to magnify the kinds of flowers I want to grow and photograph. They must have what it takes at life size and not demand an excess of peering. Even in the alps, the dazzling flowers that entrance us, though individually small, are far from modest. I have often thought that lewisias would lend themselves to bedding out, if one could get the cultural conditions right. The bed, ideally, would be vertical instead of the conventional parterre. Think how economical of space, as purchased in acres or hectares, that could be. Lewisias could occupy the south aspects, ramondas and haberleas the north, leaving us a passage just wide enough to squeeze between.

The vulgarity syndrome shows itself in colour as well as in size. A bed solid with scarlet salvias gives me no more pleasure than it probably does you, but we need bright colours in the garden all the same. Since they are so bright and draw attention to themselves so easily we don't need them in the same quantity as the cooler greys, greens and pastel shades that will set them off. The mistake in so much bedding out is to allow the scarlets, for instance, such an aggressive role. Silver foliage takes its place only as dot plants, which fidget more than they cool. The roles could be reversed, except that dot-planting is seldom a very happy arrangement.

Yellow is another colour before which people of good taste tend to quail; the bright yellow of sunflowers, gold plate achilleas and calceolarias, especially. 'In general,' Robin Lane Fox writes in a recent article, 'the art of border-planning in well-known gardens seems to be to keep yellow to a minimum or else to isolate it in a mass during late summer.' Yet what a glorious, vitalising colour it is. Why hold it at arm's length?

Writing me a postcard from the Midlands, a friend describes a visit to Chatsworth with some holidaying Germans. 'In low cloud and pelting rain the Emperor fountain appeared to go up but not come down again. The double border, strictly herbaceous, in yellows with accents of orange and red, a *great* treat as we left the house. So clever; it should instantly convert doubters to yellow.' Now just imagine if those borders had concentrated on purple. They would have looked suicidally glum, beneath sodden skies.

Not when warmed by sunlight, of course. So why not, I would plead, consciously mix your colours more often? Not in a fidgety hotch-potch but in groups and treating greens and greys as colours as much as yellows, purples and the rest.

Connoisseurs of taste avoid mixtures because they are afraid of and don't know how to handle them. They might slip up. 'Don't, I beg you, plant it,' I remember a lady saying of a certain purple pansy, 'where it can be caught in the rays of the setting sun; it sets your teeth on edge.' Such dangers are multiplied by mixtures but so are the excitements and the triumphs. It's a great thing to be able to rely on your own judgement at least as much as on other people's.

Always look at the flower first. Let that speak to you on its own terms. If you like its message then think first how to grow it well, second how to fit it in with agreeable neighbours. They won't necessarily be on the same wavelength in order to get on well.

There's always a balance to be struck. I tend to think of hybrids and cultivars as man-made flowers. They inherit the weaknesses of their breeders and selectors as well as their strengths. As a wilding, a plant may have too large a

PEEL ME A WALNUT

preponderance of leaf and stem over flower to make much impact in a garden, which must always be acknowledged as an artificial environment. So we would like a little more flower power, and this is something that the breeder will help us to achieve.

But then, given the tools and techniques at his command and his longing for uniformity, which is one of mankind's commonest aspirations, he may go too far, reducing a plant from an individual to a unit, from an identifiable shape to an amorphous mass.

Then we must administer a sharp tug to the reins. The breeder has gone too far. We must return to nature or something near (always supposing that we haven't already accidentally destroyed it in our enthusiasm). The great thing is always to keep an open mind; never to shut ourselves deliberately away from any given class of plants, of colour, size or whatever.

If I have somewhat cut myself off from the minuscule it is doubtless because my eyesight isn't as good as forty years ago and because I have a large garden in which small things are lost. I acknowledge the place of the miniaturist but I also plead to be allowed the expansive gesture and to revel in a spot of splashing around when the mood is on me, without its being considered an unfortunate lapse by my sensitive fellow-creatures.
10.10.85

PEEL ME A WALNUT

ONE of the more spectacular examples of bird display occurs when a tern presents a fish to its mate, both of them on the wing. Humans cannot emulate the panache of such gallantry, and the nearest approach to it that I can suggest is for A to peel a fresh walnut for B. It is a tedious act of devotion but the recipient can bask in the reward. If only the necessary tooth-picking that must follow could also be performed by someone else, bliss would know no bounds.

It is only when a walnut is absolutely fresh that it will peel. First the kernel must be extracted from the shell in a not too disintegrated state. Whether this is possible or not depends on the tree producing the nuts. Some yield up their kernels without a struggle. With others, they are so firmly embedded that a pick must needs be used to winkle out the fragments and no sort of expertise is possible. Having got your kernel and pulled away the septum dividing its two halves, it next requires patience and application to remove the skin from off those knotted protuberances. You are at last left with a nugget of pearly whiteness, to be savoured with salt, or not, as you please.

A walnut kernel's skin is bitter, being impregnated with tannin. That does not mean that it is inedible. The skin is largely responsible for the characteristic musty walnut flavour. But a fresh, skinned walnut is something apart and only to be enjoyed if you grow your own.

As soon as you look into the subject from this angle, you find it to be full of obstacles and complexities. Walnuts are either propagated directly from seed or by grafting a named variety on to a seedling. To get a tree of known quality and performance, it is obviously necessary to acquire a named clone; that is, a grafted plant. But grafting is a long and tedious procedure and the British climate is against a successful take. So it is normal to import grafted plants.

This is what the celebrated fruit-retailing firm of Black-moor Nurseries in Hampshire, used to do. They imported 'Franquette' and 'Parisienne': varieties that would be worth growing for their *oh là là* names if for no other quality. But, this year, no longer.

There is anyway a danger in growing foreign varieties that have been selected for cultivation in a climate different from ours. The walnut is not indigenous and it is therefore understandable to find it extremely susceptible to damage of the flowers and young foliage by late spring frosts. Some varieties are more susceptible than others, the latter having a tendency to flower and leaf late, thereby eluding the frosts.

The walnut's sex life is another peculiarity. As with the hazel, male and female flowers are borne separately but on the same tree. However, they do not necessarily flower at the same time, in which case the females (which are wind-pollinated by male catkins) will need pollen from another tree whose male flowering synchronises with their own.

To be on the safe side, then, you need several walnuts growing within wind-hailing distance, and having a different parentage and flowering habits but all on the late side, so as to avoid frost.

Probably the most sensible course is to buy seedlings and hope for the best. Treat your walnuts as ornamentals and don't worry about the fruit until it comes along, if it does, some fifteen or twenty years after planting (sooner with grafted varieties, later with seedlings). There is no question but what a walnut is a very ornamental tree, and especially in winter, when its pale grey trunk and branches are fully revealed.

If well suited, it makes a large tree up to 60 feet tall, so walnuts should not be planted less than 40 feet apart. They are tap-rooted and this has several implications. First, plant your walnut as young as you can get it. Don't buy a standard, which will take years to recover from being transplanted. Buy a whip, which is an unbranched young plant one year from grafting – or buy a seedling only two years old, and train it into a tree yourself. When planting, don't bend the tap root so as to get it into the hole. Better to shorten it to a foot, there and then. And don't grow a walnut in shallow soil. It must have depth to thrive. The best walnuts are in East Anglia. I remember, as a student in April 1950, visiting Mr Dennis Carter's fruit farm in Essex, where he had a ten-year-old plantation of beautiful young walnuts: 30 acres of them, English varieties with a French one for pollination. I wonder what happened to them.

Rooks adore walnuts and it is some compensation for losing your crop in advance to watch their urchin-like antics. When one bird goes off with a nut, his mates will chase him till he drops it.

Never wound a walnut by sawing off its branches, if you can possibly help it. They bleed fit to make you feel a murderer. Bituminous wound dressings just won't stick on a dripping surface and you must char it first with a blowlamp.
22.10.70

THE SMELL OF AUTUMN

IT is the smell of the season that so largely endears autumn to me and, I hope, to you too. It is all very fine to go primrosing in the woods in spring if you don't forget to savour their quite different offerings now. The smell of decaying leaves is so deliciously bitter-sweet as to affect our emotions strongly. What produces it? Is it the fungi that are at work? Certainly almost each of the enormous range of toadstool species that are now fruiting is worth sniffing. I only wish our noses were trained and sharp enough to seek out the truffles lurking only a little below the soil's surface.

The damps of autumn likewise bring out garden scents. It is quite confusing when you come upon several of them simultaneously as I do when passing through an archway from one part of our garden to another, walled-in area. One of these predominates. At night it is the sickly sweetness of *Cimicifuga racemosa*, the bugbane. This scent is mainly attractive to flies and bluebottles, which are its pollinators, so I don't quite know why it should remain so strong at night but at any rate I find it agreeable.

More pungent by day is the curious, musty, almost rank smell given off by a large self-sown *Euphorbia characias*, bulging over the path. Some strains of this euphorbia smell much more strongly than others. It has something of the quality of azaleas (*Rhododendron luteum*, alias *Azalea pontica*) in the spring garden whose glutinous scent is easily overdone, in my opinion, though many dote on it.

And then, above the spurge, I have the rosy umbels of *Clerodendrum bungei*, erstwhile known as *C. foetidum* on account of the pungent, though not unpleasing, odour from its bruised leaves. The flowers are quite unlike that: sweet-smelling and popular with butterflies. They are deep carmine in bud opening rosy mauve. Where you can do with a suckering coloniser in the not too heavy shade of tall trees, this sub-shrub is well worth considering, for its late flowering season is most useful, but it fails to make the grade and is prematurely destroyed in frosty situations.

Oily-aromatic scents that are carried on the air give a sensuous pleasure that is, I suspect, akin in its appeal to that of savoury food in preparation. The cistuses are many (not all) of them strong in this department; especially, just now, *Cistus × cyprius*. Its spicy maquis scent carries at least ten yards from the point of origin. Its leaves are now beginning to take on their winter cast, the pale-bluish tint of oxidised lead.

I have no pines within my garden to impart their resinous fragrance but I do have the cedarwood scent exhaled by *Hebe cupressoïdes*. It does seem extraordinary that a veronica should so closely mimic a conifer as not merely to look like one, with its tiny adpressed scale-leaves, but to smell like one also. I have a pair doing juniper duty; they flank the head of a flight of steps. Taken as cuttings from Margery Fish's garden back in the fifties (she lost her parent plant in the '63 winter), they are now become somewhat bare in the stem and long in the tooth. Unfortunately these whipcord hebes, as the conifer-mimicking types are called, do not respond by flushing reliably after a hard pruning back. I do get self-sown seedlings after a good year like the present but seedlings cannot be relied upon to have an identical habit and growth rate, which is essential where a formal pair is required, so I shall have to take cuttings again.

Another shrub that imparts a strong and intriguing odour, a little musty yet good in the main, is *Ozothamnus ledifolius*. I have written of this before but it is so little grown and known and yet such a good evergreen shrub for year-round pleasure that I shall continue to plug it until nurserymen and garden centres are forced to place it on offer from the sheer exhaustion of being battered with enquiries from frustrated would-be customers. It was introduced from Tasmania in 1930 and is also known by some authorities as *Helichrysum ledifolium*. The RHS *Dictionary*, playing safe, gives it as hardy on the south coast but its hardiness turns out to need no qualification. 'A small, globular, dense, aromatic shrub' from Hillier's manual seems to place it at once in the vegetable gnome class. I can assure readers that its denseness is not inspissated and it is a good deal less globular than Mount Kilimanjaro. About 2 foot tall and as much across, it should be planted in coveys. The small neat leaves are fresh bay-green, yellow on their undersides, which show to greatest effect on the young shoot tips. The burnt-orange colour of the flower buds in May has all our visitors agog with admiration. This colour gradually subsides into the whiteness of the full-blown inflorescence.

Well then, I've left no space for dilating on the smell of box hedging (which means nothing to me but much to many) nor of the fresh farmyard manure that is daily being spread on his fields by our neighbour nor of other seasonable country smells. They are many and mostly good.
23.10.75

OVERRATED? UNDERRATED?

THAT we should change our minds about the status and merit of the plants we live with is surely no disgrace. At any rate I hope not, because I often find my opinions to be as unstable as a weather-cock.

Elaeagnus pungens 'Maculata' used to be one of my most favourite shrubs. Such glorious variegation, such luminous colouring in winter sunshine. And yet my doubts and reservations kept increasing and I had more and more difficulty in choking them back. Then, the other day, came my let-out. John Treasure was with me on one of his rare visits and as we passed the elaeagnus he remarked, 'You know, I'm getting *tired* of that shrub.' As his voice is naturally drawling the word 'tired' evoked Atlas with the entire world burden on his shoulders. Endorsement on a doubtful issue is a great stimulus and I leapt enthusiastically to the shrub's offence. It doesn't know how to grow; its angular branch system is like a forest of in-growing toe-nails and it is always liable to die back at the tips. Often it just dies: full stop. The solution is to grow *Ilex* 'Golden King' instead. After twenty years of its company I still say that this holly has every virtue. True it is slow-growing, but even that becomes a virtue after twenty years.

Now what of *Buddleia fallowiana alba*? I gave this overpraised shrub a shrewd dismissive backward cow-kick some time ago and that should have settled its hash. I was only waiting to remove my specimen until the shrub behind it (a privet – I have a weakness for privets) had grown sufficiently to minimise the inevitable gap. This year the doomed buddleia excelled itself. It is still true, as I have often snidely remarked, that the flowers on each spike are not half of them opened before the first are already brown and withered but somehow, I now realise, this does not matter. The spikelets are slender and unobtrusive whether live or dead. They form, in a healthy specimen, a harmonious unit, a tall shimmering dome of different shades of cream and grey with the leaves, which are of even greater importance. But this buddleia's flowering season is very long and still in full swing as I write in mid-October.

What of that disputatious plant *Persicaria* (*Polygonum*) *affinis* 'Donald Lowndes'? I loathe it. It was a miserable failure in my Long Border and I shall never, I hope, attempt to grow it again and yet how can I help but admire it as seen in some (not all) gardens? A low ground-coverer with a forest of thick spikes whose colour changes from rose-red to brick-red and finally, with the foliage, to warm-brown as the season advances. How can it be so handsome and effective and yet, basically, such a horrid plant? Well, there are people like that, too.

P. affinis 'Donald Lowndes' is not just coarse; it is coarse-grained to its innermost fibre. 'Much finer flowers than the above, good ground-cover,' Bloom's catalogue tells us. 'The above' is 'Darjeeling Red'. Now it all depends on what you mean by finer. If you mean larger and having more flower power, agreed. But if you mean having greater refinement, then 'Darjeeling Red' (deep pink, really) has it every time since its spikes are slenderer and its leaves don't stare at you with bold unwinking insolence.

My latest hate is for the hybrid hosta called 'Honeybells'. Having *Hosta plantaginea* as one parent it retains that species' night scent but adds pale-lilac colouring to the dead-whiteness of *H. plantaginea*'s flower. So much for the gain (if gain it is); the losses are disastrous. 'Honeybells' has lost most of the pristine freshness so notable throughout the season in its parent's foliage. It is, moreover, far too vigorous. After two years my colony is already so thick and congested that flower spikes were produced only at the margins. This costiveness is not a lone case: other gardeners tell me of the same experience. Furthermore if there is the slightest set-back in growing conditions at the time of flowering – I mean by shortage of water – the buds drop off the stems unopened. What a wonderful rending of roots I am looking forward to, what a beautiful space for re-planting.

Plants do, of course, behave differently for different people. An acquaintance whose garden I was recently visiting for the first time led me purposefully to her specimen of wintersweet, *Chimonanthus praecox*, growing against a white wall. It was still in full leaf. I have written in the past of this shrub's 'sordid appearance in its summer dress', for the leaves are large and coarse and yet, in the instance I am describing, the leaves were large but not coarse. They held themselves with notable distinction. Very strange. On returning home I rushed out to my specimen with the same predisposition for indulgence as the father showed his prodigal son, but it was no use. My wintersweet was as scruffy and unprepossessing as an unshaven tramp. For the umpteenth time I must wait upon leaf-fall as a merciful release.

30.10.75

NOVEMBER

VEGETABLES FOR ORNAMENT

THE basic, down-to-earth question 'Can you eat it?' finishes by depressing me, after relentless repetition. Surely, having grown a rather fetching collection of ornamental gourds, let us say; surely it should be satisfaction enough to be able to stand back and admire them rather than expect to be able, having admired, to eat them as well. That smacks too much of savagery.

And yet mine is really an unreasonable objection. After all, if a red cabbage or Brussels sprout is beautiful in its growing season, is that not the more reason for growing these rather than their plain relations?

But this is an awkward dichotomy, nonetheless, because if you plant a red cabbage in your border, on account of its beauty, but, come September, decide to eat it, because you have a delicious Viennese recipe for red cabbage with vinegar and brown sugar; why, then, your border won't look quite the same afterwards, will it? On the other hand, if I tell you that you should make up your mind at the outset whether the vegetable in question is to be for carnal or spiritual degustation and sited in the border or the vegetable garden accordingly, you may fairly reply that, having no spare plot for vegetables, you fully intend to make the best of both worlds insofar as you are able, and to grow your globe artichokes in the flower border, decapitating them when the tempting moment arrives.

There was a fascinating bedding-out scheme at Kew this year, devoted entirely to ornamental vegetables. All credit to Mr Halliwell, who has brought new life and abundance of ideas to a branch of public gardening that is all too often stereotyped and boring. Not that bedding out in private gardens is often very inspiring, either.

I am not going to suggest that we should all start bedding out with vegetables alone. The snag is that some look their best in one part of the summer or autumn, some in another; seldom all together. But we could easily take elements from this Kew experiment and use them in our own gardens with flowers or other kinds of foliage.

One of the most effective edging plants, there, though it was beginning to look ragged by early September, was the lettuce called 'Salad Bowl'. This is a singularly fresh, pale-green, with crinkly foliage. Then there is *Petroselinum crispum*, better known, perhaps, as parsley, but you must admit that its botanical name rolls impressively off the tongue, after a little practice. Parsley is the most brilliant green. I have, in another garden, seen it associated with orange tagetes, with startling effect. Also, more gently, with the glaucous foliage of Jackman's blue rue. The great thing, with parsley, is to grow it really well with widely spaced plants having the chance to develop fully.

Swiss chard is a bold and comely plant, with thick white mid-ribs framed in glossy green. But I had never before seen the variety called 'Ruby', in which the mid-ribs and all the veins are red while the blades are purple. Against a background of parsley, one could scarcely do better for a summer bedding scheme. Ornamental beet, with purple or reddish foliage, is easily and quickly grown but the only time I attempted it I was foiled by slugs. At Kew, there was a delightful variety called 'Flower Garden' (from Carter's). Its leaves are so narrow and svelte as to remind one of a willow's, but their colouring is deep-purple.

Ornamental kale and cabbage are well known to flower arrangers. They are variegated in shades of cream, rosy-purple and green, and reach their climax in autumn and early winter. One seedsman foolishly lists them as *flowering* cabbage and *flowering* kale. The last thing you want from any brassica, whether grown for ornament or eating, is its tiresome yellow flower. Seakale, on the other hand, is a perennial and does flower very prettily in late spring with a dome of white, honey-scented blossom, but its pale glaucous leaves are its principal ornamental asset, and they are in condition from May till the first frosts of autumn.

Cardoons are first cousins to globe artichokes but with even showier, more deeply cut, grey leaves, and I find them reliable and hardy perennials. But they flower at 8 feet, which could be embarrassing in a small garden. The answer is not to let them flower, in that case. Just cut the stems down to the ground when they appear in summer. There will be no second attempt.

There are two principal strains of ornamental maize. My favourite – and it grows only 2 or 3 feet tall – is normally listed as *Zea mays* 'Gracillimus', and it is striped in cream and green. The other is usually called 'Quadricolor' and is good at its best but all the strains of it available are extremely badly selected. Instead of being striped with purple, green and cream, as they should, they usually come plain dull-green. Even 'Gracillimus' can be disappointing and should be grown in pots for a time until it becomes evident which seedlings are worthwhile, whereupon the rest can be summarily dismissed.
4.11.71

INDOOR COMPANIONS

A MAIDENHAIR fern greeted me in the hall of my friend's house. 'What a beautiful specimen!' I exclaimed, and then, 'Have you just got it?' She had. Furthermore she perfectly understood the implication, for her fingers are not of the greenest and maidenhair ferns do not forgive the wrong treatment. I must hasten to add that I have never kept one in my own home but feel confident that if I did my success would be complete so there is no need to put myself to the test.

Actually my house does rather suit ferns. It is very cool in winter and damp at all seasons (so much better for the antique furniture) and this suits the two I have ventured upon admirably. The larger is called *Woodwardia radicans*. It comes from South Europe and other parts of the old world but I understand that, as a wild plant, it is on the danger list. This is a large and imposing fern. I have had my plant since 1969 and its bipinnate fronds measure over 6 feet in length although, being flexible, they do not take up this much lateral space and the plant is about 10 feet across. It alarms some visitors for it gives a curious impression of reaching out for you. I like being reached out for by my ferns; it gives me a reassured and wanted feeling but those who regard plants with suspicion or even animosity feel otherwise.

Woodwardia radicans needs a lot of space. It could well occupy the north window of a cavernous and already dark hall such as, I feel sure, a large proportion of *Country Life* readers own. As long as it doesn't freeze or have to endure the indignity of an open window (draughts bruise its fronds) it is happy. I give mine a liquid feed every fortnight or so while it is putting on new fronds and it needs daily watering in summer but only once a week or ten days in winter.

My other indoor fern, *Pteris tremula*, is much more easily obtainable and is of generally manageable dimensions – perhaps 3 feet across by 2 feet tall if grown in a 6 inch pot. Its fronds are well dissected and a pale, fresh green even when quite mature. This is on the windowsill of the dining-room and faces south-east so that sunlight blazes on it all morning, if there is any sun to blaze, but the fern never scorches.

A deep windowsill is a great asset – something that house owners should insist upon as a body, for they will not get it otherwise. On the Continent, accommodation for room plants is a *sine qua non*, but in this country it is assumed that everyone has their garden and therefore there's no need to clutter up the interior with plants. Which is feeble.

It is, of course, true that if you range a lot of plants along a window ledge they will exclude a good deal of light from your rooms. But light filtered through foliage is most soothing and I regard the craze for light rooms as a passing phase. The sooner it passes the better. Light living-rooms are especially super-fluous for gardeners who spend so much of their time under the sky. It is restful to enter the green shade of a fern-fringed room.

Foliage plants give the greatest year-round pleasure though even of these many should be regarded as expendable. It is easy, in most cases, to start a youngster that will take over. The sedge, *Cyperus involucratus*, is one of the commonest of house plants (popularly known as the umbrella plant) and is certainly a favourite with me because its radiating spokes, crowning 2 foot-long naked stems, have such style. But after a year (or two at the most) I put mine in the fish pond outside in early summer, where it perishes come the first frost, but meantime a young one will either turn up as a self-sown seedling or be produced by an umbrella head dipping into water or can be induced by detaching a head and floating it in a saucer of water.

Flowering plants come and go – bowls and pans of bulbs in winter and spring, vallotas in autumn, the blue trumpets of *Streptocarpus confusus* 'Constant Nymph' from May till December. I usually replace this last, in late autumn, with *Begonia* 'Cleopatra', which has fascinating foliage, deeply incised, lopsided, as all begonia leaves are, and patterned in copper and pale-green. These markings vary in intensity at different seasons and according to how much light the plant is receiving but they are always gorgeous. Very welcome sprays of pale-pink flowers are borne in February. In spring the plants go back to the greenhouse and then stand outside – I still have some outside now, in late October; it has been so very mild.

I could grow nothing but begonias and still be a happy man but the only other one I have indoors, *B. haageana*, is a bit of a worry. As the friend who gave me my original cutting grew it, in a sunny window, the plant was translucent and of a marvellous coral-red. She starved it. I find it terribly difficult, in fact impossible, to force myself to starve my plants. Consequently this one grows enormous and its foliage is heavy and dark. There must be a moral somewhere, if not a solution.

11.11.76

Bird Behaviour in the Garden

When showing friends round the garden, recently, we passed within four or five feet of a cock blackbird who was eyeing us with a zany expression that implied he would get on with what he was doing when we had gone. We paused and looked at him while he continued to look at us. I was admiring his new plumage, actually, for Cassius (it happened to be) had been a sorry sight till recently. 'Poor thing,' murmured one of my companions. I was indignant and asked whether we must take it that any wild creature which fails to flee at man's approach is sick or wounded. That was, indeed, the inference.

Most birds, on the contrary, will become tame if you go about your business and let them go about theirs without interference. When really used to you, it becomes no embarrassment to them to be stared at, spoken to or even sworn at, on occasion. Blackbirds can swear back. That's one of the nice things about them; they meet you on equal terms.

We have a long, narrow apple shed with the door at one end and the apples at the other. There is a bench near the door at which several people will congregate, but this does not deter Blackie (a hen blackbird) from going in and out and helping herself as she pleases. But she swears at us and quite startles those who don't know her if we don't allow her much of a gap to fly out by.

In fact, she knows she's not allowed to help herself to apples in this way (there's no question of finishing one before starting on the next) and the bargain is that if we'll throw her an apple to eat outside the shed, she'll finish that completely except for the core and skin before attempting to help herself from the racks again. An apple a day suits her in most seasons.

This year she nested successfully in the potting shed. We have no cats to make this impossible. Earlier broods in the garden had been robbed by magpies, but she was safe from them in the shed. The cock was very shy and I wondered whether Blackie would have to do all the work of feeding the young, and whether she would be able to cope with that as well as with brooding them (though it was so hot that little brooding was, in fact, necessary). However, the cock plucked up sufficient courage, though his visits were accompanied by the maximum of protesting noises and I had to keep my head down attending resolutely to my business and not look up at him. I was away the weekend when the young flew, but Moffat was there at the crucial moment and tells me they all walked out of the door like a procession of ducks. We missed their company.

On the outside of the potting shed grows a large specimen of the evergreen *Ceanothus impressus* and this has one branch lying against the wall and a strong side-branch coming off it at right angles. The T formation is particularly popular with birds. Blackie has used it in former years, but always been plundered by magpies. This year a song thrush took over. She was so dreadfully shy at first that I thought she could never succeed where people are continually passing and the crowds were worst of all when she was already brooding her eggs and the ceanothus came into flower – such a display that everyone was stopping and staring. However, I was much surprised and greatly pleased to notice that she became increasingly unconcerned and successfully brought off her young. I forthwith removed the nest, as I always do, and she was soon back making another. The second brood was successfully launched in August. But the thrushes are far less apt to be tame than the blackbirds.

Roy Hay sometimes writes that he wouldn't mind sharing his fruit with the blackbirds if they would take only 20 per cent and leave him the rest. This is a difficult sort of bargain to strike and I think one should either make up one's mind to protect the fruit properly, or to let the birds eat as much as they want or, if this arrangement upsets you, not to grow fruit. To plant and then to have to prowl apoplectically with a pop-gun is bad for one's character.

I can think of at least four gardening friends who are also peacock fanciers. Peacocks, of course, have a bad name as destructive vegetarians but, as is so often the way when you come to examine a subject at close range, they're not nearly as black as they're painted. It is quite untrue to say that you must choose between peacocks and a garden. They are perfectly compatible for most of the time but you will have to protect your green vegetables, for instance. They can be netted at some expense but little trouble. Indeed, even without peacocks, I am beginning to think seriously of netting my lettuces and young brassicas, because the moorhens keep taking gashes from their leaves when the foliage is not yet sufficiently abundant to be able to cope. Peacocks will also tend to peck at anything new, but they soon lose interest.

Another fallacy about peacocks is that their voices are unbearably harsh. They are no more cacophonous than the pheasants'. The one disappointment in their respect is that they seldom take up just that position in your garden where, scenically, you feel that a peacock should be standing.

13.11.69

Only a Cat Nap

'Very autumnal,' I hear people saying with a little shudder as they scurry past looking pinched, as though they'd received a touch from the first frosts before there'd been time to lay in a store of nuts. One thing certain, about autumn, is that it will be autumnal. Hurrah for autumnal autumn, I say, but this is all a matter of temperament and does not even depend on whether you're a gardener or not.

Fallen leaves may distress you; undeniably they're a bit of a nuisance if yours is the responsibility for clearing them up. But whereas every leaf that falls on a lawn will upset some, others are content to see them all come down before having a grand clearance. And if the wind has had fun with them before you get around to it, there may be greater ease in clearing drifts rather than carpets.

There is a deliciously soothing quality about falling leaves. Especially the sound of them. As I sit at my potting bench, I can hear every leaf stalk that falls from an overhanging ash making a small tap and scutter on the roof; a confidential comment, a whisper of intimacy. When it is sunny I bask on a stone seat in the sunk garden as I make my cuttings (lavender next) and the great leaves off the Brunswick wall figs can be heard (when the noise of aircraft, tractors, chain saws and other man-made sounds have let up) descending with a rustle and a plop. There is a timelessness about autumn, a feeling of indefinite, relaxed suspension.

And it is not a death; a mere sleep and barely that, for many plants. Only a cat nap, much needed, very restoring. Chives are getting lank and tired now, but even before the end of January, this year, there were fresh young spikes showing long enough to pick. Grape hyacinths and Dutch irises have been showing new foliage for a long time. At any moment we shall be giving the rough grass its third and final cut, no later than mid-November, otherwise we shall damage the noses of new daffodil shoots.

When you cut down old peony stems you want to remove as much as you possibly can so as to avoid infection by peony botrytis from old stems to new. But there, at the base of each black stalk, is a plump pink bud, and you have to be quite careful with your secateurs. The length of the monkshoods' growing season always astonishes me. An old favourite called *Aconitum fischeri* does not flower until October; the blue of its hoods against the yellow of its ageing foliage creates a bizarre effect. By January, next year's bronze young leaves are already unfurling. Border phloxes are early afoot too, while doronicums and lupins are all making young green before January is out. Such as these should be moved, if they need moving, as soon as possible. We are lucky to have a winter that gives us some respite, but it is not a very long one, from the gardening angle.

Some plants start growing in the autumn instead of stopping then, as do the more conventional. Bulbs have already been mentioned. Cyclamen are another case in point, especially *Cyclamen hederifolium*. And then the arums. *Arum creticum* is already pushing through and once again I've left the lifting, splitting and replanting of my colony till it's too late. *A. italicum* 'Pictum' is wearing a new suit of marbled foliage – I wouldn't mind splitting this one now if I wanted to: there is no flowering to spoil. I made two large groups in the garden of the florist's arum, *Zantedeschia aethiopica*, last spring. This is another plant that insists on resting in the summer but is growing strongly now. It will, of course, get frosted but in every mild winter's spell, new leaves will try pushing up until, finally, in April, they will triumph and the plants will surge forward to their June-July flowering.

Iris unguicularis should start flowering at any moment. Indeed there are many winter pleasures of this kind to look forward to. The winter sweets, *Chimonanthus praecox*, will soon shed the last of their hideously coarse foliage. This year, in striking contrast to last (and what a contrast in the summers that made this contrast), they are thickly encrusted with their club-shaped flower buds and the first of these will open before the end of the month.

Most winter sweets are seedlings, this being far and away the easiest method of raising new stock (cuttings are extremely difficult; layers are easy but, commercially, an expensive method). Would-be winter sweet owners should appreciate that they must expect to wait six or seven years before their shrub has matured sufficiently to start flowering. As it happens I have a 6 foot-tall seedling in my border that is about to flower for the first time. I collected the seed from which I grew it in January 1964. So it will be just on ten years. When you buy a plant it is already some three years old. It is a great advantage to gardeners if they can be sedentary; then they can afford to be patient. Of course you can usually take your winter sweet with you, up to the last journey.

15.11.73

The Houseleeks in My Life

I HAVE a sneaking affection for houseleeks. Sneaking, not because I am in any way ashamed of my feelings but because, despite the group's fascination, I have never done anything about it. My earliest memory of a houseleek is still a very living, flourishing example on the steep-tiled roof of our apple shed, which was a cowshed in earlier centuries. It is the commonest species, *Sempervivum tectorum*, with largish rosettes, purple at the tips and it is an enormous, happy lump.

Seeing that houseleeks are, by their fleshy nature, exceedingly tolerant of drought, I should have thought that to water one would be a work of supererogation. Nevertheless, Romke has taken to spraying this one every time he passes with the hose in the past two summers and the houseleek has responded with a quite amazing increase in size. Visitors always notice and comment on it. It is a local personality. Quite eighty years old, which is older than the garden. We knew the cottager, old Mrs Barnes, who started it off.

It would be fun to have a roof collection of houseleeks but I've never felt secure about how to get them going on sloping tiles. Some sort of firm matrix is necessary. Cow pats are highly adhesive, as I remember from seeing them plastered against hovel walls in India, later to be used for fuel. But when I have tried a cowpat it has later dried out, shrunk and flaked off. Perhaps clay needs to be added. I have not been persistent in my efforts and deserve the hackneyed school report comment: 'Could try harder.'

Elsewhere in the garden we have a cobweb houseleek, *S. arachnoïdeum*, on a south-facing dry wall. It was installed when the wall was built, around 1911, and it and its handsome embossed label still look as well as ever.

245

When a schoolboy, I used to visit the local Rugby market of a Saturday and buy pots of houseleeks, which had been allowed to develop large rosettes, doubtless by the removal of their competitive babies. When planted on a rock garden, the rosettes dwindled in size as the babies took over. I think it is, on the whole, sensible to allow a natural, competitive development of a carpet or hillock of rosettes, enjoying them less for their size than for their texture and colouring.

My next vivid impression of this plant came in the summer of 1939 when I stayed at Silvaplana in the Engadine. Here, at 2,000 metres odd, I was amazed to find cobweb houseleeks wild in quantities in all the walls; a mass, at that season, of most attractive bright-pink star flowers. Seeing that cacti, which are comparable in their water-storing habits, are mostly frost-tender, it seemed extraordinary that the houseleeks should so manage their affairs as to succeed in an exceedingly severe climate.

Lately, my thread of sempervivum experiences has been given a further twitch by the beautiful exhibits shown us by Mr Alan Smith of Leaves Green, Keston, Kent, at the RHS shows in Westminster. Here one can get an inkling of their range and appeal in comfort and reasonably close to eye level. Mr Smith grows them for display in large hand-made pans such as you have to find second-hand at a price, for they are no longer being made.* But they are the ideal receptacle for many small plants and, being only very slightly permeable to water, are far more resistant to frost than even machine-made clay pans. But these have anyway yielded to universal plastic.

There are two groups of houseleek, not one, as I had previously supposed. The genus *Sempervivum* comprises some fifty species, mainly European. Their flowers are star-shaped and include ten to seventeen petals. They increase by offsets (as well as by seed) which are sent out into the world on stolons. The other genus, *Jovibarba*, comprises only five species. Its leaf rosettes are very similar to the sempervivum's, but its flowers are bell-shaped or tubular and have only five to nine petals. Furthermore, the young rosettes in this genus are

* They are now, I'm glad to say.

never at the ends of stolons. They are either formed by fission into two of a single unit or they develop in the axils of outer leaves. These leaves break away from the parent plant before the young rosette has rooted and get moved to a distance by wind or water, extending the species' range.

Houseleeks love an open, sunny situation, where they can develop their full colouring. They detest shade or the drip from trees. Neither (except with the object in winter of protecting the cobwebs on *arachnoïdeum* types) should they ever be kept under glass, where they lose compactness and colouring and are subject to attack by aphids. They look beautiful in troughs and sinks; or a garden can be made for them on a well-drained, sunny slope. Don't overdo the labelling. I remember a collection at Wisley that looked like a garden of remembrance, so thick was it with handsome, clearly lettered plaques.

If you are growing houseleeks in pans, you will be conscious of the gaps left after flowering, for a flowered rosette dies. The gap allows more water to percolate than is good for the colony and it may suffer from rotting. Mr Smith therefore prefers to repot his collection every year, in spring or in autumn.

The finest colouring is often assumed in winter and retained in spring, but in some of the best cultivars it holds right through the year. There is infinite variety, here.

17.11.77

THE SWEET DISEASE

WRITING a news letter for the Wisconsin unit of the Herb Society of America, Mrs Geist gave impressions of the places and people that a party of them saw in England last summer, including Dixter and myself. Of me she writes that I am often 'quoted as saying, "I just have to have that plant," which I could relate to instantly.'

I hadn't appreciated my involvement in this sentiment but I don't deny it. 'The sweet disease' is how a fellow horticulturist/gardener describes our condition. When you're suddenly overwhelmed by the beauty of a plant, a fever takes you over. From that point, anything can happen.

Nowadays this fever takes me only rarely – one result of advancing years, no doubt. In a way I'm rather sorry about that. I find new plants more resistible. It's chiefly in the fern department that I still find myself weak and trembly. But I'm less acquisitive than I was (my friends may not have noticed it) and perhaps a welcome corollary is that I can, more and more, enjoy plants enthusiastically without necessarily feeling bound to possess them. Possessiveness is not always a charming quality. All the same, an almost savage delight in a new plant provides some of the great moments in a gardener's life.

It is the uncontrolled desire to possess which leads to garden thefts. People are rarely open on this subject, especially in print. I suppose that's understandable if you're ashamed of yourself but it is unattractive and results in a kind of humbug, the public image quite different from the reality.

I have pinched cuttings to which I had no right myself, and I can remember most such occasions with more glee than shame. There was, for instance, *Daphne tangutica*. This must have been around 1950. It was growing in a totally neglected area of rock garden at the bottom of Chilham Castle gardens, in Kent and was clearly an almost lone survivor from pre-wartime glories. When you've never seen *D. tangutica* before, it is something of a knockout; those clusters of seductive flowers so appropriately highlighted by a tremendous airborne scent, immoral and irresistible.

I don't find *Daphne tangutica* particularly easy from cuttings. Nowadays I raise scores of them every year from seed, which germinates freely and gives rise to a beautiful, stocky plant. However, the Chilham Castle daphne was flowering, not seeding, and I succeeded in rooting a cutting, which occasioned in me much pride and joy. I planted it out and within a few weeks a visitor (for we were open to the public even in those days) had nicked it. I was mortified.

I do not exactly remember why I was not on the spot when a replacement cutting was taken, this time by my mother (a staunch confederate with a minimal conscience) at Wisley. Lunchtime was the moment chosen, when garden staff were absent, and John Treasure, who was staying with us, vividly remembers being made to keep *cave* while my mother did the deed. All went well the second time and the resulting bush, though rather long in the tooth by now, is the oldest daphne I have ever possessed.

Let me say, before others say it for me, that this was disgraceful behaviour. Thefts at Wisley are a very serious matter – the orchid house had to be closed for a long time following a big raid. Visitors have far less conscience about helping themselves from public or society's, or from National Trust gardens (that word National is so deceptive, with its totally false suggestion of 'After all, it belongs to me; I'm paying for it') than from those that are private and merely open for a charity. Continual thefts are a pestilential scourge.

I've taken nothing from Wisley without permission these thirty years, I promise. They are, after all, most sympathetic to properly placed requests from members. In fact I think I can truly say that I never take bits from any garden. I ask. But then I have to admit that I'm now in a much stronger position and more likely to be granted my request than I was when I was young and unknown (I hope that doesn't sound conceited) and I have some sympathy for those who are less well placed.

The trouble is, I really enjoyed those unregenerate days (I wonder how St Augustine looked back on his profligate youth; was it with unmitigated disgust or did he occasionally chuckle over a discreditable incident recalled?). There was that time at Eastwell Park – I don't believe the house was lived in, in 1949, but the garden was kept going. There was a huge plant of *Lespedeza thunbergii* in full bloom in October; cascades of rich purple pea blossom arching its rod-like stems into graceful parabolas. One can be terribly fickle over plants but I've never got over my love affair with that one. It always gets me. That time I got it, a whole 3 foot rod which I stuffed down my trouser leg. I was walking like a war wounded after that. Peter Hamer, a fellow Wye student, was with me.

One really needs a confederate for the full flavour of the triumph. It was John Treasure, again, at Hidcote when we raped 'Madame Julia Correvon'. (He's old enough now to be able to stand the exposure.) This must have been in the late fifties because I remember having my first Sweetie Pie, a much-loved dachshund, on a lead. John had to hold her while I took the cuttings. We were starting to collect and to propagate clematis at that time and this, so far as I know, was the only specimen extant in England then. Graham Thomas had shown an irresistible (that word again) slide of it at a London lecture. I asked him afterwards if there was any chance . . . but he was evasive. 'We must propagate it,' he said, but that didn't help me any. Well, we rooted our cuttings and went on from there. That 'Madame Julia' is now widely obtainable (twelve sources are listed in *The Plant Finder*) was thanks to our enterprise.

If you must pinch cuttings from my garden, please take them neatly and not where it shows and don't let me catch you, particularly if the plant is on sale in my nursery. That's plain mean.

26.11.87

FIG YEARS PAST AND FUTURE

IT must be quite five years since I had any crop of figs, let alone a good one. Seeing that green figs are my favourite fruit, this is a notable deprivation. But so long as you (or I) have a fig tree in your possession and, for preference, happy past experiences of its potential, hope will always be beckoning just around the corner.

There have been local (to me in Sussex) figs around this year. I met some in a Hastings greengrocer's last September and included them in a large fresh fruit salad. No doubt they contributed, but I later decided that I'd have done better to eat them on their own and by myself. Pleasures of this kind need concentrating, not dispersing. It's no good trying to stir a fig addict's conscience by telling him he's being selfish. That is a part of the enjoyment.

I might indeed have had a few figs of my own had I chased them singly with ladder and protective bags (I use perforated lettuce bags) before blackbirds weighed in, which they do just as the fruit is beginning to change from green to puce. I don't resent the blackbirds' intrusion at all. Like me, they know a good fruit when they see one. It's a question of pitting my perseverance and wits against theirs. Generally they win, being more single-minded. But I find a certain vicarious pleasure even from watching a blackbird enjoying my fig – our fig.

Anyway, I didn't bag the figs because there weren't enough of them to make the ladder and bag work worthwhile. When there is a heavy crop, as in 1975 and 1976, for instance, and such years usually occur one in three, it is worth working over the figs every three days. To fix bags prematurely is unwise. Even with perforated plastic, much condensation accumulates within them. Better to wait until you see a fruit just beginning to turn, adjust a bag over it, making your twist tie take in the branch behind; then return in three days' time (given decent weather). The fruit will be ripe with mouth-watering long-itudinal slits down its skin. Never pick a fig before entirely ripe; it's not worth eating. The bags you remove can immediately be fixed on the next lot of ripening fruits, and so on for several weeks.

1989 could be a fig year. If you look at a shoot made this year, it ends in a sharp, acute-angled tip. That is a leaf bud. But in the few inches below this bud and just above a leaf scar, you'll see tiny rounded protuberances. These are next summer's potential crop. Any that are larger than a pea will not survive the winter. All those several-inches-long figs that are still hanging on but can never ripen in our climate because formed too late, are no better than a health hazard. As they wither and rot, they will often set up rotting in the healthy shoot behind. It is worth rubbing them all off now, before this can happen.

But any sort of pruning of a fig should only be entered upon after consideration of what results you're aiming at. You may have no higher aspirations than a handsome foliar clothing to a wall, as along the front of the National Gallery. At Dixter, five wall figs were sited by Lutyens for this specific purpose and the variety, 'Brunswick', was also chosen advisedly, first for its vigour and capacity to cover a big area and second for the deep, handsome indentations to its leaf.

But in a good year it bears the largest and most luscious fruits. Edward Bunyard describes it as 'a large and rather gross-looking fruit formerly known as the Madonna, but upon the arrival of George I it was rechristened. It is not recorded if His Majesty accepted this as a compliment, but it has a certain Hanoverian lustiness.' He adds that it attains a great age and seems to thrive on neglect.

And that's the point, for the less you prune a fig the more of those fruit-bearing shoot tips it will retain. So, thin out its branches if you must (we find this necessary every third year) but let those that are spared remain intact to their very tips.
29.11.88

DECEMBER

THE GARDEN IN WINTER

WINTER is not a season on which I should wish to write a gardening book. But if I did, at least I should not cheat. Each season is three months long; those of winter are December, January and February. March, however chill, is a spring month. November, in which we still are as I write, is clearly autumn, even though we did have an inch of snow two days ago. There is abundance of foliage on all the oaks. Their winter has not started.

So I was irritated by a book which came out in the autumn called *The Winter Flower Garden*, in which winter's domain is extended to include half of November at one end and of March at the other, allowing the author to cite the hardy plumbago, *Ceratostigma willmottianum* as a winter flower and early tulips also. They feature on the dust jacket. It is true that, given frost-free weather, the ceratostigma *can* go on flowering late, though its colour is wan and pasty then, compared with its summer and early autumn complexion. And it is true that, in a mild season, spring bulbs may flower early; almond blossom also. But to anyone with the courage of their convictions about the beauties of the winter season, they do not belong there, neither do they need to.

A year without its winter would seem all wrong to me, as a countryman. It is a necessity, not just a necessary evil. There is evil for humans far more than for plants. We get diseases and die more freely in winter than at other seasons and we have to spend heavily on keeping ourselves warm.

In the garden we are likely to lose plants which we knew all along were on the fringes of or, indeed, way outside their natural climatic range. Those are calculated risks and we have no right to complain of losses that were wholly predictable. But the cool temperate plants that comprise the bulk of our gardens' contents and the whole of the countryside are not only well adapted to winter; they need and could not do without this season. You have only to see what a poor account of themselves roses give in the tropics (even at high altitudes) and how short-lived they are, to realise that without their winter, plants such as these burn themselves out. Others, which need cold in order to bring about the physiological changes that enable them to break dormancy in the following spring, are lost without it, remaining dormant for ever more.

To think of leaf fall and the onset of winter as sad is anthropomorphic; the usual silly way we have of looking at things from our own point of view. I should, however, be a hypocrite if I pretended that I was longing to be out in the garden on this cold and drizzly day on which I write, rather than bound to my desk (armchair, actually) meeting a deadline with my regular piece. I am happy to be where I am.

There are, I know, more dedicated winter gardeners than myself. Margery Fish was certainly one, Graham Thomas, Rosemary Verey.

It is because of Rosemary Verey that I am writing on this subject. 'I am just embarking on a book I've had in mind for some time – the garden in winter' she tells me in a letter and asks me to put down some thoughts which might be quotable, to encourage the doubtful to take the winter garden seriously. What, she asks, do I enjoy most about my garden in winter, what do I do in it and which plants give me greatest pleasure?

I love my winter garden because of its silence and emptiness; the slow pace, not dead, not even merely ticking over – there is always a forward impulse – but a gentle stirring. Even when the weather is rough, there is a feeling throughout of inner calm. In particular, the ponds seem to be in a state of reverie.

I notice the birds more in winter, and other creatures. There was a squirrel in our apricot, against the house, just now. It sat there looking at me and I stood, returning its stare for quite a while. Then I moved on and it continued on its apricot business. In summer there would surely have been an interruption.

The birds are all in their fullest plumage, against the cold. The blackbirds are my favourites. One shouldn't have favourites, but there they are, so close at hand always, smart, querulous sometimes, demanding and bossy at others, each one with an individual personality.

The song thrushes will be singing in every mild spell; even in cold weather, they cannot hold back by the time it is February and they will have been joined by mistle thrushes, chaffinches, blue and great tits; then the blackbirds themselves with their gloriously liquid notes, *sotto voce* at first, then strengthening.

The flowers I love best are those that everyone loves best, because they are there in winter. Deservedly they are written about more than all the rest and there is always something fresh to be said about them.

Some of the evergreens are very beautiful, especially when their foliage is wet and gleaming and also those, like many conifers, whose colouring changes to rich purple, now. And the grasses that finished flowering long since retain a wonderful warmth of personality. Grey foliage plants are not enlivening now, however, but bamboos, especially the *Phyllostachys* are superb.

There are berries. The skimmias hold theirs right through and I find a shiny black berry, like that of *Sarcococca confusa*, as cheering as a red one.

What I do in the garden? Mostly pruning and training. I like to get the roses done before spring's arrival. Our sheltered rose garden, the frostiest spot of all yet so warm when the sun slants in, is the place I think of most in my winter garden and there is great satisfaction when it has all been organised once more.

5.12.85

COMPENSATIONS FOR DROWNING

MANY of us must have the feeling (as I write, at least) that it has rained, if not non-stop at any rate on every day for the past three months. It has been impossible to get on with the majority of clearing and planting jobs that await our attention at our main season of renewal. This does at least give us the chance of staring around us and taking note of our surroundings. And what could be more beautiful, at any time of year, then the scene presented to us when the sun breaks through between downpours?

It has often be remarked that the Western Scottish Highlands owe a large part of their magic to the appalling weather that habitually bombards them from off the Atlantic. To this they owe their mantle of ferns, lichens and mosses and then, when the clouds break, the whole land sparkles, distances seem near enough to touch and the very wetness of the objects confronting us (notably of rocks) adds intensity to their colouring. In these short days we have the bonus of low sunlight of a particularly mellow quality. Unfortunately I have never visited the Highlands later than September or earlier than March but we can, following our recent drenchings, enjoy some of the consequent vitality that animates quite ordinary objects in our own undramatic lowland countryside and gardens.

This low sunlight has a way of getting in underneath an overhanging canopy of trees or large shrubs so as to illuminate their trunks, which would otherwise remain, so to speak, dormant. Our native Scots pines are famed for the rufous colouring on the bark of mature trees, but when the sun strikes them almost at right-angles, as now, and when the trunks are still wet and glistening from rain, their richness, heightened and offset by a setting of glaucous foliage, is startling.

So it was in a friend's garden that I visited recently and another star performance by trunks that took my eye was contributed by a trio of old rhododendrons: 'Cornish Cross', a Loderi cultivar and *Rhododendron falconeri*. The first was smooth, silky and blotched in various shades according to where the rind had most recently peeled. Loderi was a mixture of smooth and rough: rough where old bark still clung, smooth where it had peeled off. These Loderis, in their season, carry trusses of white or blush, fruitily scented blossoms that are each some 5 inches across at the mouth of their open funnels. And yet, because of the looseness of the truss and the open habit of the bush that wears them, there is no question of them appearing outsize or bloated. Young specimens display their charms most effectively at close range. As they age, the display is carried aloft and may be missed although, if cunningly placed, they may then make their mark as seen from a distance, rising in a billowing cumulus cloud behind a foreground of azaleas, perhaps, or other lower shrubs. At this stage, as you saunter point blank among your rhododendrons, you must either submit to a crick in the neck or accept compensation from their mature trunks, and these are at their most remarkable in winter. In *R. falconeri* the surface is all rugged, and in fitting contrast to the warm rust colouring revealed by the felted underside of old leaves.

Some evergreens are better suited by the light of winter than others. The grey or glaucous tones of many eucalypts can strike a trifle chill and dismal. So can similarly coloured conifers like the popular hedging cultivar of Lawson's cypress called 'Allumii', while the matt and lifeless substance of *Chamaecyparis nootkatensis* 'Pendula' is rendered even more lugubrious by its heavily weeping habit.

A leavening of yellow makes all the difference. I think *Chamaecyparis obtusa* 'Crippsii' is my favourite of the medium-large golden conifers. In addition to its lively colouring, seen against the green of second-year foliage, its broad-based spire with drooping tips to young branches is both sturdy and graceful. Another variant within the same species,

'Tetragona Aurea', is enchanting in youth, forming mossy encrustations of gold-green shoots. With age it is apt to become woody and ungainly.

In the same garden already mentioned, there are huge colonies of old, many of them self-sown, tree heaths: *Erica arborea alpina*, and I was surprised how much light and life there was in the yellow-green of their young shoots when the sun touched them.

One of my favourite small shrubs for evergreen winter effect is the little known *Ozothamnus ledifolius*. It is a composite from Tasmania and yet perfectly hardy, and the leaves at the tips of young shoots point upwards, thus revealing the bright-yellow colouring of their under-surfaces. In spring the dense umbels of flower buds are tawny-orange, much the same colouring as *Euphorbia griffithii*, which I accidentally grow near at hand. A happy accident.

Most of my gardening friends go into agonies of hate when I point out my young spotted laurel to them. For those who are lucky enough to be able to contemplate *Aucuba japonica* without disturbance to their blood pressure, let me remark that the commonest form of the spotted laurel is not really spotted enough. Its flecks of yellow sink into their green matrix if seen at any distance. It is worth hunting out a more vigorously spotted form and the well-named 'Crotonifolia' is just that. Both its green and its gold are at their most effective now.
12.12.74

LONG-FLOWERING PLANTS

WE are naturally grateful (though gratitude is a terribly exhausting virtue) to those of our plants which keep on flowering, on and on and on, but is there not a kind of relief bordering on the vindictive when we can at last get at them with sheers or secateurs and wipe the smirk off their silly faces?

Those shrubby hypericums, for instance. I would have called them *Hypericum patulum*, in the old days, but the pundits seem to have done away with that species. Anyway, it's the one that seeds itself into the walls and floor of my sunk garden. I admit that it quite often puts itself where it would have been too difficult to plant anything myself and there it goes on flowering. Not that anyone really notices a plant like that. Like a utilitarian piece of furniture, you take it for granted right from its first appearance.

The ubiquitous 'Hidcote' is similar. Always an insistent shade of not quite clean yellow. Try growing a hedge of 'Hidcote' with pink hydrangeas and red 'Floribunda' roses alongside it, but you needn't ask me along to admire the result as I have an example in a front garden that I constantly pass in my own village.

A plant that I'm frequently expected to admire for its steadfast qualities is *Polygonum* (now *Persicaria*) *amplexicaulis* 'Atrosanguinea'. On a 3 foot plant, its small, crimson pokers are borne untiringly for several months in late summer and autumn. But it tires me, even if it doesn't tire itself. It is uncharmingly coarse and it is invasive, surreptitiously elbowing out its neighbours. No doubt it keeps weeds at bay and it does a job, if that's the sort of job you want done. I know I'm being unfair and that you could show me an example in your own garden to which I should have to admit every kind of accolade, but nothing will persuade me to be fair on its behalf.

I have never been altogether at ease with *P. affine*, though I do grow the clone 'Superbum'. That is a mat former, again suppressive of any but the most serious weeds, and it produces a succession of 9 inch-tall pokers from July to November. At first they are anaemic pink but they gradually deepen to rich crimson. The mixture of shades as more spikes keep on being produced is pretty good. The leaves are uninspiring, but this wins high marks as a landscape plant to be seen on undulating ground from some distance. Take a look at the planting at Wakehurst Place, in mid-Sussex.

If you cut your colony hard back now . . . no, let's say trim, which sounds more civilised . . . you'll kill it outright. This is a rather sweet, while unaccountable revenge by one, in a partnership, who loathes the plant, while the other insists upon doting on it. After all, you were only tidying up. If you like the plant, delay tidying up operations until the spring, when signs of renewed life have become apparent.

It's the same with the really pretty *P. vaccinifolium*, whose leaves are tiny and whose cushiony habit is not too uniform. I killed most of mine by shearing it at the wrong time, which is how I come to be an authority on the subject. *P. vaccinifolium* is moisture-loving and I have failed to satisfy it in this respect for several years, but I shall keep on trying a while longer, as its forest of tiny pinky mauve spikes are just what I want between my hedges of the Michaelmas daisy, *Aster lateriflorus* 'Horizontalis' and the flagstone path in front of them. Both for colour and season, the match is perfect. Admittedly the polygonum is madly un-ground-covering and constantly requires hand weeding but sometimes I'm obstinate.

I have been an enthusiastic advocate of shrubby potentillas, in my time – that is *Potentilla fruticosa* in its scores of cultivars, of which 'Red Ace' was the most highly acclaimed, at its first bombshell appearance, only to be reviled for bad behaviour a year or two later. Still, a moment of having been carried away is precious enough not to deserve subsequent resentment, even though it was under false pretences. 'Red Ace' was the first in this colour to present itself to an astonished public, but when you come to grow it, a pasty, raddled shade of orange is only too normal, at least for those of us living in the south.

Shrubby potentillas are at their best in northern climes. They grow better (making excellent 3 foot hedges), flower better and are of a richer colouring. Grey skies and chilly temperatures are exactly what they enjoy. I still think that rich, buttercup-yellow shades suit them best, but the reds will flower red (not bleaching, as in the south) and the orange and pastel-pink shades, however nasty, will at least flower as intended and some of them are good.

These potentillas will start flowering in May, if not pruned, and will never be without some blossom for the rest of the growing season. But they'll probably look pretty weak for much of it. Best treatment is to do some fairly hard pruning, each spring. This will delay the onset of flowering but it will be a lot more wholehearted once it does start. The treatment not to give your shrubby potentillas is to allow them their head for a number of years, until they are unbearably scruffy, and then to cut them hard back. That is apt to maim them permanently.

In hydrangeas, I do wholeheartedly welcome a flowering season prolonged into four months. Only some of them do it and then only if they are growing healthily and are constantly rejuvenated by sensible pruning each spring. At the top of my admiration list would be 'Preziosa' – if only I could grow it well. For some ununderstood reason, I cannot. But many gardeners can and do.

This hydrangea goes through a colour sequence similar to *Polygonum affine* 'Superbum', starting pale and pasty but increasing in richness over a long period and producing a succession of not very large inflorescences. Add to its flower colour rich-red tones in stems and foliage and you have quite a feature. If only it liked me.

17.12.92

OTHER MEN'S WEEDS

I AM feeling particularly pleased at receiving a letter from a lady in Ohio expressing her own pleasure in a book of mine that has come her way. Obviously we click. When I ask myself what I mean by that I think the chief necessary ingredient for clicking is a shared sense of what is funny. If you've got that, you're more than halfway there. One is always being told how different the Americans are from ourselves and how recognition of this fact is dangerously masked by our common language. So when I, who have never visited America, receive a letter from so distant a place and alien a culture as Ohio, quite clearly indicating we're on the same wavelength, it is warming.

Her last paragraph introduces a situation that every gardener will recognise, unless he is the cause of it. Having written of her neighbour, whose rose bushes apparently attract all the devastating Japanese beetles away from her own garden, my correspondent continues with: 'A complaint and a rhetorical question. How would you feel if every time she came into your yard to see what was blooming, she always had to stop some place and start pulling your weeds? At first I figured that I should be glad to have someone pulling my weeds because that was that many fewer for me to pull. But now I must say it is beginning to annoy me no end. It is as if she is saying to me, "You have a nice garden BUT . . . I really can't be satisfied with what you are doing, and I must interject my personality." I know some areas of my yard always need weeding, and I do get around to it eventually. That's the way it is.'

Of course, we always claim we get around to it eventually, even if we don't. If we didn't believe that, we shouldn't be able to continue gardening. One must have faith. But even if we have lost control, or our friends have, that's a matter between ourselves and Destiny and no excuse for insensitive interference by third party do-gooders.

Margery Fish latterly found her garden a bit much to cope with although, brave spirit that she was, she never admitted it or gave in. The last time I saw her, she told me how riled she'd been by a relation who declared that she liked weeds. The last time he'd stayed, he had set himself to weed a certain piece, like it or not, and had virtuously applied himself to it throughout the visit. 'And it was just the piece,' Margery told me, 'that I like to keep for weeding when I'm waiting for a visitor to arrive.' And if she never would have got it weeded herself, so what?

It is true that, if you're going round a friend's garden with your host and you see a weed that, in your own, would make you leap forward, it may be difficult to restrain the leap. But stop to consider. If you're on very intimate terms, no harm will be done nor offence given. Always ask yourself, honestly, how would you react if the situation was reversed?

Many visitors come to my garden and most are strangers or quite casual acquaintances but it is surprising how they love to draw attention to my weeds. It gives them a feeling of superiority and I cannot retaliate by visiting and commenting on their gardens. 'Your lawns are weedy,' was the direct approach of one. Actually, they're not very, so I was a bit mystified. I don't use weedkillers regularly, but often enough to keep down the plantains and daisies if not the creeping buttercups and certainly not the clover. However, it turned out that my tormentor was referring to our patches of rough grass as lawns and as we encourage every sort of wild flower to have its way in these, it is small wonder that she (doubtless accustomed to trim beds and orderly surroundings) was shocked. 'You do grow parsley,' was a male comment, referring to our cow parsley. 'We like it,' from me and a savage grunt from him ended that exchange; a clear case of not being on the same wavelength.

Some visitors, seeing this rough grass, are kind and pitying. 'Labour must be very hard to come by,' they say sympathetically or, if it happens to have been cut recently, 'I see you're gradually pulling the garden back into shape.' If I am accompanying the visitor along my borders, she is liable to dart at the groundsel or whatever, with the arch remark, 'I never can resist groundsel.' She would, though, if I weren't there to witness its extraction.

I'm not denying that weeds are a blot. They or anything that's spoiling the scene give particular pain to one close friend. The pain is genuine; I know it. He, Lanning Roper, lets me pull the first weed, however, and then sets to with such thoroughness and devotion that I feel like my father did towards my mother: 'Are we going round the garden or are we weeding?' the first proposition having been the original intent.

When Mr and Mrs Patrick Gibson kindly allowed me to visit their garden at Penns in the Rocks, he, one of the busiest of men with many irons in many fires, managed to save some of the inevitable waste of time I was causing by making our tour in the company of a large weed sack on wheels. Whenever we stopped to look and comment he improved the moment by weeding or dead-heading his roses. But when I decided that I'd looked at that rose bush for long enough, I had only to make a show of joining him in his exercise and he immediately moved on. I enjoy that sort of game.
19.12.74

A QUESTION OF UPBRINGING

A FRIEND who is a garden designer asks me to devote an article to a subject near my heart: 'Wild flowers as well as bulbs naturalised in rough grass and the subsequent difficulties of mowing and how to overcome them. As you know,' his letter continues, 'I am quite a hundred per cent on your side about this, but find I am a very bad advocate when it comes to convincing clients!'

I appreciate his difficulty only too well. Many of our potential customers for viewing the gardens at Great Dixter when they are open between April and October take one look over the front gate at the waste of weed-infested unmown grass (as they consider it) that immediately confronts them and depart forthwith. I'm glad they go as I'm sure I shouldn't enjoy meeting them but my brother and sister-in-law get worried and she has suggested that I should put up a notice explaining the rough grass to visitors (bring in Conservation, with a capital C), and give them a list of wild flowers in their seasons that should be looked out for. Shan't. The more notices you put up the less private and personal a garden becomes.

If people can't appreciate this relaxed and informal style of wild gardening they'll never be persuaded. If they can, they don't need persuading. I believe it's a question of upbringing, how you react, and that your attitudes are fixed for life at a very early age. If at an early age you enjoyed moving between walls of flowering grasses and moon daisies higher than yourself, if you enjoyed pulling stems of meadow foxtail out of their sockets and nibbling the sweet soft end, or getting your shoes yellow with pollen as you walked through a buttercup field, or making daisy chains, or making rice puddings with heaped-up fallen apple blossom petals, or telling the time with a dandelion clock. If you enjoyed picnics when you sat on the ground and not on seats and could bury your face in the growing plants and instinctively take in the smell of them; if you did and enjoyed these things you'll quite naturally take to the concept of wild grass gardening. It will need no advocate.

But if you were told never to sit on the ground because it is damp and dirty; if you have always been surrounded by trim lawns and find anything wilder repulsive if not actually frightening; if, in short, your suburban or urban upbringing divorced you from contact with the countryside so that you never got used to it as a part of your life and of you, then no advocacy of actually letting grass get rough in a garden, thereby negating your entire concept of what a garden should be, will make on you the slightest impression.

In rough grass or meadow gardening, you retain control but you relax it. You give the grasses, the other plants that naturally inhabit grassland and the alien but compatible plants which you introduce the chance not only to flower but also to set and scatter their seed. Only then do you cut them down but by then you have allowed them the opportunity to increase. In this way you gradually build up a varied tapestry of colour that changes continually but lasts for many months.

Starting with the crocuses and snowdrops of January and February, the daffodils soon follow, then anemones, snakeshead fritillaries and dandelions in April, primroses and lady's smock in damp places, cow parsley under trees, quickly to be followed by buttercups and red clover, the earlier-flowering grasses, various native orchids in succession, common daisies. And so to the climax of early June with a high tide of grasses in flower, white clover, moon daisies, hawksbeards – the tally is legion. And these are followed by meadow cranesbill, tufted vetch and meadow sweet in early July.

By now the display is waning and all should be cut down and cleared away to the compost heap. A second close cut in late August precedes the flowering of colchicums and autumn crocuses and a final cut in late autumn leaves the set ready for the reappearance of short-stemmed winter-flowering crocuses.

In this kind of gardening the wild flowers do a large part of the work and your introductions can be many or few, more one year, less in another, according to your energy and mood. There are no demands on you apart from your management of the turf.

This side of it, however, is vital. When the first cut has to be faced, in July, you must put your back into the job and you must have the right tools.
21.12.78

BETWEEN SCYLLA AND CHARIBDIS

AT least it is socially acceptable to be a gardener or horticulturist (which is the grander entry I make in my passport). I can believe a friend who tells me that the fact of his being a physicist is a complete and instant conversation stopper. 'Heat, light, mirrors, pulleys, oh dear!' must subconsciously run through the back of the desperate interrogator's mind and even if we can rise to the nuclear, scope for intelligent conversation is likely to be prescribed.

Doctors and lawyers get caught in a different trap. They risk an immediate query or detailed case history on matters that will be supposed to interest them and will, it is hoped, elicit free advice or information. Which is an unmitigated bore. 'I never give opinion without a fee,' was one lawyer's stuffy riposte in this situation, which must arouse latent sympathy in many similarly caught, though generally less ruthless, victims.

The professional gardener, however, being implicated in our country's most popular hobby, generally meets with some responsive spark in conversation with strangers and he is expected to react with sunny and genial co-operation to questions of the 'What should I?' and 'What would you?' variety.

And as most gardeners, professional or otherwise, love talking about gardening, this generally works very well. How fortunate when your profession is also your chief recreation.

The lady on my right, at dinner, couldn't understand why the delphiniums, which she raised from seed, died when she planted them out in the autumn but lived if she waited till the next spring. This is a textbook outcome arising from a textbook case but I nonetheless had to come up with a clear and convincing explanation. Delphinium roots, I told her, although they appear to make a fibrous mat are in reality rather fragile. When handled they easily drop off. If this happens in the autumn, when the plant is dormant, it is unable to make good its losses by putting out new roots. On the contrary, those with broken ends will tend to rot in the cold wet ground that surrounds them and that'll be their grave. In the spring, however (and a delphinium's spring starts early), the plant is active; broken roots can soon be replaced by new ones and recovery is assured.

This seemed to make sense to my neighbour and I next tried if I couldn't improve her methods of raising delphiniums in other ways. It appeared that she was sowing the seed as late as May – the hunting season and its aftermath fully preoccupies her till then – and left the seedlings interlocked in their container (I couldn't quite make out if she pricked them off) until she was ready to plant them out in the autumn. Whether before or after cubbing I forgot to enquire.

If, I suggested, you could sow them in April, prick them off into a box and then line them out to grow on for the remainder of the growing season, you'd have large flowering plants by the time the autumn arrived. They could be lifted then with such a bulky ball of soil that the roots wouldn't notice, and be planted in their permanent positions to make a splendid display in the next summer. Indeed, they would already have made a pretty good show in their first autumn.

She was flatteringly amazed; I could have been a magician waving my wand. But there was a snag. She had no spare plot of ground in which to line them out. Except for the raspberry and strawberry cage, which was in the shade of a tree so that the strawberries in particular did not thrive, the whole of their walled garden had been grassed down and turned over to her husband's rams (whether they were hunting rams I again forgot to enquire).

Was the tree a valuable one? I asked. She thought it did look rather nice. Was the cage's framework of wood? No, of metal. Then could she not move the cage to a sunnier part of the walled garden and at the same time filch a piece of ground from the rams in which to line out seedlings that were growing on?

This was a splendid idea in theory, but in practice her husband always had a good and unanswerable reason for not carrying out such a proposition when she suggested it. Would I not come over to visit them some time and make the suggestion myself? It would be more likely to carry weight and at the same time she wished I would persuade Derek to move her greenhouse, it being in a position protected by the house and a wall so that it received no sunlight at all in the winter and was consequently covered with green stuff – algae, no doubt.

By now, however, I felt myself to be wading in rather deep water, so I turned to my other neighbour. She, a little playfully, I suspect, and knowing full well that I am a bachelor of long standing with little experience of children and even less, come to that, of horses and hounds, pressingly invited me to witness a children's meet that was shortly to take place at her home. My haste in declining may have verged on the impolite.

Life in the country is not always straightforward.
31.12.81

INDEX OF BOTANICAL NAMES

A Note on the Author and the Editor

Christopher Lloyd was born in 1921 at Great Dixter, Northiam, East Sussex. He took a B.Sc. degree in horticulture at Wye College, University of London, and stayed on for four years as assistant lecturer in decorative horticulture. In 1954 he returned to Dixter, where he started a nursery for clematis and other plants that he believes in and enjoys. Here he wrote *The Mixed Border* (1957), *Clematis* (1965, revised edition with Tom Bennett 1989), *Shrubs and Trees for Small Gardens* (1965), *Hardy Perennials* (1967), *Gardening on Chalk and Lime* (1969), *The Well-Tempered Garden* (1970, revised edition 1985), *Foliage Plants* (1973, revised edition 1985), *The Adventurous Gardener* (1983), *The Year at Great Dixter* (1987), *Garden Flowers from Seed* (with Graham Rice, 1992) and *Christopher Lloyd's Flower Garden* (1993).

Frank Ronan was born in Ireland in 1963. His fourth novel, *Dixie Chicken*, will be published in the spring of 1994.